RYAN **PARROTT** • MARCO **RENNA** • DAN **MORA** • WALTER **BAIAMONTE** • RAÚL **ANGULO**

VOLUME THREE

Published by

BOOM!
S T U D I O S

SERIES DESIGNER
MADISON GOYETTE

COLLECTION DESIGNER
CHELSEA ROBERTS

ASSISTANT EDITOR
GWEN WALLER

EDITOR
DAFNA PLEBAN

HASBRO SPECIAL THANKS
ED LANE, **BETH ARTALE**,
AND **MICHAEL KELLY**

Ross Richie Chairman & Founder
Matt Gagnon Editor-in-Chief
Filip Sablik President, Publishing & Marketing
Stephen Christy President, Development
Lance Kreiter Vice President, Licensing & Merchandising
Bryce Carlson Vice President, Editorial & Creative Strategy
Kate Henning Director, Operations
Elyse Strandberg Manager, Finance
Michelle Ankley Manager, Production Design
Sierra Hahn Executive Editor
Dafna Pleban Senior Editor
Shannon Watters Senior Editor
Eric Harburn Senior Editor
Elizabeth Brei Editor
Kathleen Wisneski Editor
Sophie Philips-Roberts Editor
Jonathan Manning Associate Editor
Allyson Gronowitz Associate Editor
Gavin Gronenthal Assistant Editor
Gwen Waller Assistant Editor
Ramiro Portnoy Assistant Editor
Kenzie Rzonca Assistant Editor
Rey Netschke Editorial Assistant
Marie Krupina Design Lead
Grace Park Design Coordinator
Chelsea Roberts Design Coordinator
Madison Goyette Production Designer
Crystal White Production Designer
Samantha Knapp Production Design Assistant
Esther Kim Marketing Lead
Breanna Sarpy Marketing Lead, Digital
Amanda Lawson Marketing Coordinator
Grecia Martinez Marketing Assistant, Digital
José Meza Consumer Sales Lead
Ashley Troub Consumer Sales Coordinator
Morgan Perry Retail Sales Lead
Harley Salbacka Sales Coordinator
Megan Christopher Operations Coordinator
Rodrigo Hernandez Operations Coordinator
Zipporah Smith Operations Coordinator
Jason Lee Senior Accountant
Sabrina Lesin Accounting Assistant
Lauren Alexander Administrative Assistant

Licensed by:

BOOM! Studios, 5670 Wilshire Boulevard, Suite 400, Los Angeles, CA 90036-5679. Printed in Canada. First Printing.

ISBN: 978-1-68415-752-5, eISBN: 978-1-64668-330-7

WRITTEN BY
RYAN PARROTT

ILLUSTRATED BY
**MARCO RENNA
& DAN MORA** (CHAPTER 10)

COLORS BY
WALTER BAIAMONTE
WITH ASSISTANCE BY **KATIA RANALLI & SARA ANTONELLINI**
& RAÚL ANGULO
WITH ASSISTANCE BY **JOSE ENRIQUE FERNÁNDEZ** (CHAPTER 10)

LETTERS BY
ED DUKESHIRE

COVER BY
INHYUK LEE

ELTARIAN, GREEN RANGER, BANDORIAN MONK, AND
DARK SPECTER'S ASSASSIN CHARACTER DESIGNS BY
DAN MORA

CHAPTER NINE

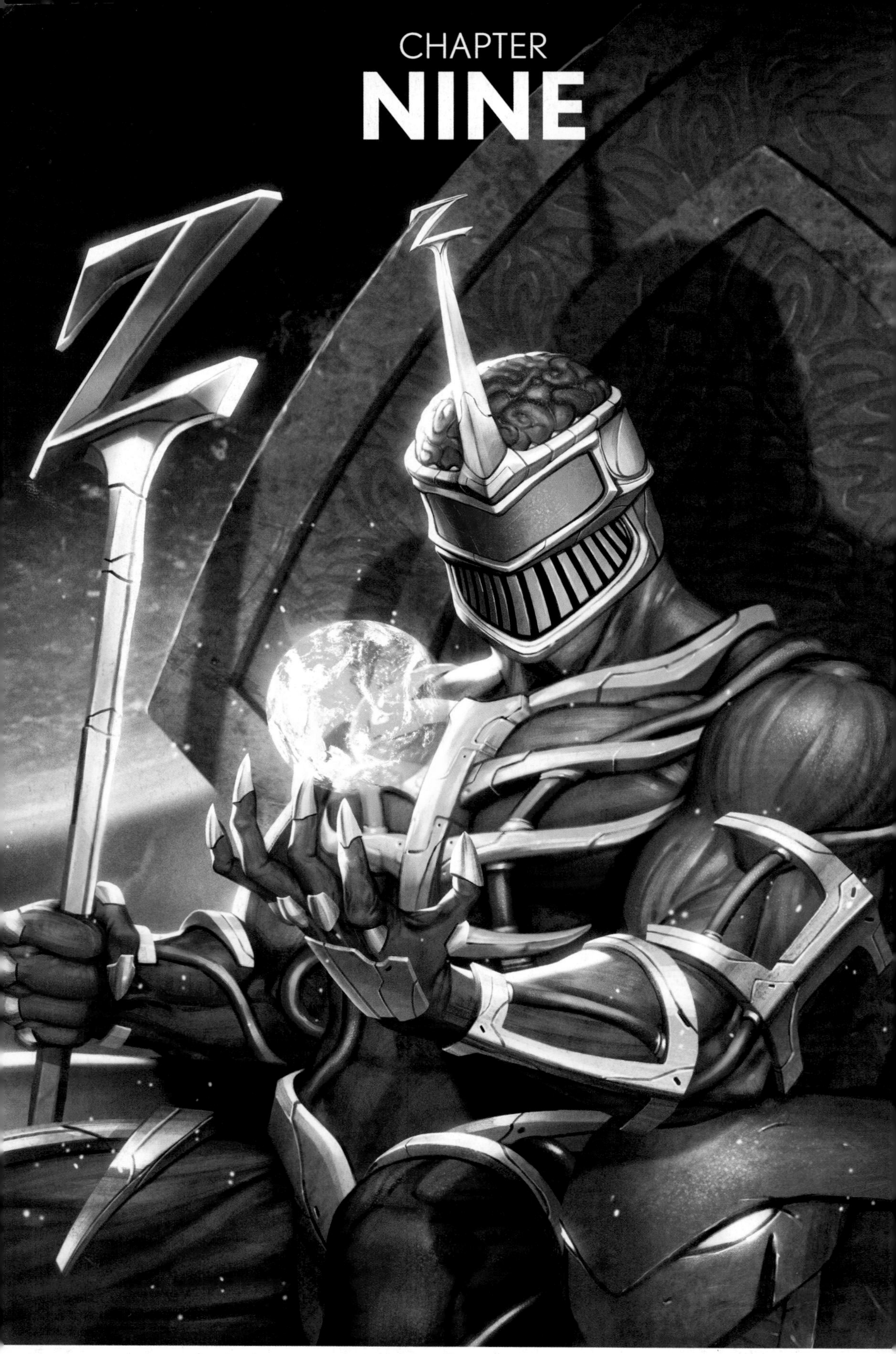

INHYUK LEE | ISSUE NINE COVER

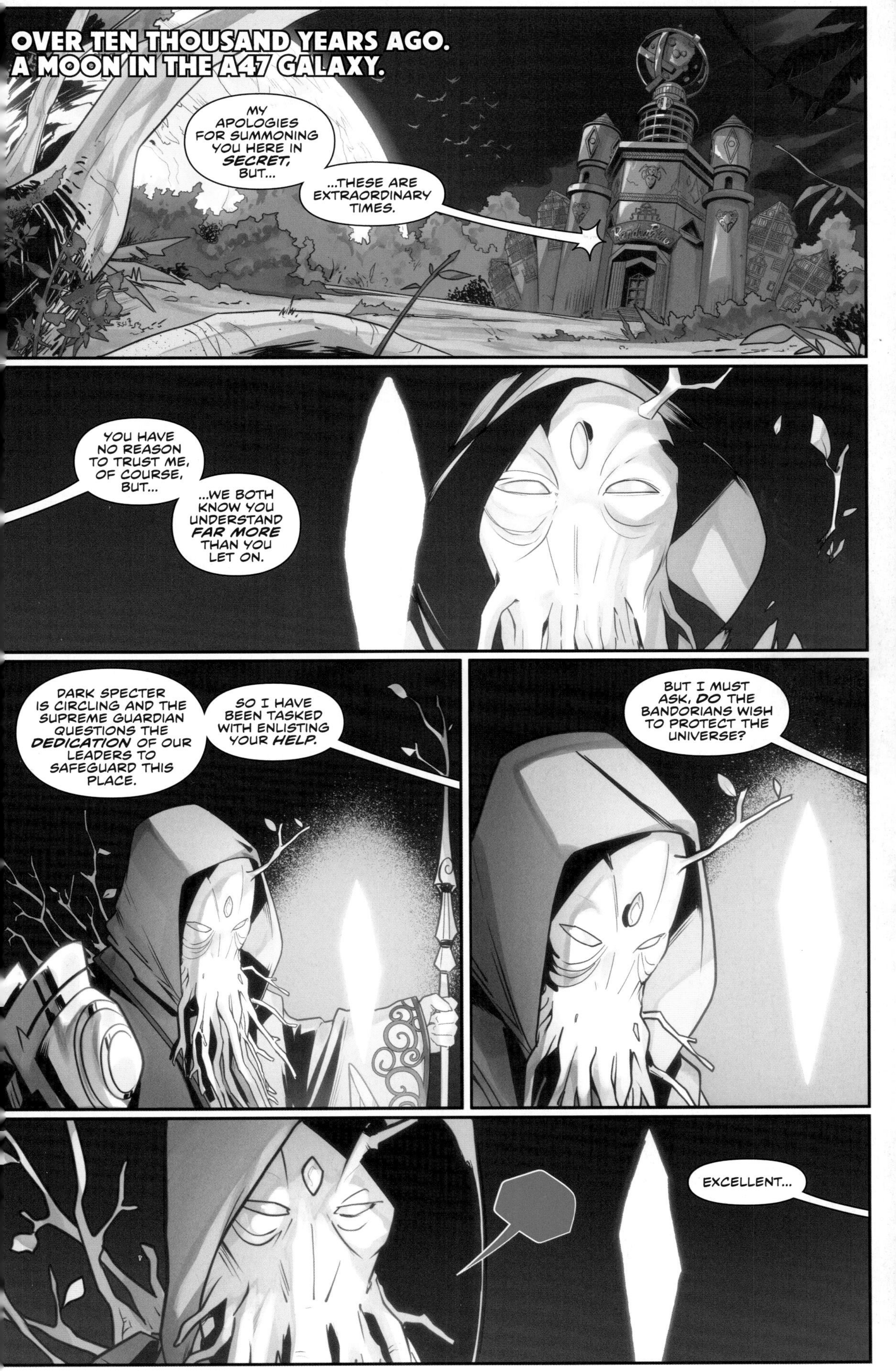
OVER TEN THOUSAND YEARS AGO.
A MOON IN THE A47 GALAXY.
MY APOLOGIES FOR SUMMONING YOU HERE IN SECRET, BUT...
...THESE ARE EXTRAORDINARY TIMES.
YOU HAVE NO REASON TO TRUST ME, OF COURSE, BUT...
...WE BOTH KNOW YOU UNDERSTAND FAR MORE THAN YOU LET ON.
DARK SPECTER IS CIRCLING AND THE SUPREME GUARDIAN QUESTIONS THE DEDICATION OF OUR LEADERS TO SAFEGUARD THIS PLACE.
SO I HAVE BEEN TASKED WITH ENLISTING YOUR HELP.
BUT I MUST ASK, DO THE BANDORIANS WISH TO PROTECT THE UNIVERSE?
EXCELLENT...

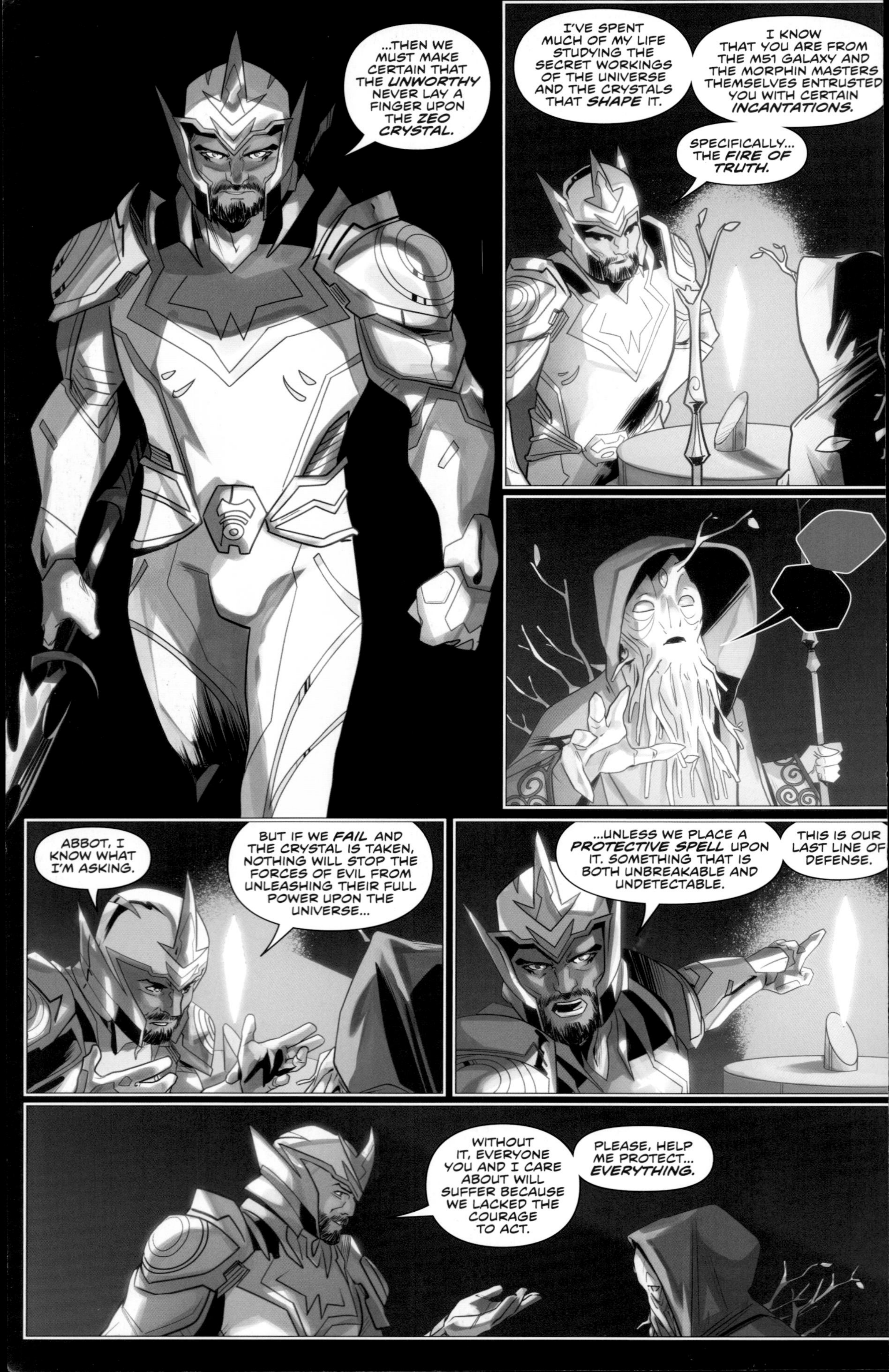
...THEN WE MUST MAKE CERTAIN THAT THE UNWORTHY NEVER LAY A FINGER UPON THE ZEO CRYSTAL.
I'VE SPENT MUCH OF MY LIFE STUDYING THE SECRET WORKINGS OF THE UNIVERSE AND THE CRYSTALS THAT SHAPE IT.
I KNOW THAT YOU ARE FROM THE M51 GALAXY AND THE MORPHIN MASTERS THEMSELVES ENTRUSTED YOU WITH CERTAIN INCANTATIONS.
SPECIFICALLY... THE FIRE OF TRUTH.
ABBOT, I KNOW WHAT I'M ASKING.
BUT IF WE FAIL AND THE CRYSTAL IS TAKEN, NOTHING WILL STOP THE FORCES OF EVIL FROM UNLEASHING THEIR FULL POWER UPON THE UNIVERSE...
...UNLESS WE PLACE A PROTECTIVE SPELL UPON IT. SOMETHING THAT IS BOTH UNBREAKABLE AND UNDETECTABLE.
THIS IS OUR LAST LINE OF DEFENSE.
WITHOUT IT, EVERYONE YOU AND I CARE ABOUT WILL SUFFER BECAUSE WE LACKED THE COURAGE TO ACT.
PLEASE, HELP ME PROTECT... EVERYTHING.

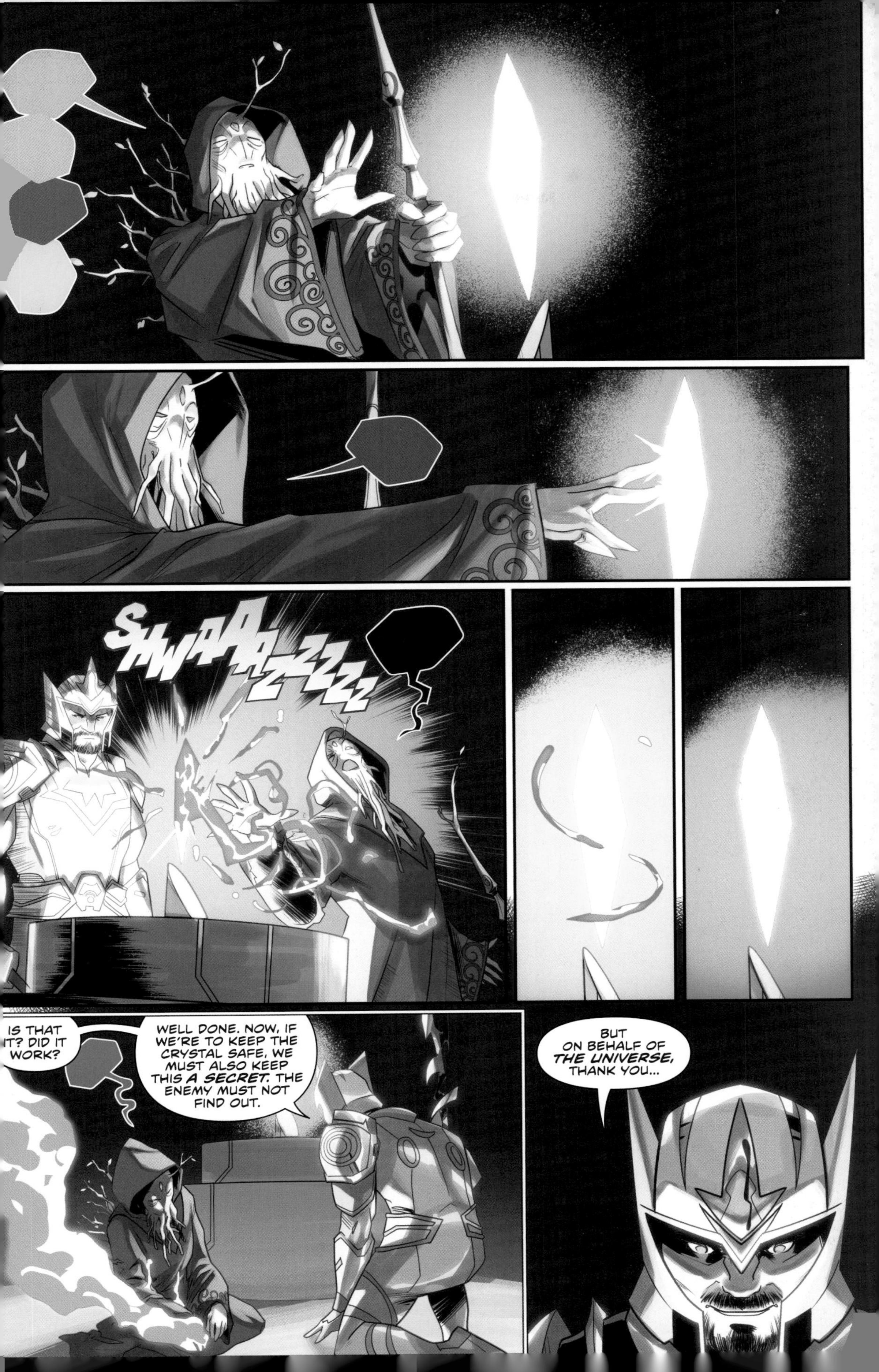
SHWAAAZZZZZZ
IS THAT IT? DID IT WORK?
WELL DONE. NOW, IF WE'RE TO KEEP THE CRYSTAL SAFE, WE MUST ALSO KEEP THIS A SECRET. THE ENEMY MUST NOT FIND OUT.
BUT ON BEHALF OF THE UNIVERSE, THANK YOU...

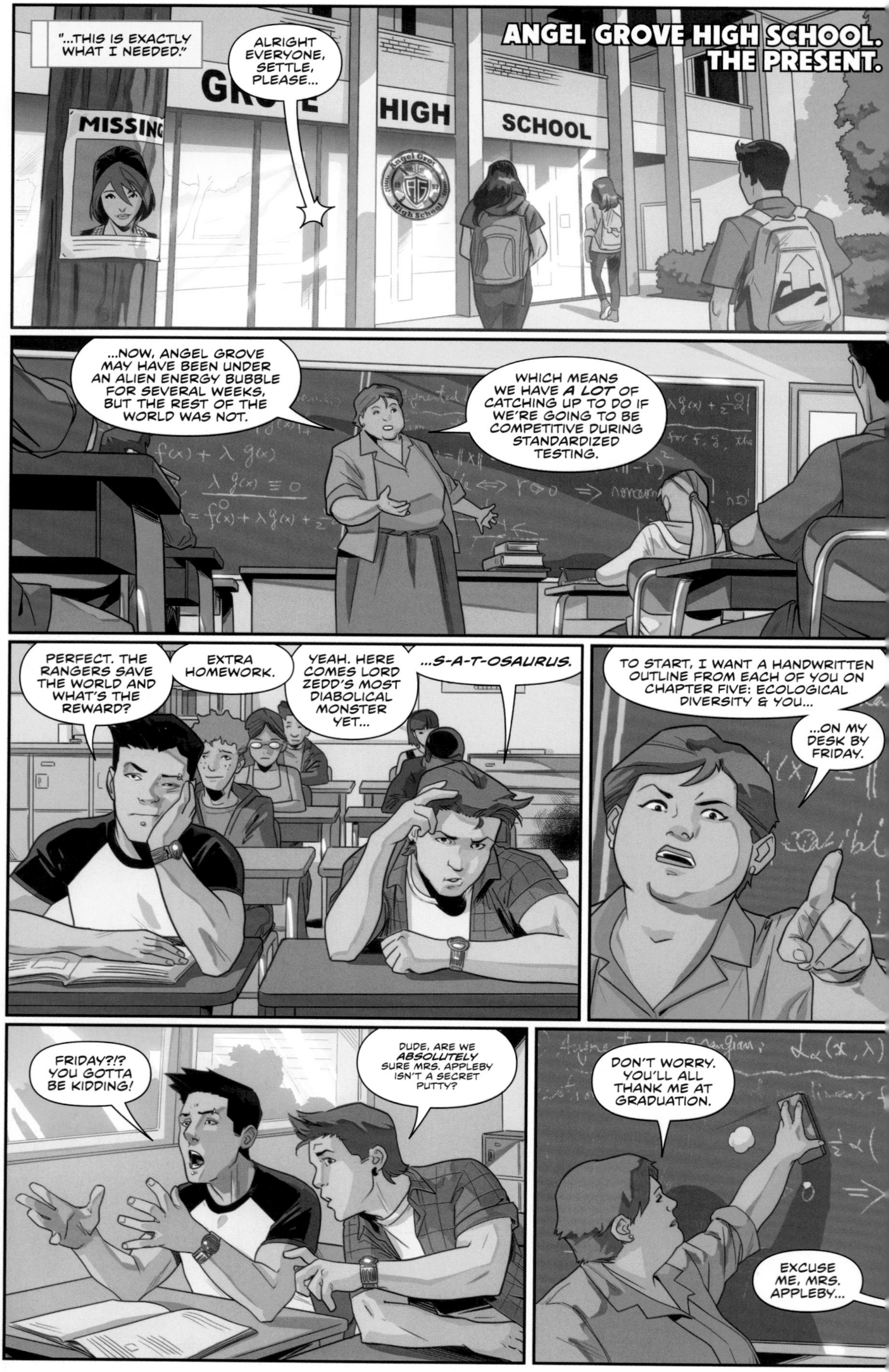
"...THIS IS EXACTLY WHAT I NEEDED."
ALRIGHT EVERYONE, SETTLE, PLEASE...
ANGEL GROVE HIGH SCHOOL. THE PRESENT.
MISSING
GRO E HIGH SCHOOL
...NOW, ANGEL GROVE MAY HAVE BEEN UNDER AN ALIEN ENERGY BUBBLE FOR SEVERAL WEEKS, BUT THE REST OF THE WORLD WAS NOT.
WHICH MEANS WE HAVE A LOT OF CATCHING UP TO DO IF WE'RE GOING TO BE COMPETITIVE DURING STANDARDIZED TESTING.
PERFECT. THE RANGERS SAVE THE WORLD AND WHAT'S THE REWARD?
EXTRA HOMEWORK.
YEAH. HERE COMES LORD ZEDD'S MOST DIABOLICAL MONSTER YET...
...S-A-T-OSAURUS.
TO START, I WANT A HANDWRITTEN OUTLINE FROM EACH OF YOU ON CHAPTER FIVE: ECOLOGICAL DIVERSITY & YOU...
...ON MY DESK BY FRIDAY.
FRIDAY?!? YOU GOTTA BE KIDDING!
DUDE, ARE WE ABSOLUTELY SURE MRS. APPLEBY ISN'T A SECRET PUTTY?
DON'T WORRY. YOU'LL ALL THANK ME AT GRADUATION.
EXCUSE ME, MRS. APPLEBY...

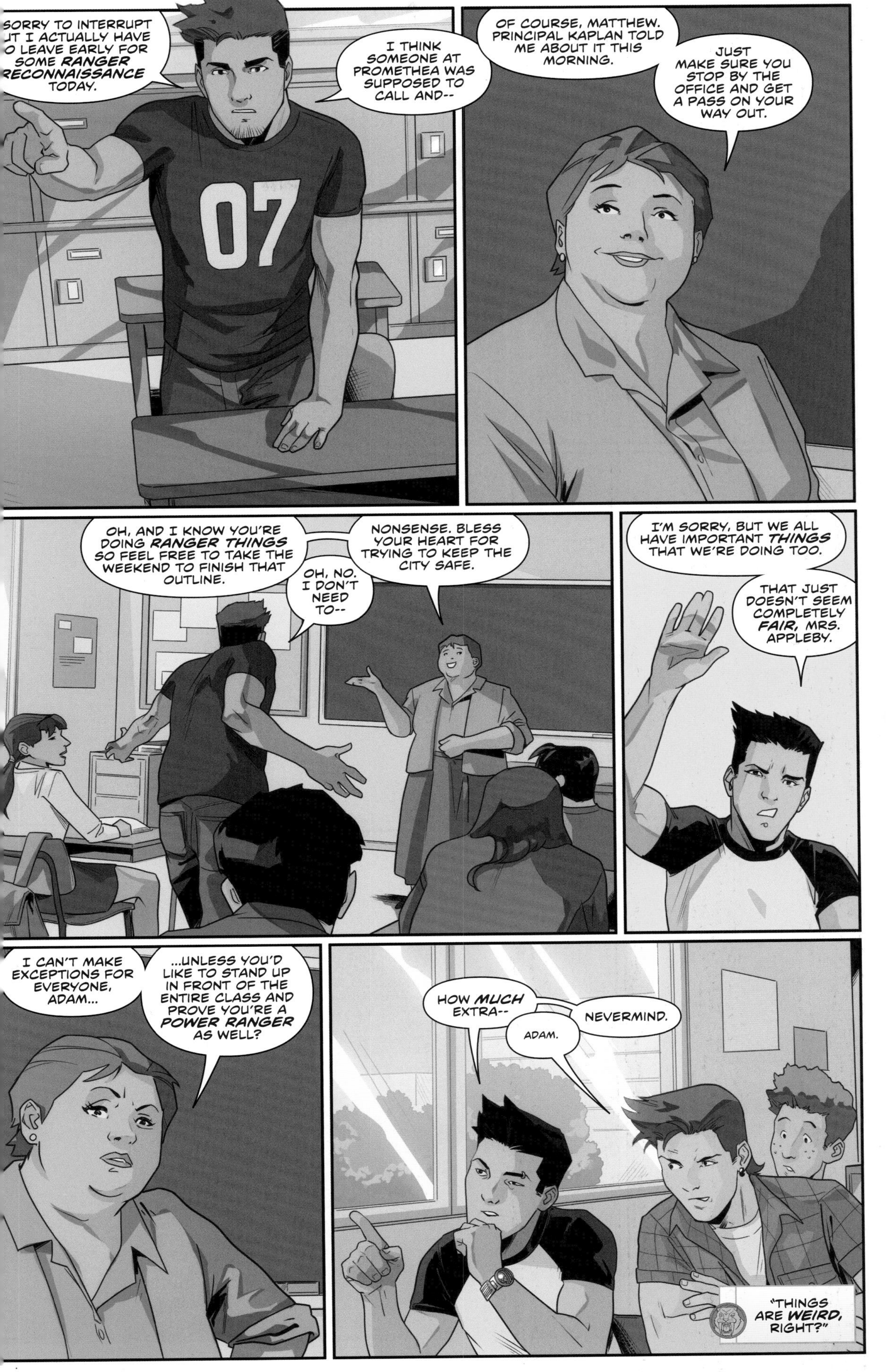
SORRY TO INTERRUPT BUT I ACTUALLY HAVE TO LEAVE EARLY FOR SOME RANGER RECONNAISSANCE TODAY.
I THINK SOMEONE AT PROMETHEA WAS SUPPOSED TO CALL AND--
OF COURSE, MATTHEW. PRINCIPAL KAPLAN TOLD ME ABOUT IT THIS MORNING.
JUST MAKE SURE YOU STOP BY THE OFFICE AND GET A PASS ON YOUR WAY OUT.
OH, AND I KNOW YOU'RE DOING RANGER THINGS SO FEEL FREE TO TAKE THE WEEKEND TO FINISH THAT OUTLINE.
OH, NO. I DON'T NEED TO--
NONSENSE. BLESS YOUR HEART FOR TRYING TO KEEP THE CITY SAFE.
I'M SORRY, BUT WE ALL HAVE IMPORTANT THINGS THAT WE'RE DOING TOO.
THAT JUST DOESN'T SEEM COMPLETELY FAIR, MRS. APPLEBY.
I CAN'T MAKE EXCEPTIONS FOR EVERYONE, ADAM...
...UNLESS YOU'D LIKE TO STAND UP IN FRONT OF THE ENTIRE CLASS AND PROVE YOU'RE A POWER RANGER AS WELL?
HOW MUCH EXTRA--
ADAM.
NEVERMIND.
"THINGS ARE WEIRD, RIGHT?"

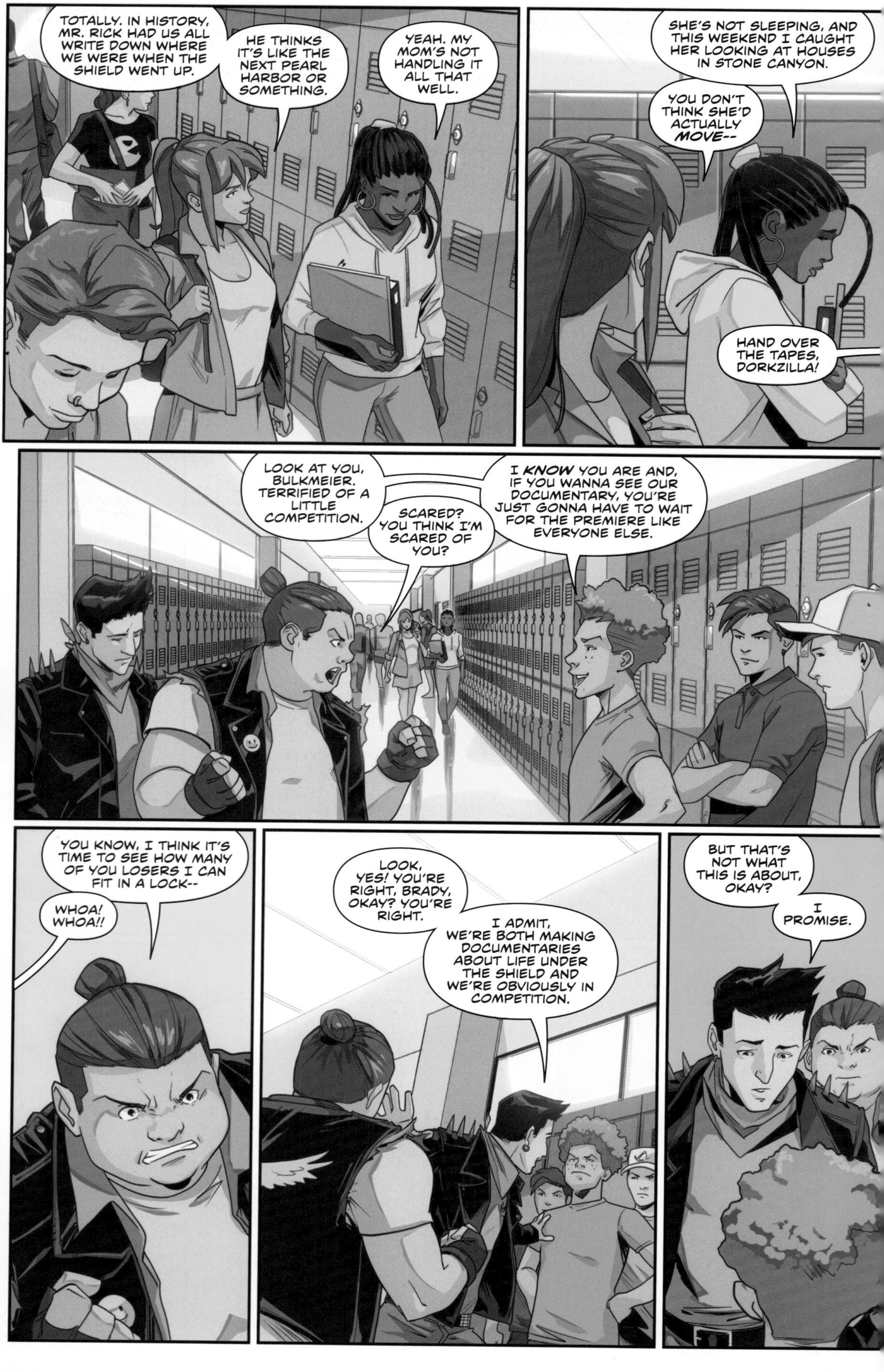
TOTALLY. IN HISTORY, MR. RICK HAD US ALL WRITE DOWN WHERE WE WERE WHEN THE SHIELD WENT UP.
HE THINKS IT'S LIKE THE NEXT PEARL HARBOR OR SOMETHING.
YEAH. MY MOM'S NOT HANDLING IT ALL THAT WELL.
SHE'S NOT SLEEPING, AND THIS WEEKEND I CAUGHT HER LOOKING AT HOUSES IN STONE CANYON.
YOU DON'T THINK SHE'D ACTUALLY *MOVE--*
HAND OVER THE TAPES, DORKZILLA!
LOOK AT YOU, BULKMEIER. TERRIFIED OF A LITTLE COMPETITION.
SCARED? YOU THINK I'M SCARED OF YOU?
I *KNOW* YOU ARE AND, IF YOU WANNA SEE OUR DOCUMENTARY, YOU'RE JUST GONNA HAVE TO WAIT FOR THE PREMIERE LIKE EVERYONE ELSE.
YOU KNOW, I THINK IT'S TIME TO SEE HOW MANY OF YOU LOSERS I CAN FIT IN A LOCK--
WHOA! WHOA!!
LOOK, YES! YOU'RE RIGHT, BRADY, OKAY? YOU'RE RIGHT.
I ADMIT, WE'RE BOTH MAKING DOCUMENTARIES ABOUT LIFE UNDER THE SHIELD AND WE'RE OBVIOUSLY IN COMPETITION.
BUT THAT'S NOT WHAT THIS IS ABOUT, OKAY?
I PROMISE.

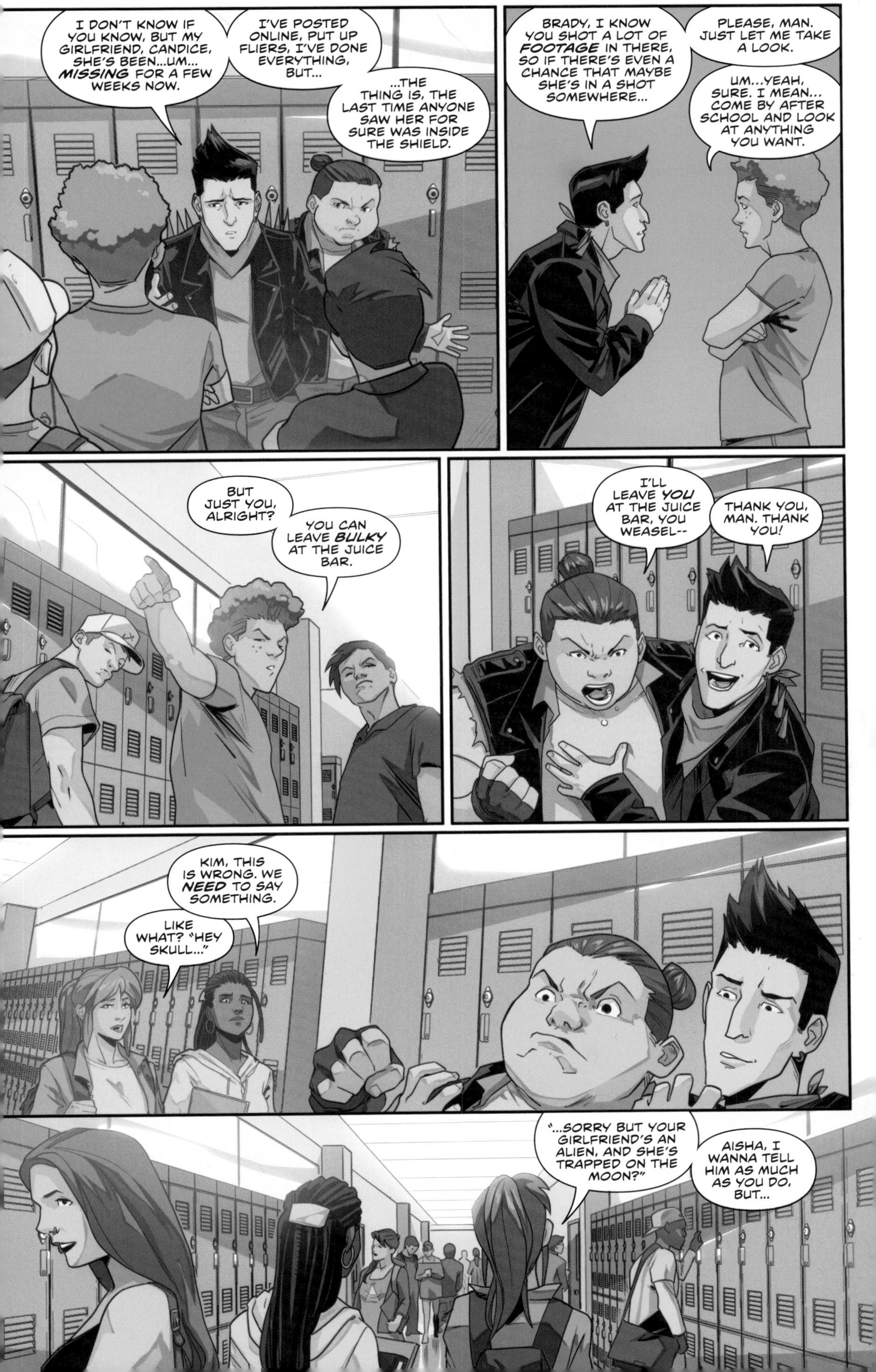
I DON'T KNOW IF YOU KNOW, BUT MY GIRLFRIEND, CANDICE, SHE'S BEEN...UM... MISSING FOR A FEW WEEKS NOW.
I'VE POSTED ONLINE, PUT UP FLIERS, I'VE DONE EVERYTHING, BUT...
...THE THING IS, THE LAST TIME ANYONE SAW HER FOR SURE WAS INSIDE THE SHIELD.
BRADY, I KNOW YOU SHOT A LOT OF FOOTAGE IN THERE, SO IF THERE'S EVEN A CHANCE THAT MAYBE SHE'S IN A SHOT SOMEWHERE...
PLEASE, MAN. JUST LET ME TAKE A LOOK.
UM...YEAH, SURE. I MEAN... COME BY AFTER SCHOOL AND LOOK AT ANYTHING YOU WANT.
BUT JUST YOU, ALRIGHT?
YOU CAN LEAVE BULKY AT THE JUICE BAR.
I'LL LEAVE YOU AT THE JUICE BAR, YOU WEASEL--
THANK YOU, MAN. THANK YOU!
KIM, THIS IS WRONG. WE NEED TO SAY SOMETHING.
LIKE WHAT? "HEY SKULL..."
"...SORRY BUT YOUR GIRLFRIEND'S AN ALIEN, AND SHE'S TRAPPED ON THE MOON?"
AISHA, I WANNA TELL HIM AS MUCH AS YOU DO, BUT...

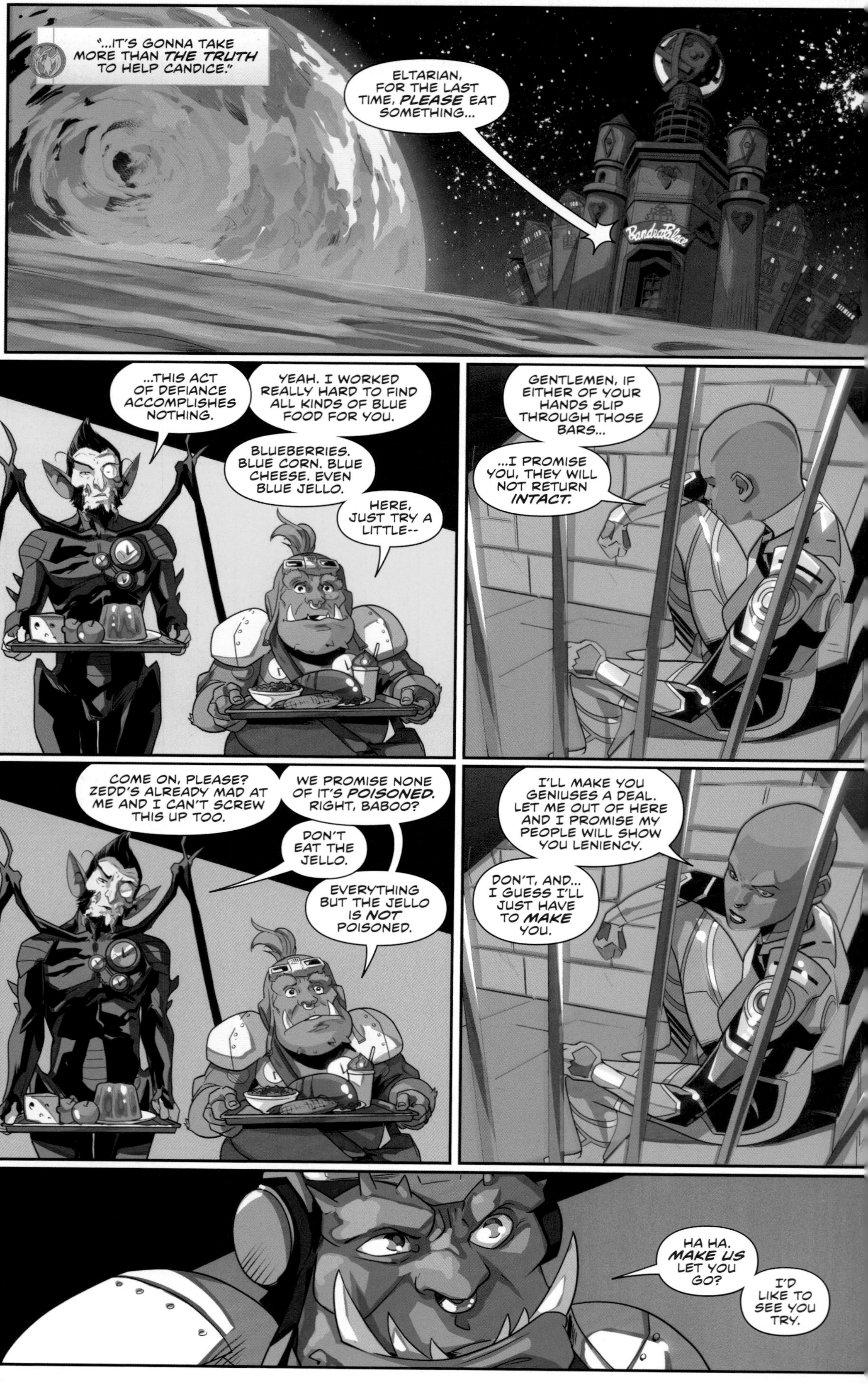
"...IT'S GONNA TAKE MORE THAN THE TRUTH TO HELP CANDICE."
ELTARIAN, FOR THE LAST TIME, PLEASE EAT SOMETHING...
BandeaPalace
...THIS ACT OF DEFIANCE ACCOMPLISHES NOTHING.
YEAH. I WORKED REALLY HARD TO FIND ALL KINDS OF BLUE FOOD FOR YOU.
BLUEBERRIES. BLUE CORN. BLUE CHEESE. EVEN BLUE JELLO.
HERE, JUST TRY A LITTLE--
GENTLEMEN, IF EITHER OF YOUR HANDS SLIP THROUGH THOSE BARS...
...I PROMISE YOU, THEY WILL NOT RETURN INTACT.
COME ON, PLEASE? ZEDD'S ALREADY MAD AT ME AND I CAN'T SCREW THIS UP TOO.
WE PROMISE NONE OF IT'S POISONED. RIGHT, BABOO?
DON'T EAT THE JELLO.
EVERYTHING BUT THE JELLO IS NOT POISONED.
I'LL MAKE YOU GENIUSES A DEAL. LET ME OUT OF HERE AND I PROMISE MY PEOPLE WILL SHOW YOU LENIENCY.
DON'T, AND... I GUESS I'LL JUST HAVE TO MAKE YOU.
HA HA. MAKE US LET YOU GO?
I'D LIKE TO SEE YOU TRY.

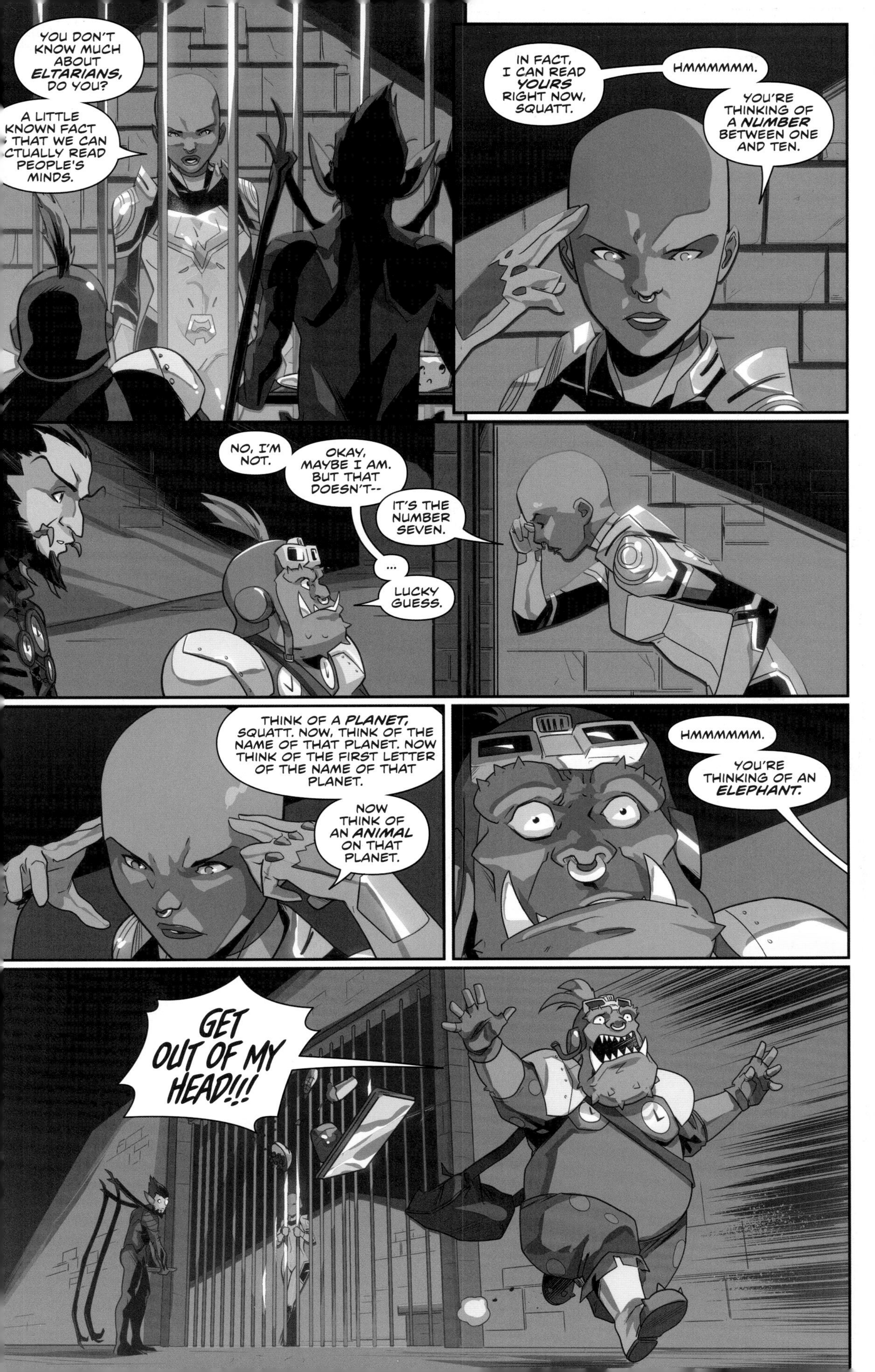
YOU DON'T KNOW MUCH ABOUT ELTARIANS, DO YOU?
A LITTLE KNOWN FACT IS THAT WE CAN ACTUALLY READ PEOPLE'S MINDS.
IN FACT, I CAN READ YOURS RIGHT NOW, SQUATT.
HMMMMMM.
YOU'RE THINKING OF A NUMBER BETWEEN ONE AND TEN.
NO, I'M NOT.
OKAY, MAYBE I AM. BUT THAT DOESN'T--
IT'S THE NUMBER SEVEN.
...
LUCKY GUESS.
THINK OF A PLANET, SQUATT. NOW, THINK OF THE NAME OF THAT PLANET. NOW THINK OF THE FIRST LETTER OF THE NAME OF THAT PLANET.
NOW THINK OF AN ANIMAL ON THAT PLANET.
HMMMMMM.
YOU'RE THINKING OF AN ELEPHANT.
GET OUT OF MY HEAD!!!

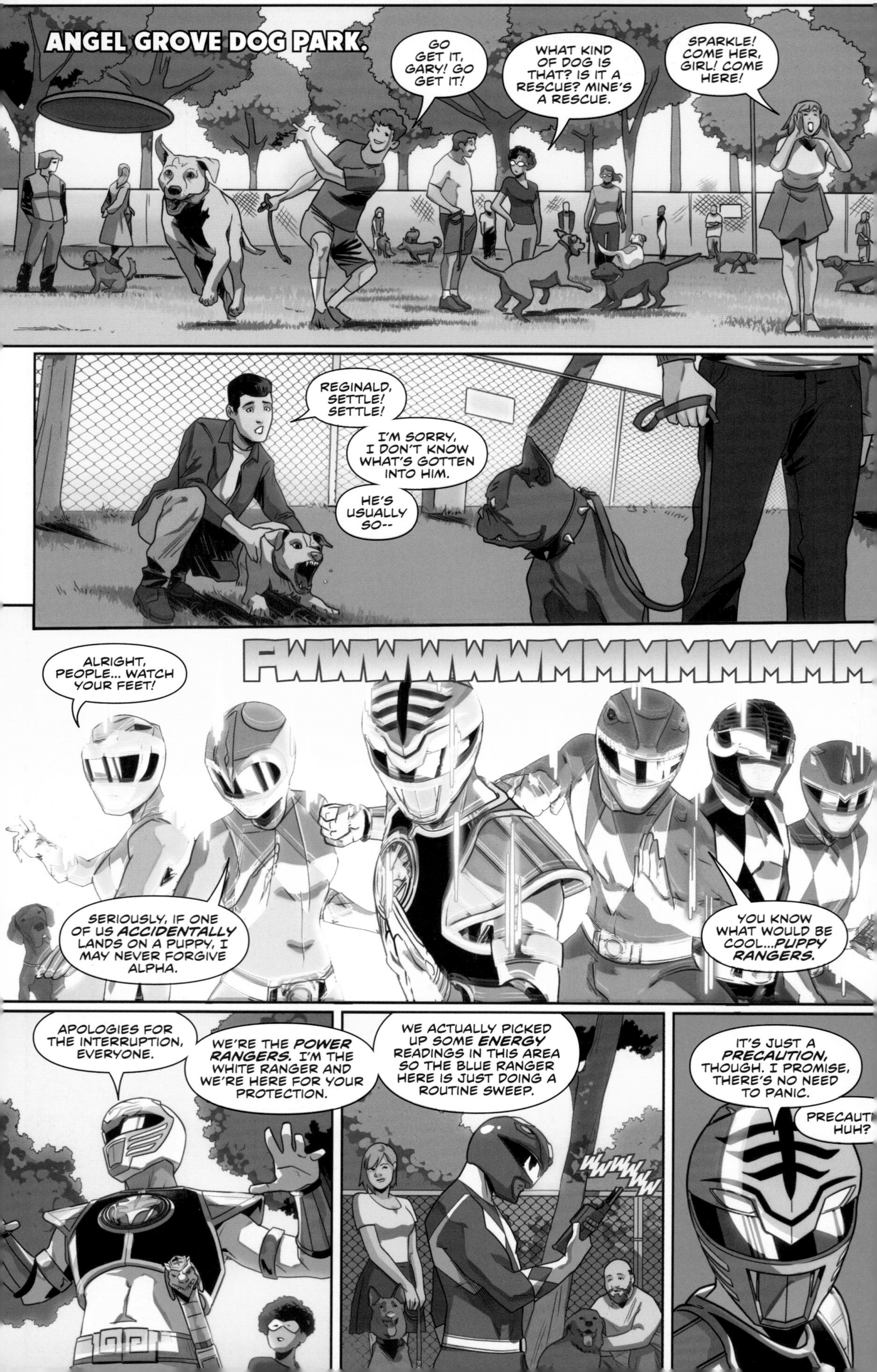

ANGEL GROVE DOG PARK.
GO GET IT, GARY! GO GET IT!
WHAT KIND OF DOG IS THAT? IS IT A RESCUE? MINE'S A RESCUE.
SPARKLE! COME HER, GIRL! COME HERE!
REGINALD, SETTLE! SETTLE!
I'M SORRY, I DON'T KNOW WHAT'S GOTTEN INTO HIM.
HE'S USUALLY SO--
FWWWWWWWMMMMMMMMM
ALRIGHT, PEOPLE... WATCH YOUR FEET!
SERIOUSLY, IF ONE OF US ACCIDENTALLY LANDS ON A PUPPY, I MAY NEVER FORGIVE ALPHA.
YOU KNOW WHAT WOULD BE COOL...PUPPY RANGERS.
APOLOGIES FOR THE INTERRUPTION, EVERYONE.
WE'RE THE POWER RANGERS. I'M THE WHITE RANGER AND WE'RE HERE FOR YOUR PROTECTION.
WE ACTUALLY PICKED UP SOME ENERGY READINGS IN THIS AREA SO THE BLUE RANGER HERE IS JUST DOING A ROUTINE SWEEP.
WWWWWW
IT'S JUST A PRECAUTION, THOUGH. I PROMISE, THERE'S NO NEED TO PANIC.
PRECAUT HUH?

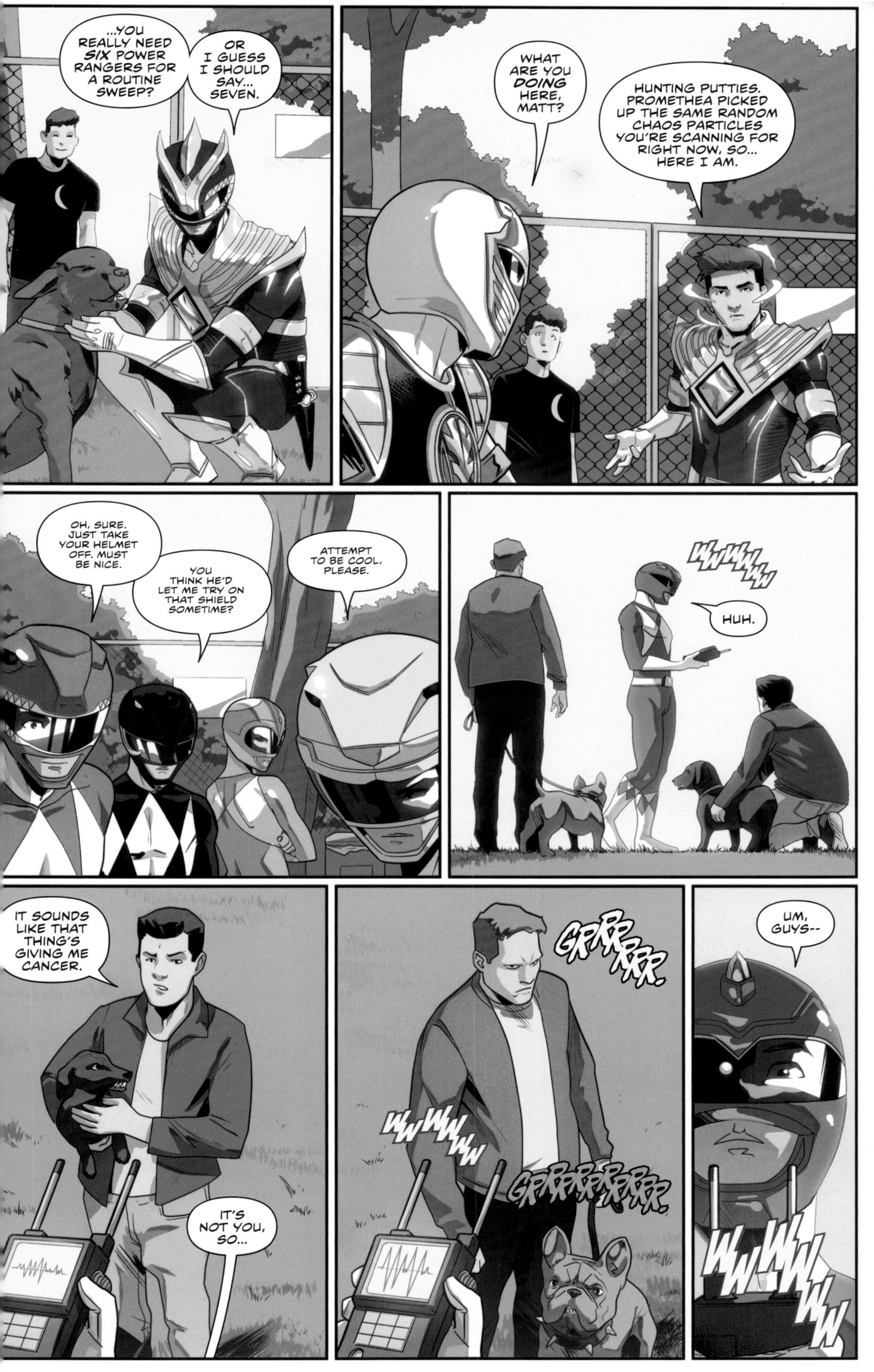
...YOU REALLY NEED SIX POWER RANGERS FOR A ROUTINE SWEEP?
OR I GUESS I SHOULD SAY... SEVEN.
WHAT ARE YOU DOING HERE, MATT?
HUNTING PUTTIES. PROMETHEA PICKED UP THE SAME RANDOM CHAOS PARTICLES YOU'RE SCANNING FOR RIGHT NOW, SO... HERE I AM.
OH, SURE. JUST TAKE YOUR HELMET OFF. MUST BE NICE.
YOU THINK HE'D LET ME TRY ON THAT SHIELD SOMETIME?
ATTEMPT TO BE COOL, PLEASE.
WWWWWW
HUH.
IT SOUNDS LIKE THAT THING'S GIVING ME CANCER.
IT'S NOT YOU, SO...
GRRRRRR.
WWWWWW
GRRRRRRRRRR.
UM, GUYS--
WWWWWW

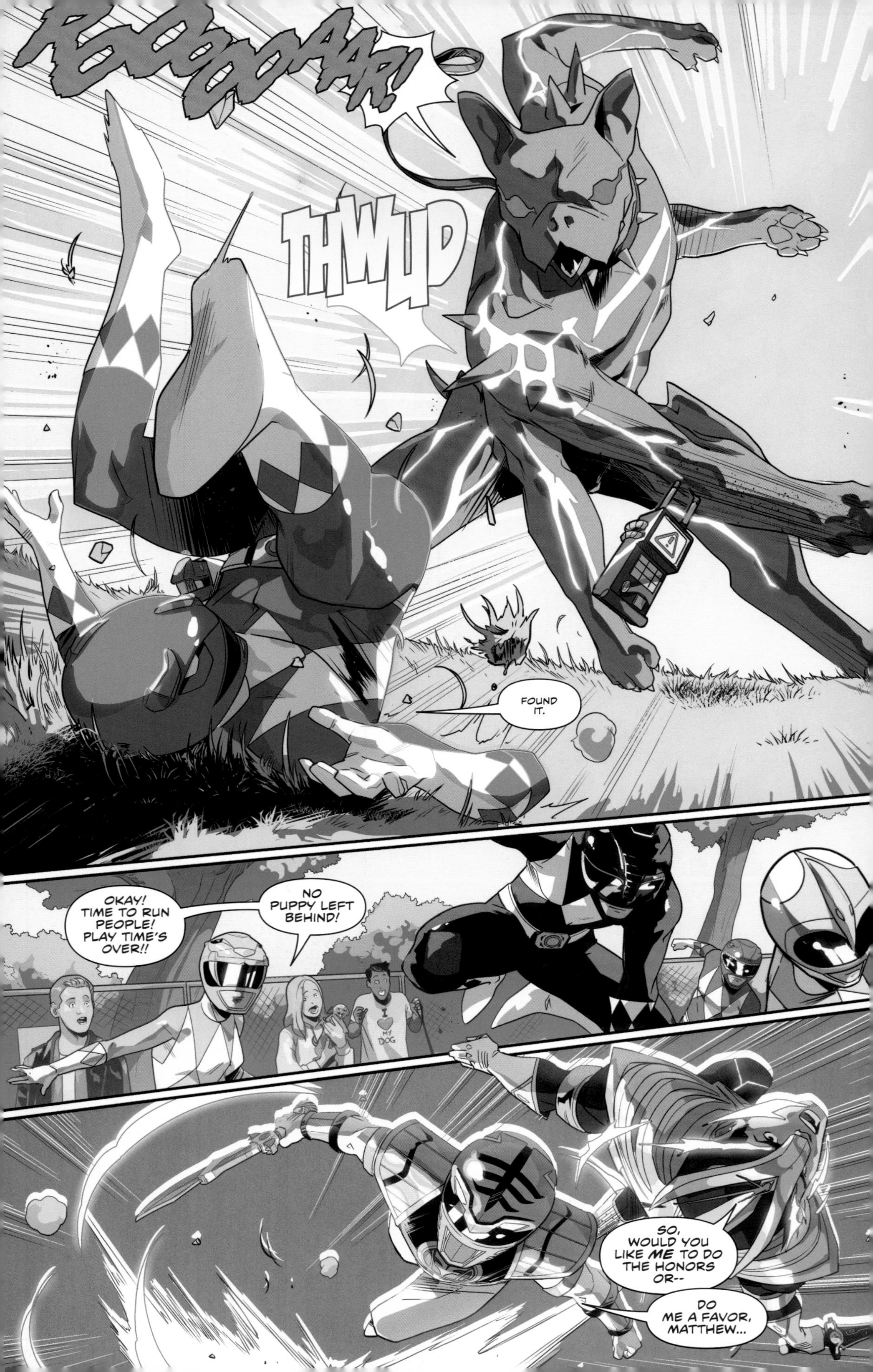
REOOOOOAAR!
THWUD
FOUND IT.
OKAY! TIME TO RUN PEOPLE! PLAY TIME'S OVER!!
NO PUPPY LEFT BEHIND!
I ♥ MY DOG
SO, WOULD YOU LIKE ME TO DO THE HONORS OR--
DO ME A FAVOR, MATTHEW...

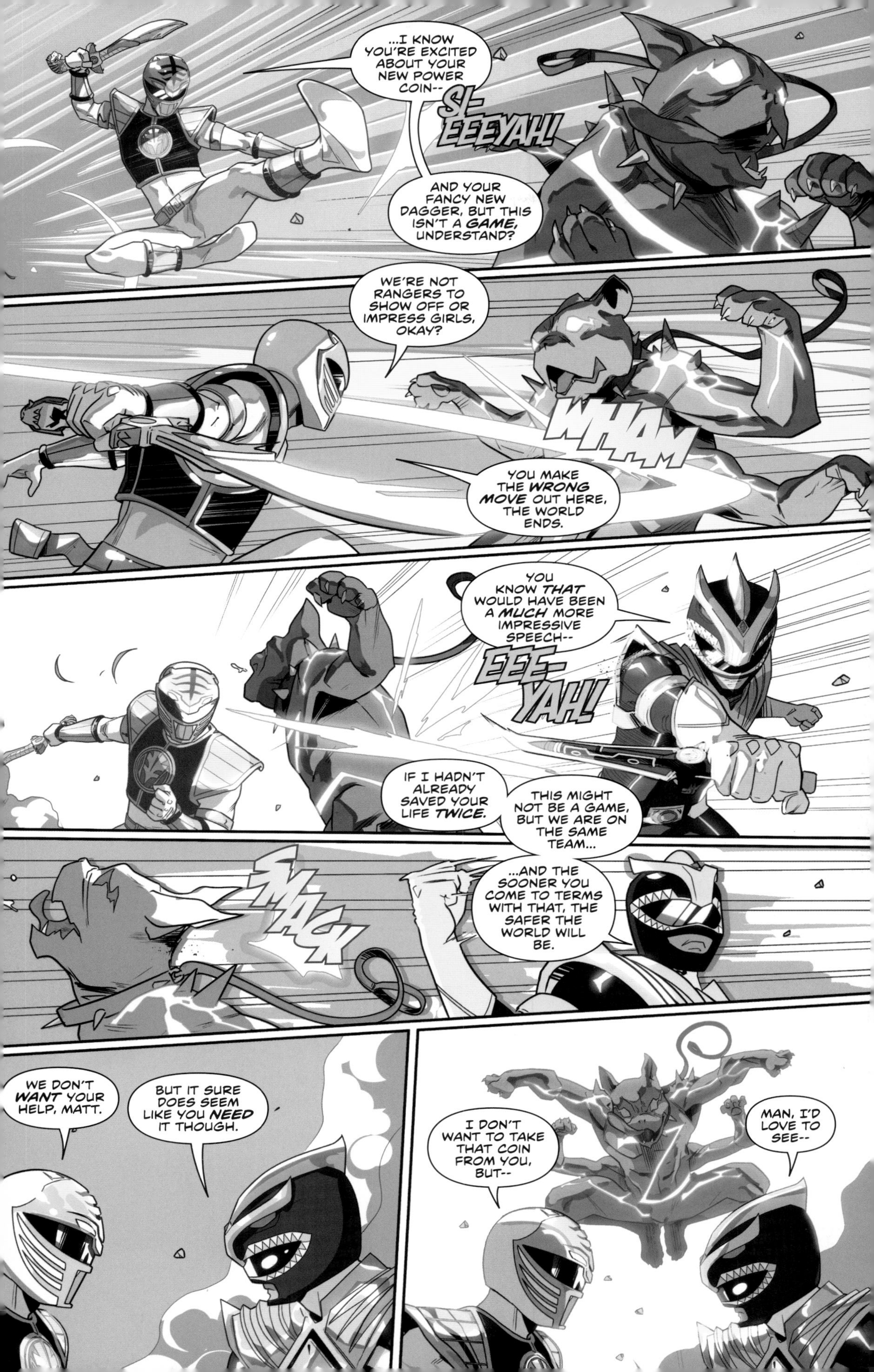
...I KNOW YOU'RE EXCITED ABOUT YOUR NEW POWER COIN--
SI-EEEYAH!
AND YOUR FANCY NEW DAGGER, BUT THIS ISN'T A GAME, UNDERSTAND?
WE'RE NOT RANGERS TO SHOW OFF OR IMPRESS GIRLS, OKAY?
WHAM
YOU MAKE THE WRONG MOVE OUT HERE, THE WORLD ENDS.
YOU KNOW THAT WOULD HAVE BEEN A MUCH MORE IMPRESSIVE SPEECH--
EEE-YAH!
IF I HADN'T ALREADY SAVED YOUR LIFE TWICE.
THIS MIGHT NOT BE A GAME, BUT WE ARE ON THE SAME TEAM...
SMACK
...AND THE SOONER YOU COME TO TERMS WITH THAT, THE SAFER THE WORLD WILL BE.
WE DON'T WANT YOUR HELP, MATT.
BUT IT SURE DOES SEEM LIKE YOU NEED IT THOUGH.
I DON'T WANT TO TAKE THAT COIN FROM YOU, BUT--
MAN, I'D LOVE TO SEE--

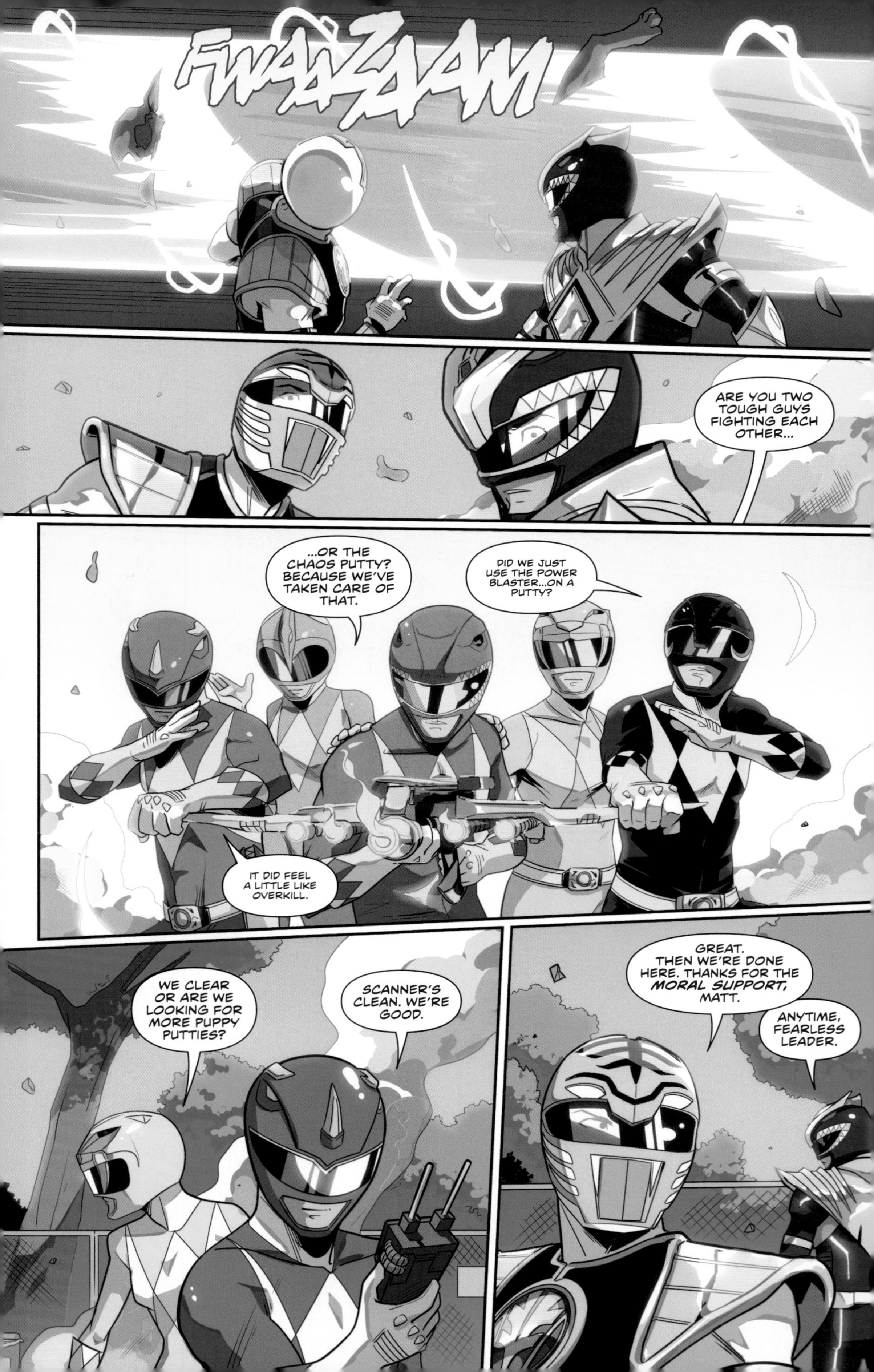
FWAAZAAM
ARE YOU TWO TOUGH GUYS FIGHTING EACH OTHER...
...OR THE CHAOS PUTTY? BECAUSE WE'VE TAKEN CARE OF THAT.
DID WE JUST USE THE POWER BLASTER...ON A PUTTY?
IT DID FEEL A LITTLE LIKE OVERKILL.
WE CLEAR OR ARE WE LOOKING FOR MORE PUPPY PUTTIES?
SCANNER'S CLEAN. WE'RE GOOD.
GREAT. THEN WE'RE DONE HERE. THANKS FOR THE *MORAL SUPPORT,* MATT.
ANYTIME, FEARLESS LEADER.

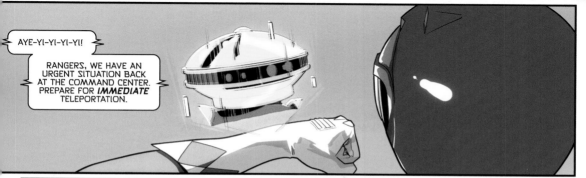

AYE-YI-YI-YI-YI!

RANGERS, WE HAVE AN URGENT SITUATION BACK AT THE COMMAND CENTER. PREPARE FOR *IMMEDIATE* TELEPORTATION.

LATER, DRAGON DUDE.

THAT WAS WAY TOO MUCH DRAMA FOR ONE PUTTY.

YEAH, I CAN'T IMAGINE WHAT THAT WAS *ACTUALLY* ABOUT.

FWWWWWWWMMMMMMM

HUH.

SO THIS... UM...*ZORGON* GUY'S STILL PISSED AT YOU, HUH?

ZORDON.

RIGHT... AND THAT'S BECAUSE OF *ME*?

...

NO, IT'S BECAUSE OF ME.

"RANGERS, AFTER MUCH DELIBERATION..."

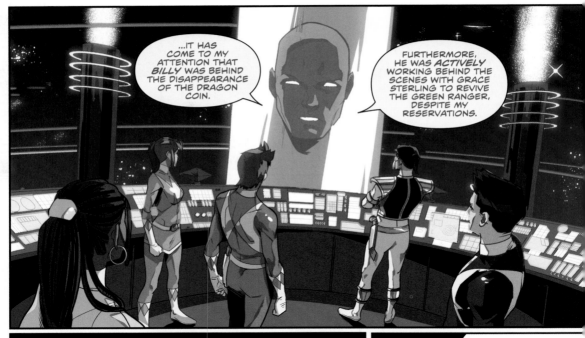

...IT HAS COME TO MY ATTENTION THAT *BILLY* WAS BEHIND THE DISAPPEARANCE OF THE DRAGON COIN.

FURTHERMORE, HE WAS *ACTIVELY* WORKING BEHIND THE SCENES WITH GRACE STERLING TO REVIVE THE GREEN RANGER, DESPITE MY RESERVATIONS.

WHAT? BILLY...BUT...NO. I MEAN...NO, RIGHT?

WHOA.

AND WE'RE 100% SURE ABOUT THIS? THERE'S NO WAY--

IT'S TRUE. I SAW HIM TALKING TO THE GREEN RANGER AT *ANGEL GROVE*, AND WHEN I CONFRONTED HIM ABOUT IT...

...HE ADMITTED IT.

REALLY?

AND YOU DIDN'T FEEL *THE REST OF US* NEEDED TO KNOW THAT?

IT'S BILLY. I GAVE HIM THE BENEFIT OF THE DOUBT.

PLUS, I TOLD HIM HE HAD TO COME FORWARD...OR I WOULD.

WHOA, HOLD ON. I MEAN, I KNOW THIS KINDA LOOKS BAD, BUT...

...SHOULDN'T BILLY BE HERE TO DEFEND HIMSELF?

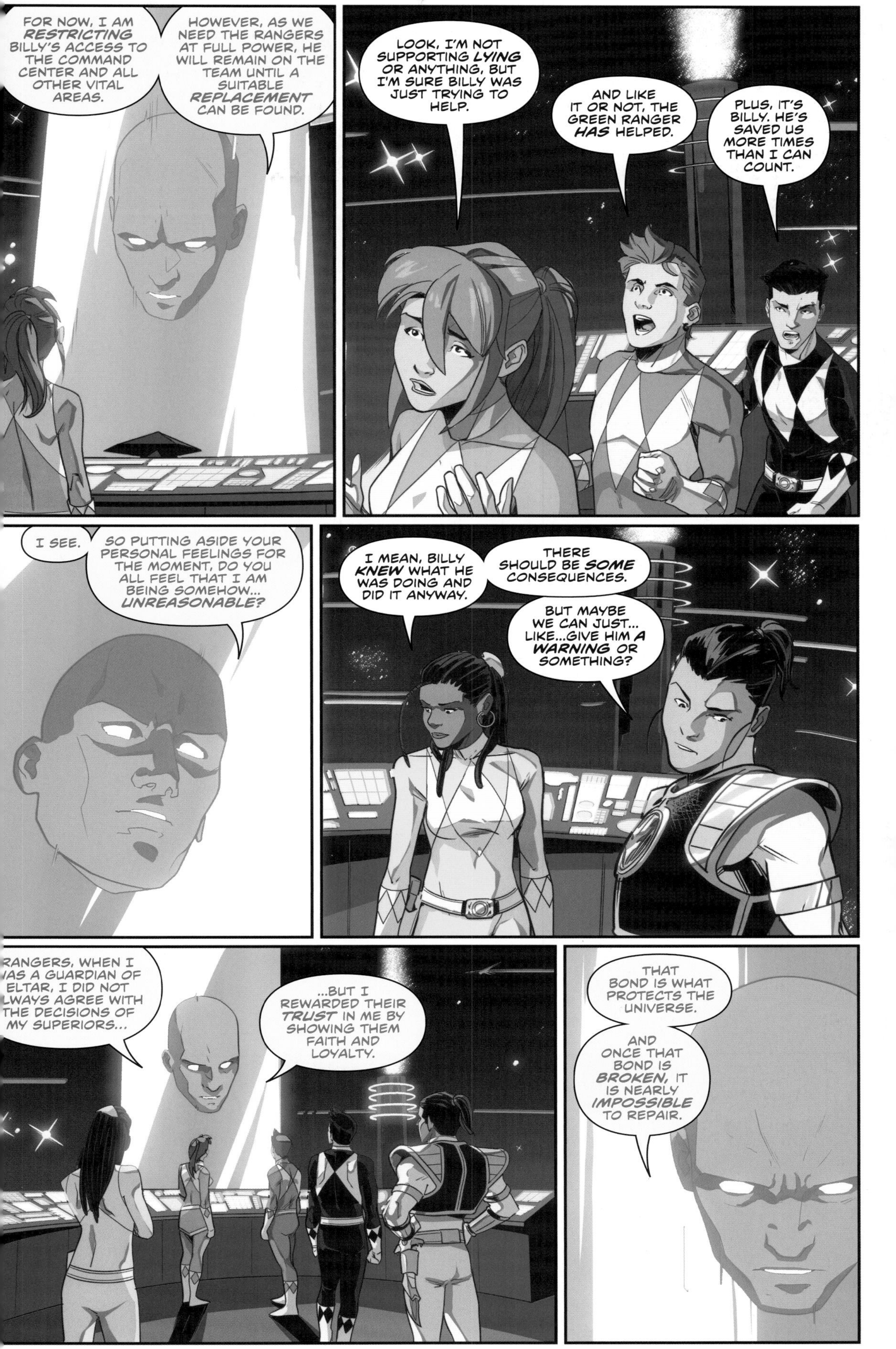
FOR NOW, I AM RESTRICTING BILLY'S ACCESS TO THE COMMAND CENTER AND ALL OTHER VITAL AREAS.
HOWEVER, AS WE NEED THE RANGERS AT FULL POWER, HE WILL REMAIN ON THE TEAM UNTIL A SUITABLE REPLACEMENT CAN BE FOUND.
LOOK, I'M NOT SUPPORTING LYING OR ANYTHING, BUT I'M SURE BILLY WAS JUST TRYING TO HELP.
AND LIKE IT OR NOT, THE GREEN RANGER HAS HELPED.
PLUS, IT'S BILLY. HE'S SAVED US MORE TIMES THAN I CAN COUNT.
I SEE.
SO PUTTING ASIDE YOUR PERSONAL FEELINGS FOR THE MOMENT, DO YOU ALL FEEL THAT I AM BEING SOMEHOW... UNREASONABLE?
I MEAN, BILLY KNEW WHAT HE WAS DOING AND DID IT ANYWAY.
THERE SHOULD BE SOME CONSEQUENCES.
BUT MAYBE WE CAN JUST... LIKE...GIVE HIM A WARNING OR SOMETHING?
RANGERS, WHEN I WAS A GUARDIAN OF ELTAR, I DID NOT ALWAYS AGREE WITH THE DECISIONS OF MY SUPERIORS...
...BUT I REWARDED THEIR TRUST IN ME BY SHOWING THEM FAITH AND LOYALTY.
THAT BOND IS WHAT PROTECTS THE UNIVERSE.
AND ONCE THAT BOND IS BROKEN, IT IS NEARLY IMPOSSIBLE TO REPAIR.

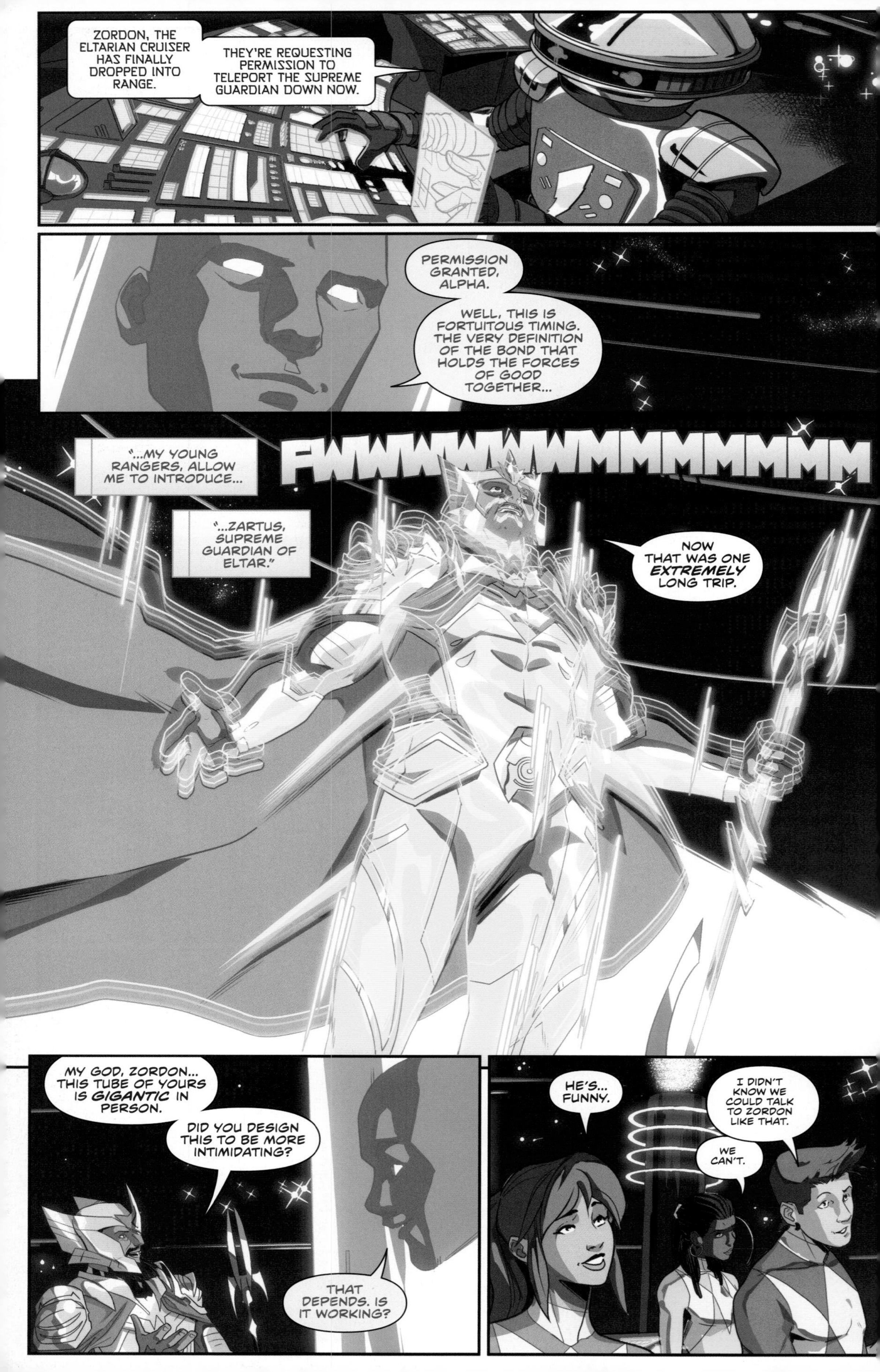
ZORDON, THE ELTARIAN CRUISER HAS FINALLY DROPPED INTO RANGE.
THEY'RE REQUESTING PERMISSION TO TELEPORT THE SUPREME GUARDIAN DOWN NOW.
PERMISSION GRANTED, ALPHA.
WELL, THIS IS FORTUITOUS TIMING. THE VERY DEFINITION OF THE BOND THAT HOLDS THE FORCES OF GOOD TOGETHER...
"...MY YOUNG RANGERS, ALLOW ME TO INTRODUCE...
FWWWWWWMMMMMMMM
"...ZARTUS, SUPREME GUARDIAN OF ELTAR."
NOW THAT WAS ONE *EXTREMELY* LONG TRIP.
MY GOD, ZORDON... THIS TUBE OF YOURS IS *GIGANTIC* IN PERSON.
DID YOU DESIGN THIS TO BE MORE INTIMIDATING?
THAT DEPENDS. IS IT WORKING?
HE'S... FUNNY.
I DIDN'T KNOW WE COULD TALK TO ZORDON LIKE THAT.
WE CAN'T.

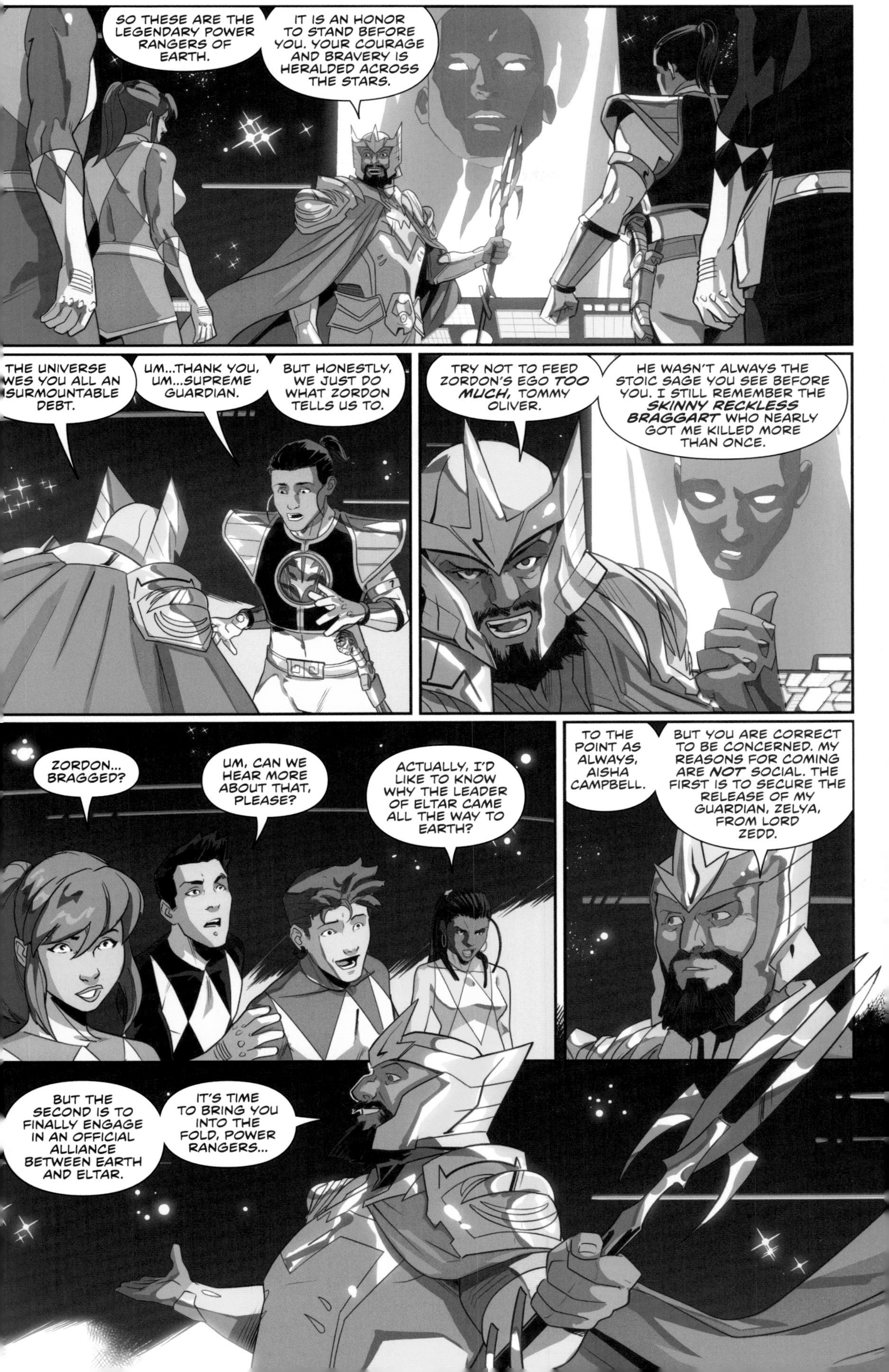
SO THESE ARE THE LEGENDARY POWER RANGERS OF EARTH.
IT IS AN HONOR TO STAND BEFORE YOU. YOUR COURAGE AND BRAVERY IS HERALDED ACROSS THE STARS.
THE UNIVERSE WES YOU ALL AN SURMOUNTABLE DEBT.
UM...THANK YOU, UM...SUPREME GUARDIAN.
BUT HONESTLY, WE JUST DO WHAT ZORDON TELLS US TO.
TRY NOT TO FEED ZORDON'S EGO TOO MUCH, TOMMY OLIVER.
HE WASN'T ALWAYS THE STOIC SAGE YOU SEE BEFORE YOU. I STILL REMEMBER THE SKINNY RECKLESS BRAGGART WHO NEARLY GOT ME KILLED MORE THAN ONCE.
ZORDON... BRAGGED?
UM, CAN WE HEAR MORE ABOUT THAT, PLEASE?
ACTUALLY, I'D LIKE TO KNOW WHY THE LEADER OF ELTAR CAME ALL THE WAY TO EARTH?
TO THE POINT AS ALWAYS, AISHA CAMPBELL.
BUT YOU ARE CORRECT TO BE CONCERNED. MY REASONS FOR COMING ARE NOT SOCIAL. THE FIRST IS TO SECURE THE RELEASE OF MY GUARDIAN, ZELYA, FROM LORD ZEDD.
BUT THE SECOND IS TO FINALLY ENGAGE IN AN OFFICIAL ALLIANCE BETWEEN EARTH AND ELTAR.
IT'S TIME TO BRING YOU INTO THE FOLD, POWER RANGERS...

"...YOU HAVE BEEN FIGHTING *ALONE* FOR TOO LONG."

FORTY-SIX, FORTY-SEVEN, FORTY-EIGHT...

YOU READY TO HAV ME READ YOUR MIN AGAIN, LITTLE BOY BLUE?

BY ALL MEANS, READ AWAY...

...BUT I'M FAIRLY CERTAIN YOU WON'T LIKE WHAT YOU FIND.

SQUATT IS A WORTHLESS LITTLE MORSEL OF A MINION, BUT YOU DIDN'T HAVE TO SCARE THE BOY SO BADLY.

IMAGINE IF I'D PULLED THE WHOLE DISAPPEARING THUMB TRICK.

I KNOW WHO YOU ARE, CANDICE. OR SHOULD I SAY...

...ZELYA OF ELTAR.

THEN YOU SHOULD HAVE KNOWN BETTER TO COME IN HERE ALONE AND UNARMED.

BECAUSE I KNOW A FEW *REAL* MAGIC TRICKS--

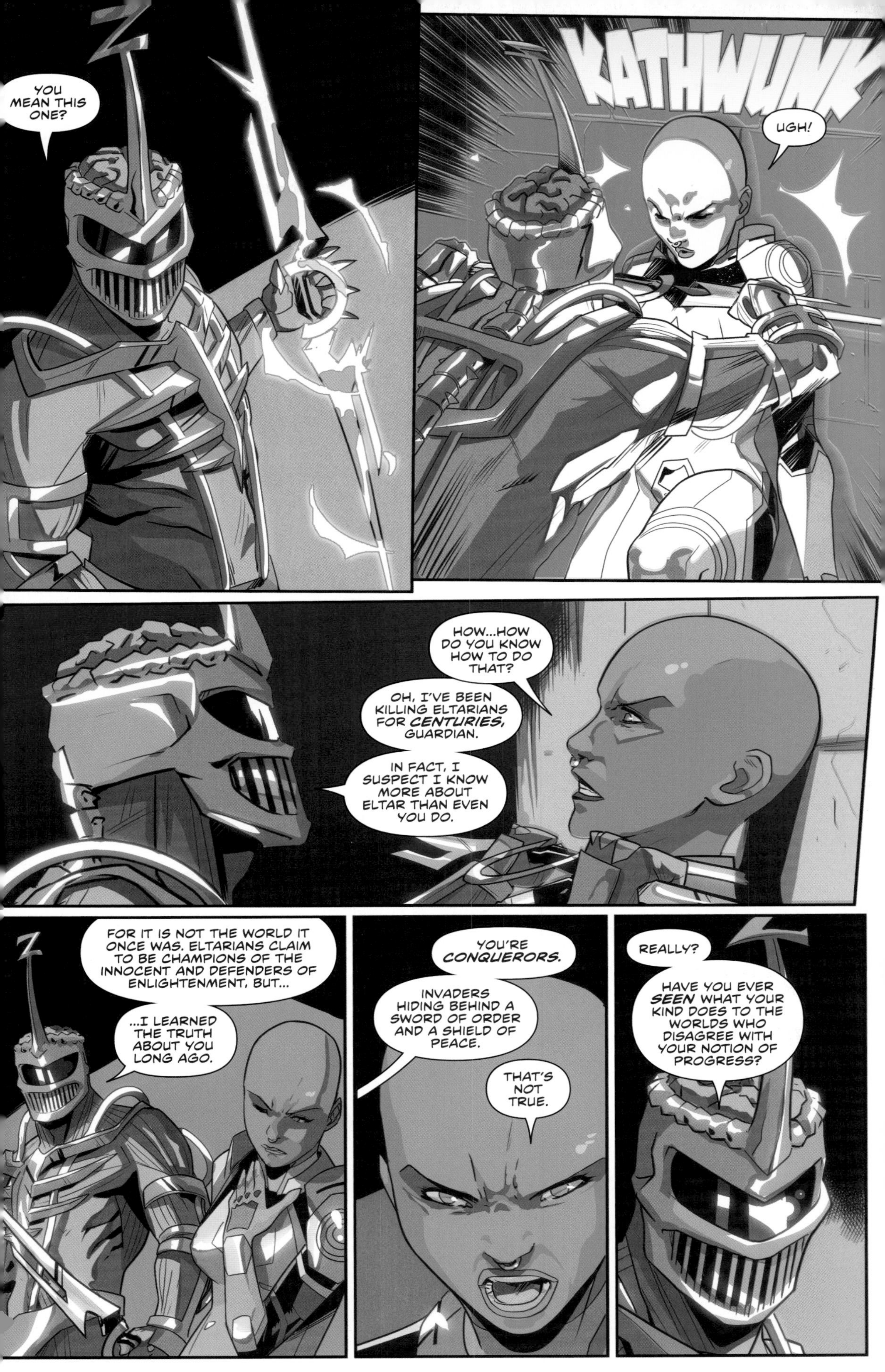
YOU MEAN THIS ONE?
KATHWUNK
UGH!
HOW...HOW DO YOU KNOW HOW TO DO THAT?
OH, I'VE BEEN KILLING ELTARIANS FOR CENTURIES, GUARDIAN.
IN FACT, I SUSPECT I KNOW MORE ABOUT ELTAR THAN EVEN YOU DO.
FOR IT IS NOT THE WORLD IT ONCE WAS. ELTARIANS CLAIM TO BE CHAMPIONS OF THE INNOCENT AND DEFENDERS OF ENLIGHTENMENT, BUT...
...I LEARNED THE TRUTH ABOUT YOU LONG AGO.
YOU'RE CONQUERORS.
INVADERS HIDING BEHIND A SWORD OF ORDER AND A SHIELD OF PEACE.
THAT'S NOT TRUE.
REALLY?
HAVE YOU EVER SEEN WHAT YOUR KIND DOES TO THE WORLDS WHO DISAGREE WITH YOUR NOTION OF PROGRESS?

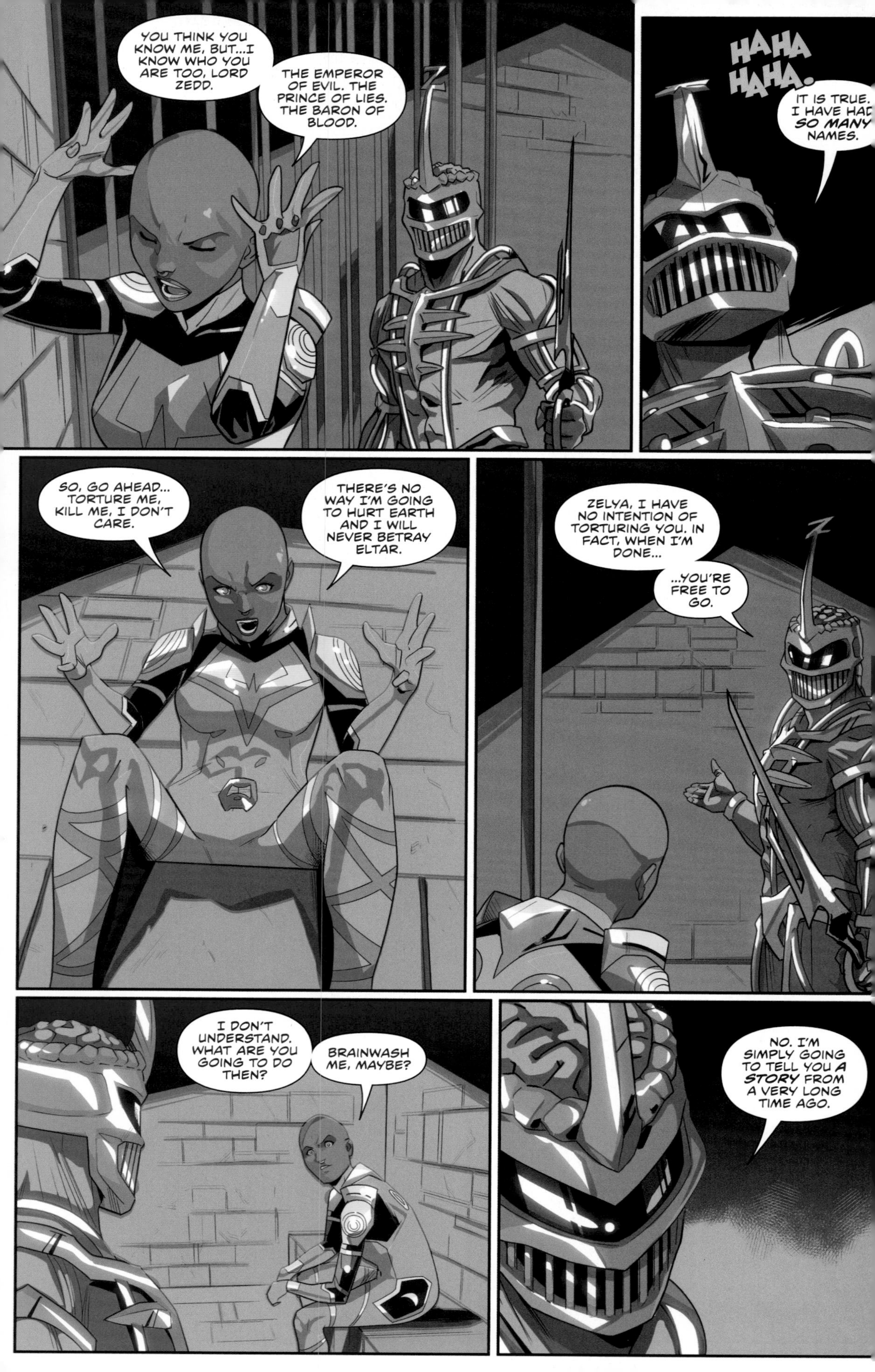
YOU THINK YOU KNOW ME, BUT...I KNOW WHO YOU ARE TOO, LORD ZEDD.
THE EMPEROR OF EVIL. THE PRINCE OF LIES. THE BARON OF BLOOD.
HAHA HAHA.
IT IS TRUE. I HAVE HAD SO MANY NAMES.
SO, GO AHEAD... TORTURE ME, KILL ME, I DON'T CARE.
THERE'S NO WAY I'M GOING TO HURT EARTH AND I WILL NEVER BETRAY ELTAR.
ZELYA, I HAVE NO INTENTION OF TORTURING YOU. IN FACT, WHEN I'M DONE...
...YOU'RE FREE TO GO.
I DON'T UNDERSTAND. WHAT ARE YOU GOING TO DO THEN?
BRAINWASH ME, MAYBE?
NO. I'M SIMPLY GOING TO TELL YOU A STORY FROM A VERY LONG TIME AGO.

CHAPTER TEN

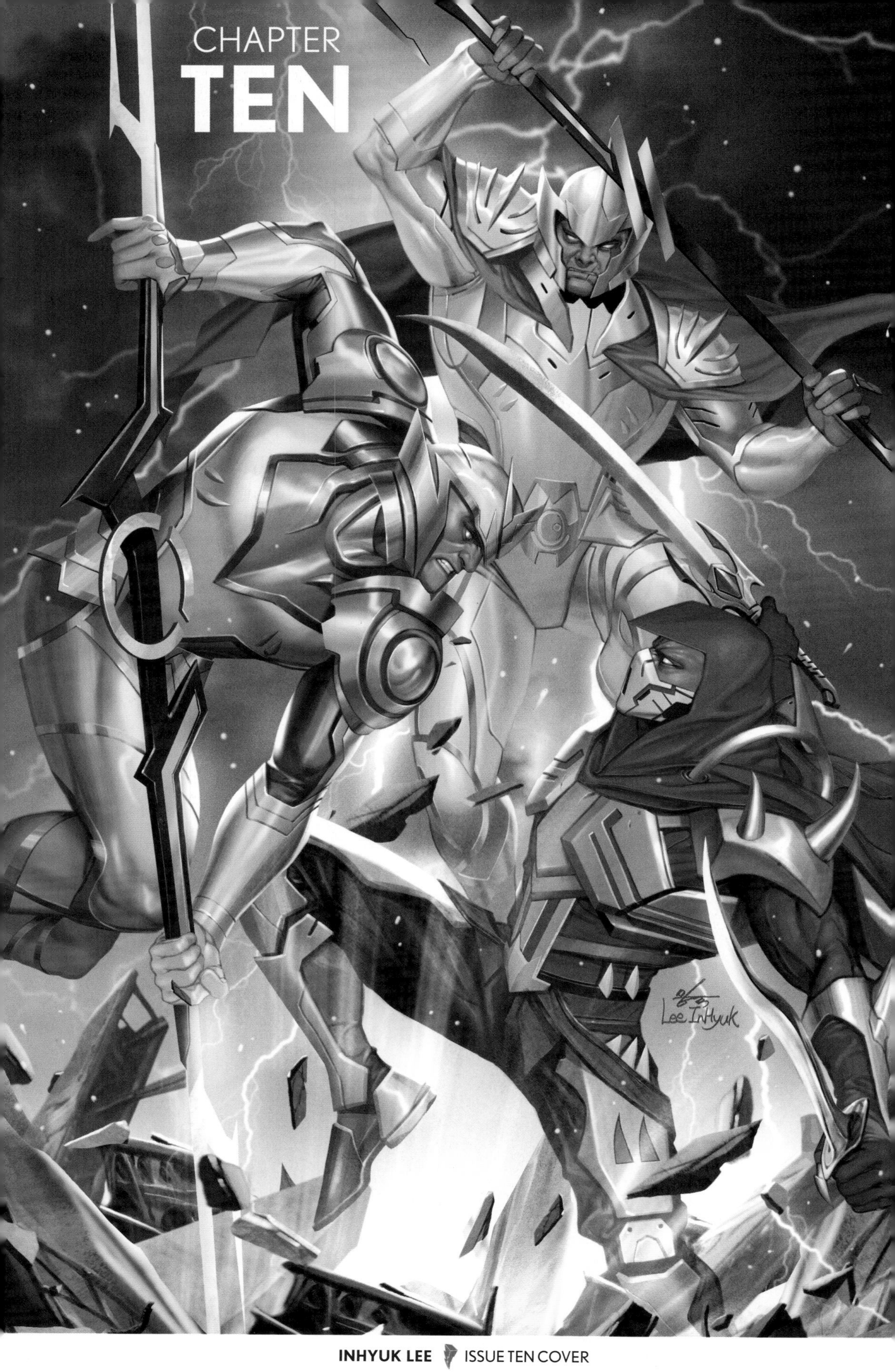
Lee InHyuk

INHYUK LEE | ISSUE TEN COVER

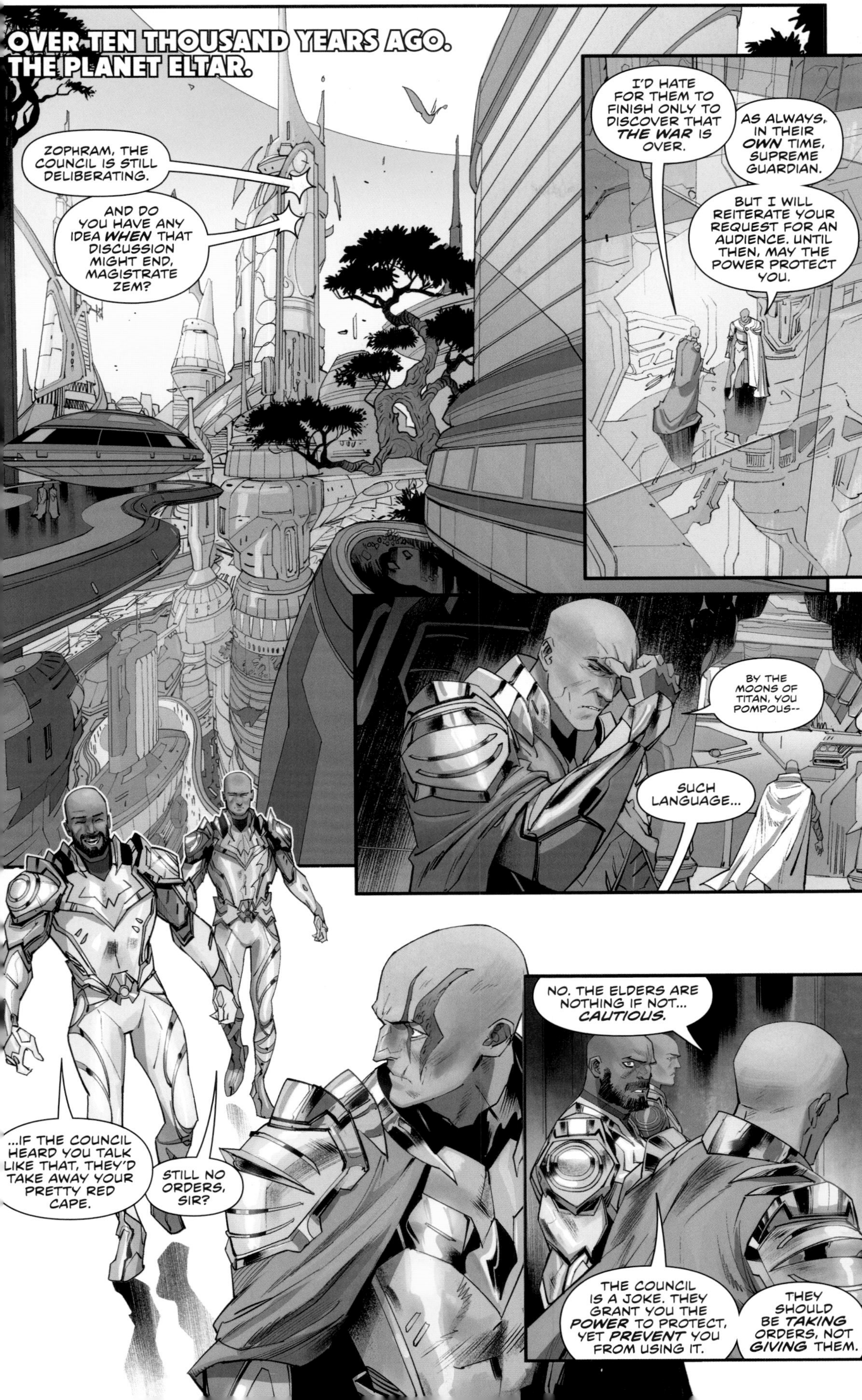
OVER TEN THOUSAND YEARS AGO. THE PLANET ELTAR.
ZOPHRAM, THE COUNCIL IS STILL DELIBERATING.
AND DO YOU HAVE ANY IDEA WHEN THAT DISCUSSION MIGHT END, MAGISTRATE ZEM?
I'D HATE FOR THEM TO FINISH ONLY TO DISCOVER THAT THE WAR IS OVER.
AS ALWAYS, IN THEIR OWN TIME, SUPREME GUARDIAN.
BUT I WILL REITERATE YOUR REQUEST FOR AN AUDIENCE. UNTIL THEN, MAY THE POWER PROTECT YOU.
BY THE MOONS OF TITAN, YOU POMPOUS--
SUCH LANGUAGE...
...IF THE COUNCIL HEARD YOU TALK LIKE THAT, THEY'D TAKE AWAY YOUR PRETTY RED CAPE.
STILL NO ORDERS, SIR?
NO. THE ELDERS ARE NOTHING IF NOT... CAUTIOUS.
THE COUNCIL IS A JOKE. THEY GRANT YOU THE POWER TO PROTECT, YET PREVENT YOU FROM USING IT.
THEY SHOULD BE TAKING ORDERS, NOT GIVING THEM.

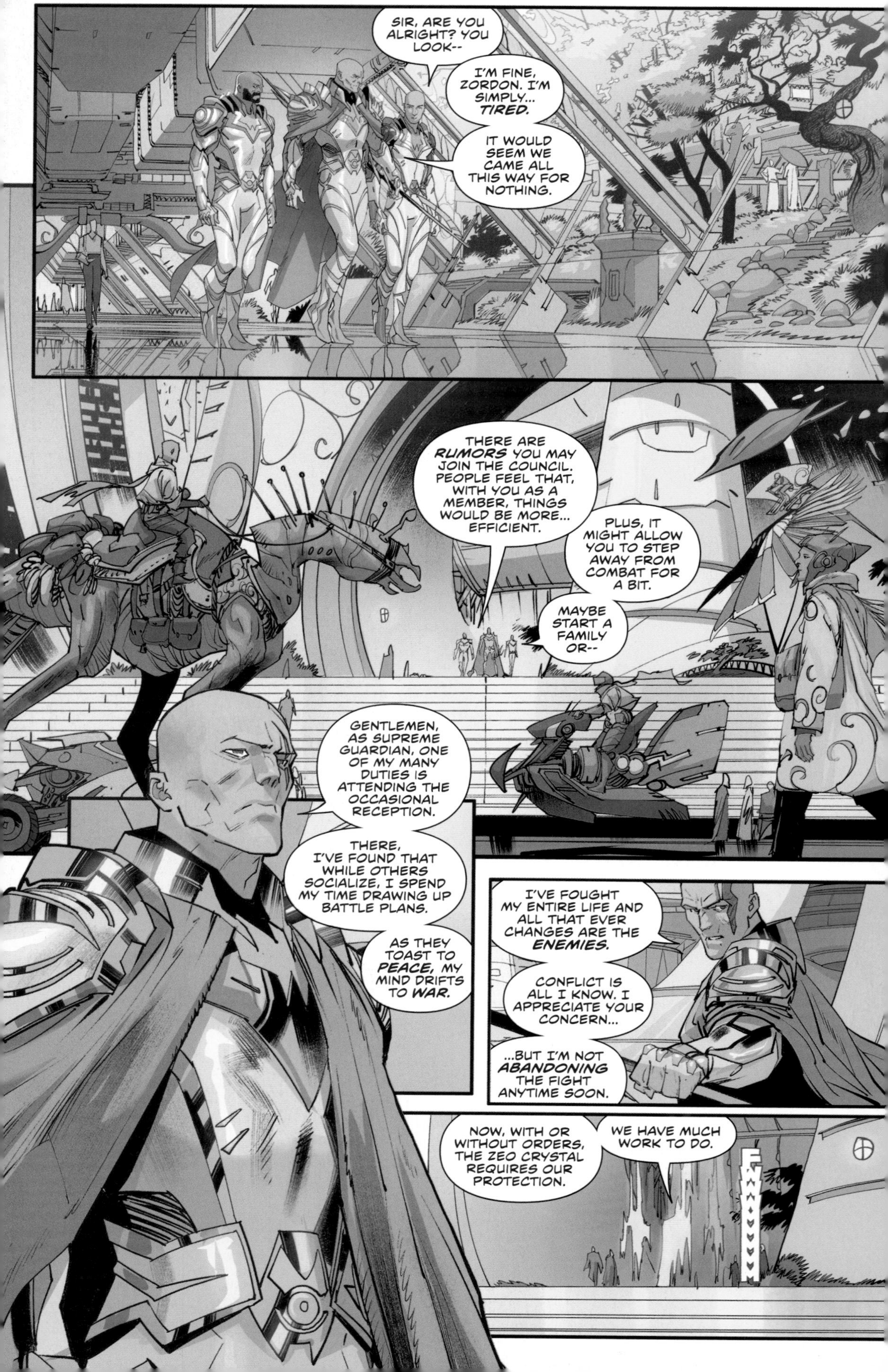
SIR, ARE YOU ALRIGHT? YOU LOOK--
I'M FINE, ZORDON. I'M SIMPLY... *TIRED.*
IT WOULD SEEM WE CAME ALL THIS WAY FOR NOTHING.
THERE ARE *RUMORS* YOU MAY JOIN THE COUNCIL. PEOPLE FEEL THAT, WITH YOU AS A MEMBER, THINGS WOULD BE MORE... EFFICIENT.
PLUS, IT MIGHT ALLOW YOU TO STEP AWAY FROM COMBAT FOR A BIT.
MAYBE START A FAMILY OR--
GENTLEMEN, AS SUPREME GUARDIAN, ONE OF MY MANY DUTIES IS ATTENDING THE OCCASIONAL RECEPTION.
THERE, I'VE FOUND THAT WHILE OTHERS SOCIALIZE, I SPEND MY TIME DRAWING UP BATTLE PLANS.
AS THEY TOAST TO *PEACE,* MY MIND DRIFTS TO *WAR.*
I'VE FOUGHT MY ENTIRE LIFE AND ALL THAT EVER CHANGES ARE THE *ENEMIES.*
CONFLICT IS ALL I KNOW. I APPRECIATE YOUR CONCERN...
...BUT I'M NOT *ABANDONING* THE FIGHT ANYTIME SOON.
NOW, WITH OR WITHOUT ORDERS, THE ZEO CRYSTAL REQUIRES OUR PROTECTION.
WE HAVE MUCH WORK TO DO.
FWAAAAAAA

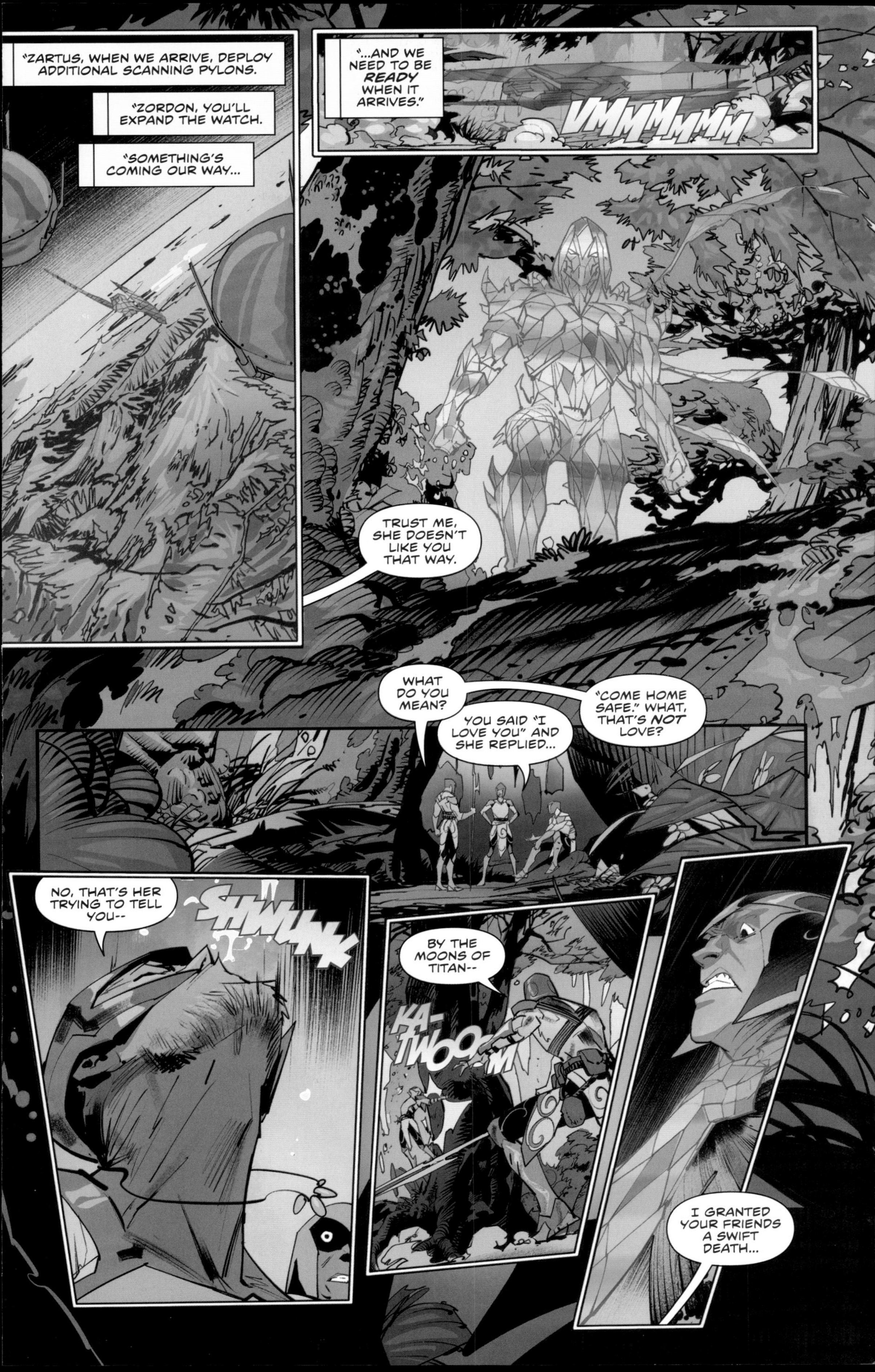
"ZARTUS, WHEN WE ARRIVE, DEPLOY ADDITIONAL SCANNING PYLONS.
"ZORDON, YOU'LL EXPAND THE WATCH.
"SOMETHING'S COMING OUR WAY...
"...AND WE NEED TO BE READY WHEN IT ARRIVES."
VMMMMMM
TRUST ME, SHE DOESN'T LIKE YOU THAT WAY.
WHAT DO YOU MEAN?
YOU SAID "I LOVE YOU" AND SHE REPLIED...
"COME HOME SAFE." WHAT, THAT'S NOT LOVE?
NO, THAT'S HER TRYING TO TELL YOU--
SHWUNK
BY THE MOONS OF TITAN--
KA-TWOOOM
I GRANTED YOUR FRIENDS A SWIFT DEATH...

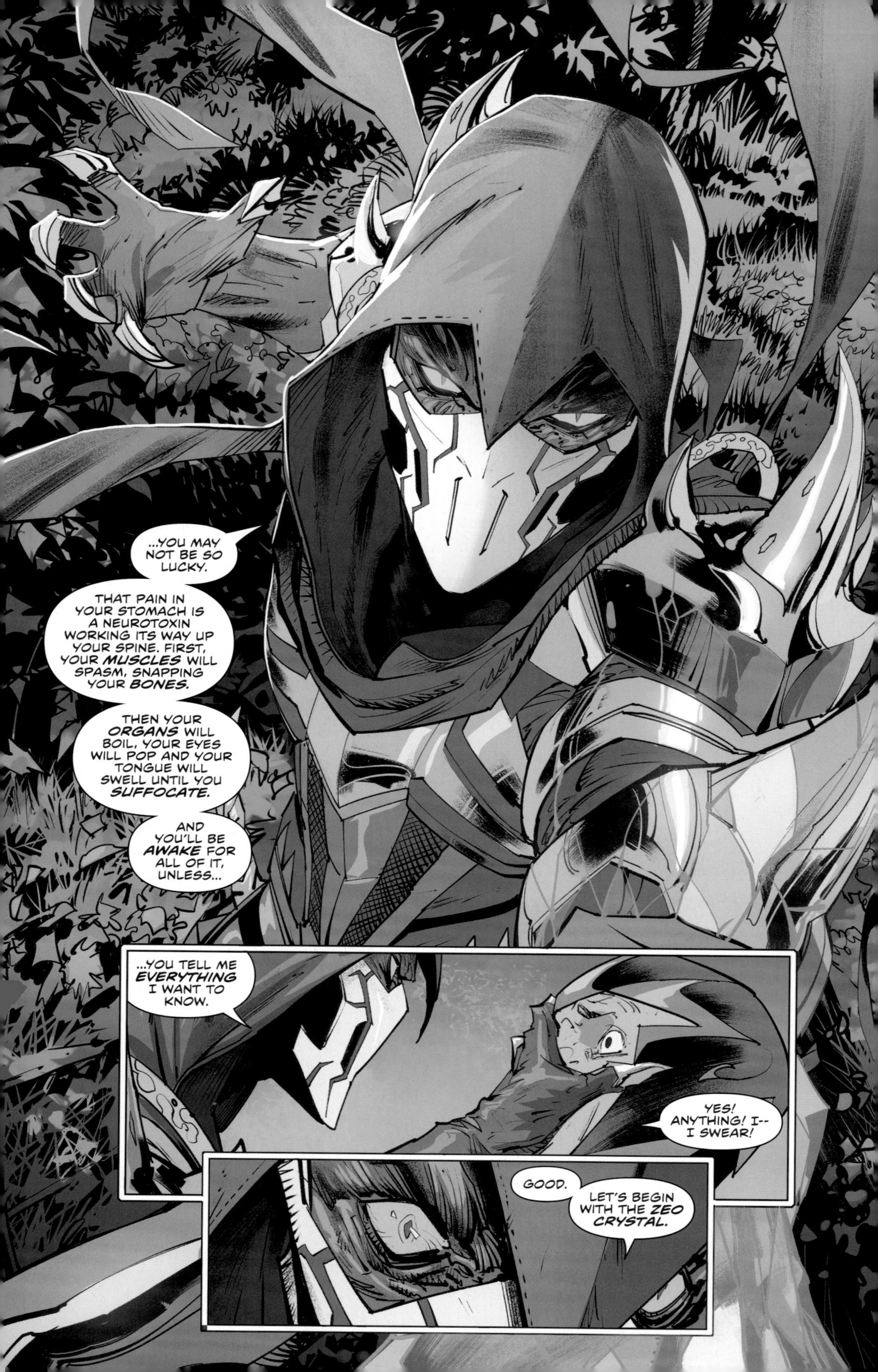
...YOU MAY NOT BE SO LUCKY.
THAT PAIN IN YOUR STOMACH IS A NEUROTOXIN WORKING ITS WAY UP YOUR SPINE. FIRST, YOUR MUSCLES WILL SPASM, SNAPPING YOUR BONES.
THEN YOUR ORGANS WILL BOIL, YOUR EYES WILL POP AND YOUR TONGUE WILL SWELL UNTIL YOU SUFFOCATE.
AND YOU'LL BE AWAKE FOR ALL OF IT, UNLESS...
...YOU TELL ME EVERYTHING I WANT TO KNOW.
YES! ANYTHING! I-- I SWEAR!
GOOD.
LET'S BEGIN WITH THE ZEO CRYSTAL.

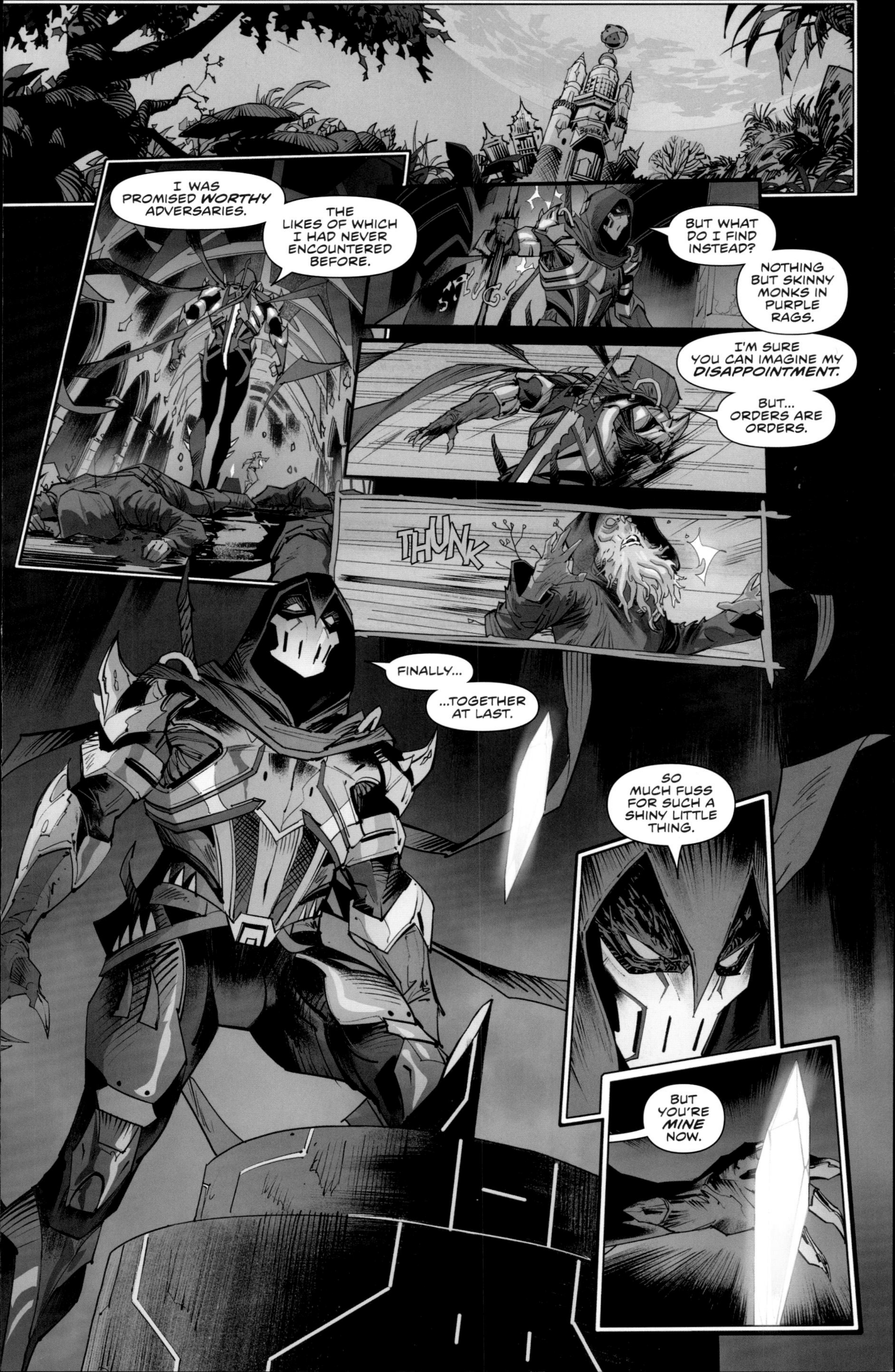
I WAS PROMISED WORTHY ADVERSARIES.
THE LIKES OF WHICH I HAD NEVER ENCOUNTERED BEFORE.
BUT WHAT DO I FIND INSTEAD?
NOTHING BUT SKINNY MONKS IN PURPLE RAGS.
I'M SURE YOU CAN IMAGINE MY DISAPPOINTMENT.
BUT... ORDERS ARE ORDERS.
THUNK
FINALLY...
...TOGETHER AT LAST.
SO MUCH FUSS FOR SUCH A SHINY LITTLE THING.
BUT YOU'RE MINE NOW.

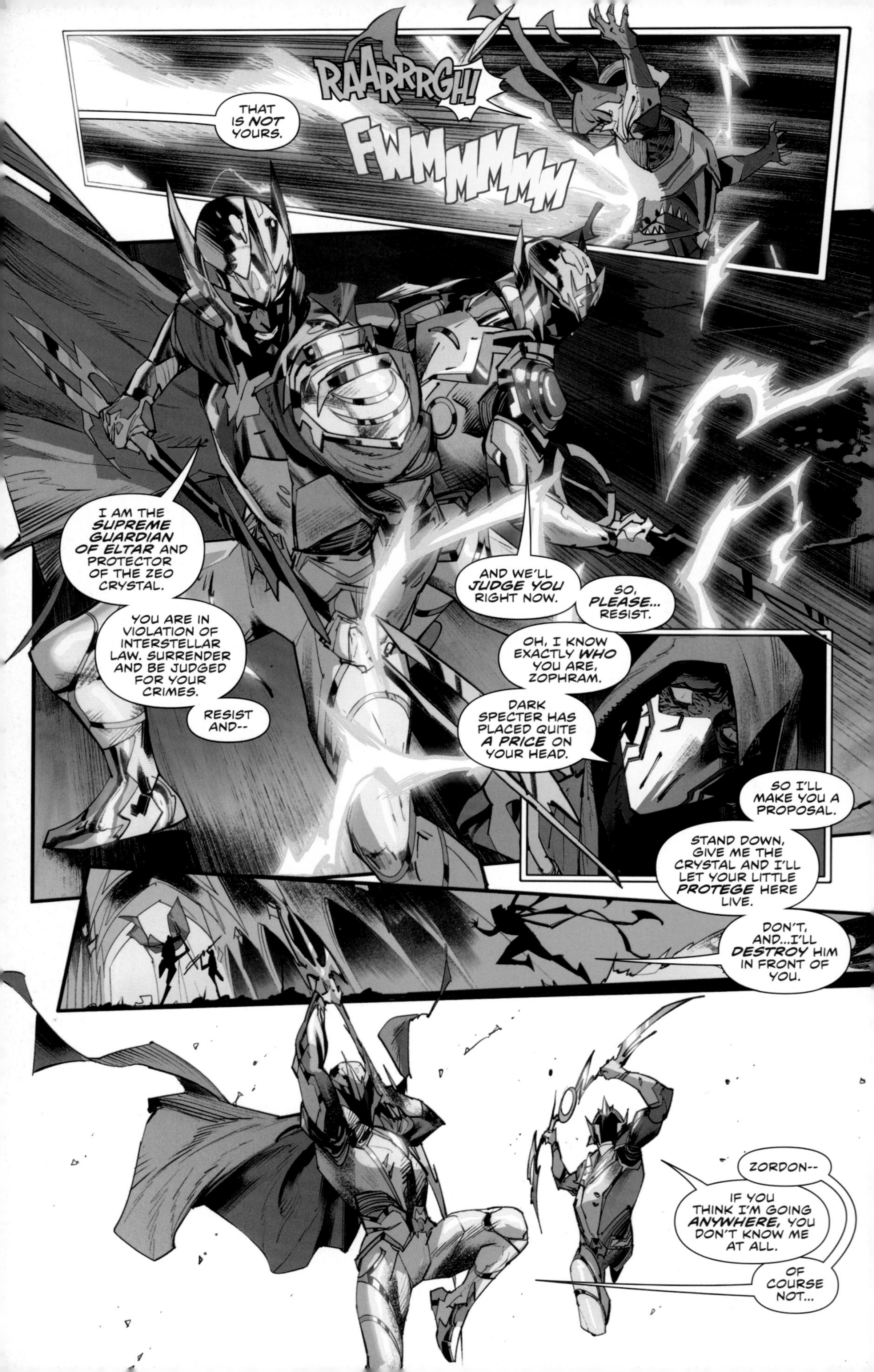

RAARRRGH!
THAT IS NOT YOURS.
FWMMMMMM
I AM THE SUPREME GUARDIAN OF ELTAR AND PROTECTOR OF THE ZEO CRYSTAL.
YOU ARE IN VIOLATION OF INTERSTELLAR LAW. SURRENDER AND BE JUDGED FOR YOUR CRIMES.
RESIST AND--
AND WE'LL JUDGE YOU RIGHT NOW.
SO, PLEASE... RESIST.
OH, I KNOW EXACTLY WHO YOU ARE, ZOPHRAM.
DARK SPECTER HAS PLACED QUITE A PRICE ON YOUR HEAD.
SO I'LL MAKE YOU A PROPOSAL.
STAND DOWN, GIVE ME THE CRYSTAL AND I'LL LET YOUR LITTLE PROTEGE HERE LIVE.
DON'T, AND...I'LL DESTROY HIM IN FRONT OF YOU.
ZORDON--
IF YOU THINK I'M GOING ANYWHERE, YOU DON'T KNOW ME AT ALL.
OF COURSE NOT...

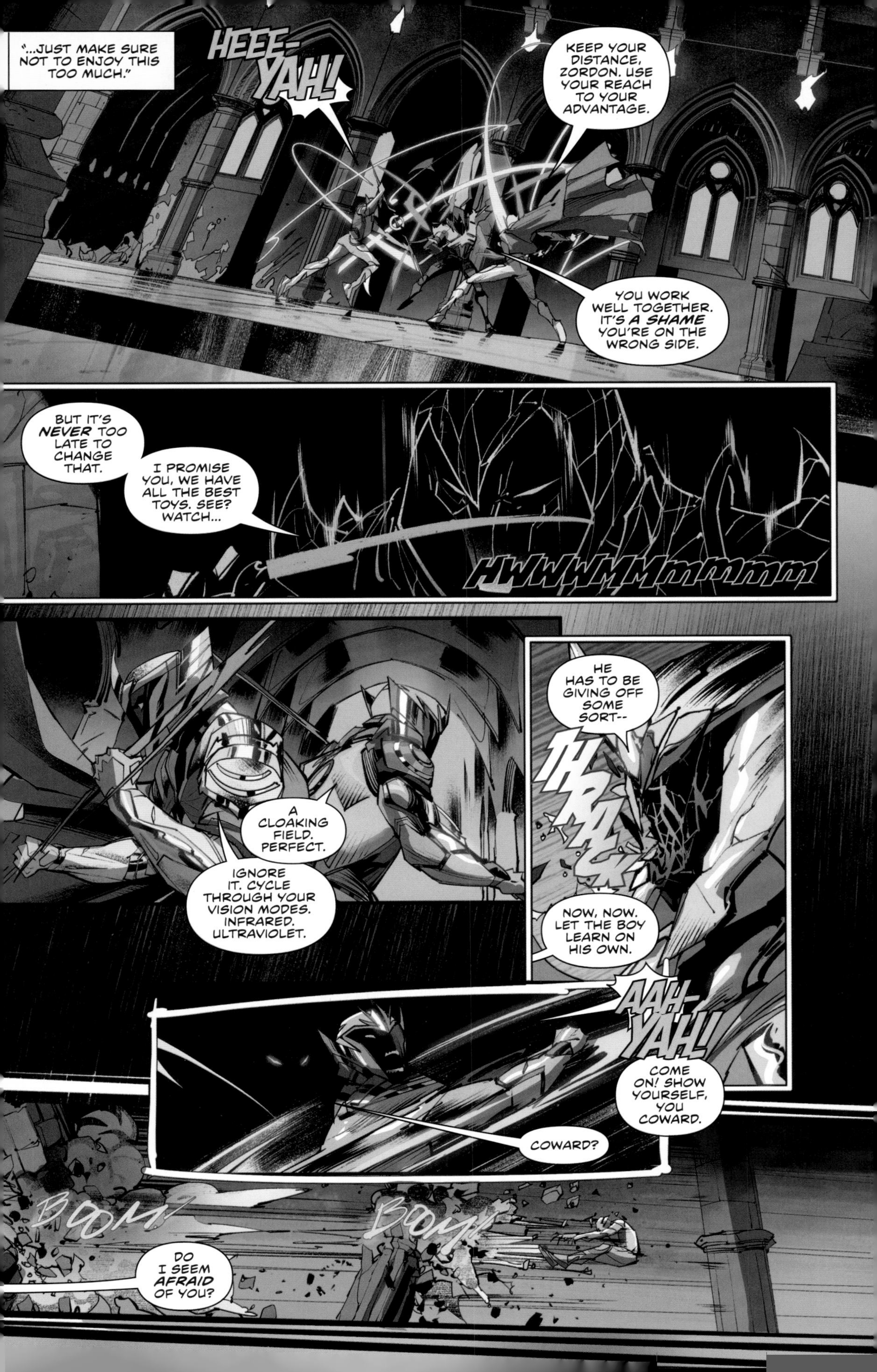
"...JUST MAKE SURE NOT TO ENJOY THIS TOO MUCH."
HEEE-YAH!
KEEP YOUR DISTANCE, ZORDON. USE YOUR REACH TO YOUR ADVANTAGE.
YOU WORK WELL TOGETHER. IT'S A SHAME YOU'RE ON THE WRONG SIDE.
BUT IT'S NEVER TOO LATE TO CHANGE THAT.
I PROMISE YOU, WE HAVE ALL THE BEST TOYS. SEE? WATCH...
HWWWMMmmmmm
A CLOAKING FIELD. PERFECT.
IGNORE IT. CYCLE THROUGH YOUR VISION MODES. INFRARED. ULTRAVIOLET.
HE HAS TO BE GIVING OFF SOME SORT--
THRACK
NOW, NOW. LET THE BOY LEARN ON HIS OWN.
AAH-YAH!
COME ON! SHOW YOURSELF, YOU COWARD.
COWARD?
BOOM!
BOOM!
DO I SEEM AFRAID OF YOU?

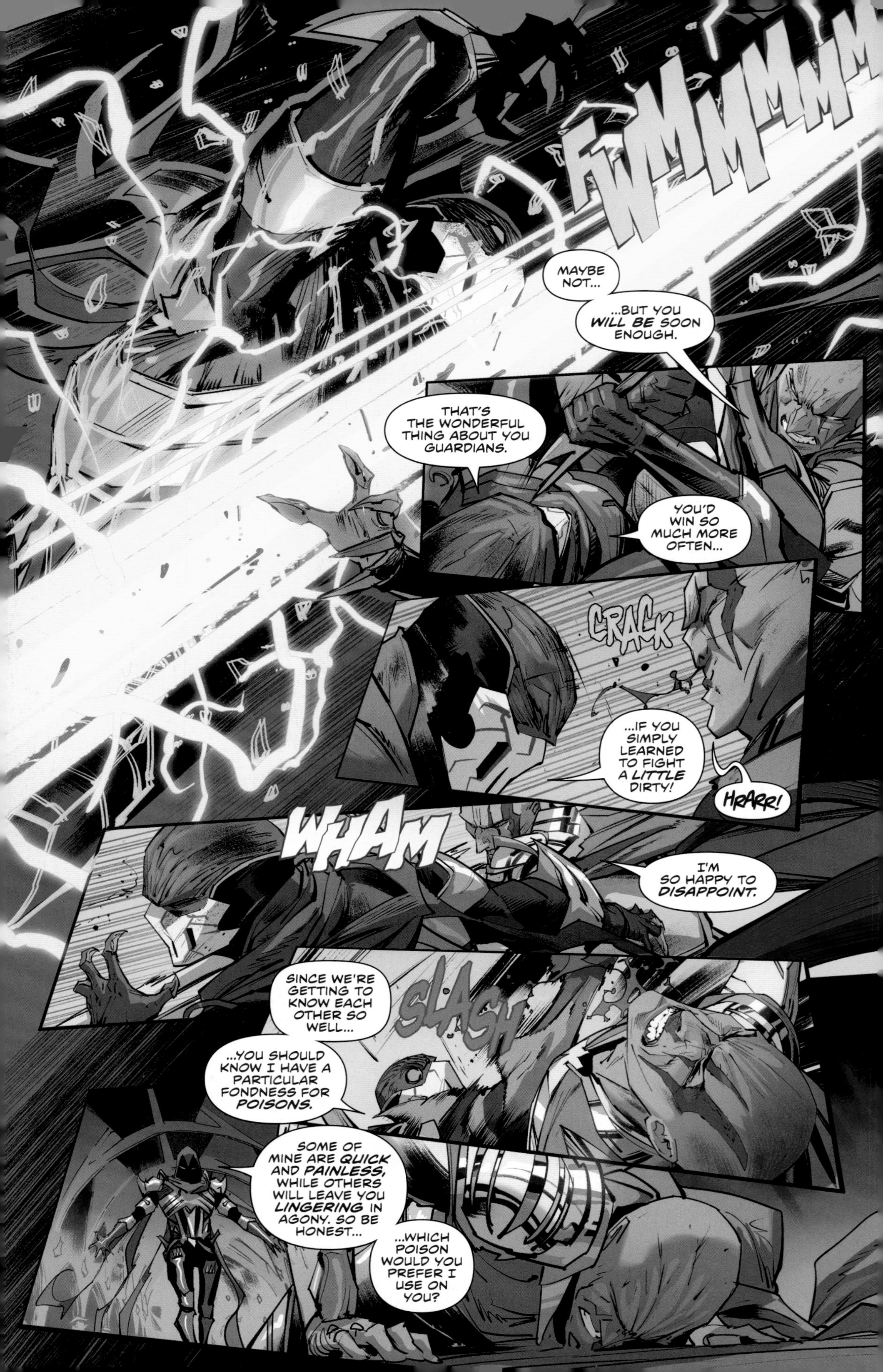
FWMMMMM
MAYBE NOT...
...BUT YOU WILL BE SOON ENOUGH.
THAT'S THE WONDERFUL THING ABOUT YOU GUARDIANS.
YOU'D WIN SO MUCH MORE OFTEN...
CRACK
...IF YOU SIMPLY LEARNED TO FIGHT A LITTLE DIRTY!
HRARR!
WHAM
I'M SO HAPPY TO DISAPPOINT.
SINCE WE'RE GETTING TO KNOW EACH OTHER SO WELL...
SLASH
...YOU SHOULD KNOW I HAVE A PARTICULAR FONDNESS FOR POISONS.
SOME OF MINE ARE QUICK AND PAINLESS, WHILE OTHERS WILL LEAVE YOU LINGERING IN AGONY. SO BE HONEST...
...WHICH POISON WOULD YOU PREFER I USE ON YOU?

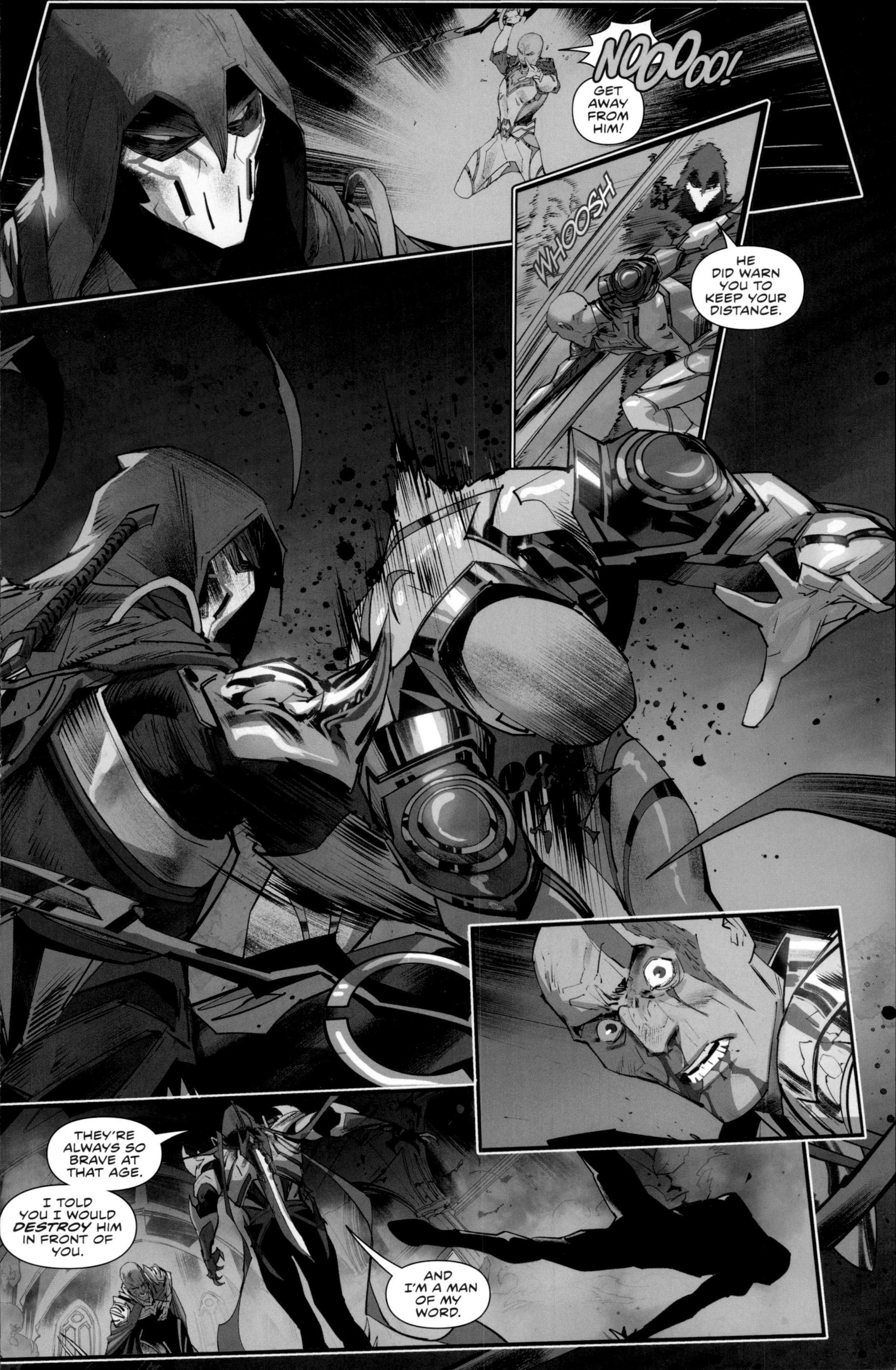
NOOOOO!
GET AWAY FROM HIM!
WHOOSH
HE DID WARN YOU TO KEEP YOUR DISTANCE.
THEY'RE ALWAYS SO BRAVE AT THAT AGE.
I TOLD YOU I WOULD DESTROY HIM IN FRONT OF YOU.
AND I'M A MAN OF MY WORD.

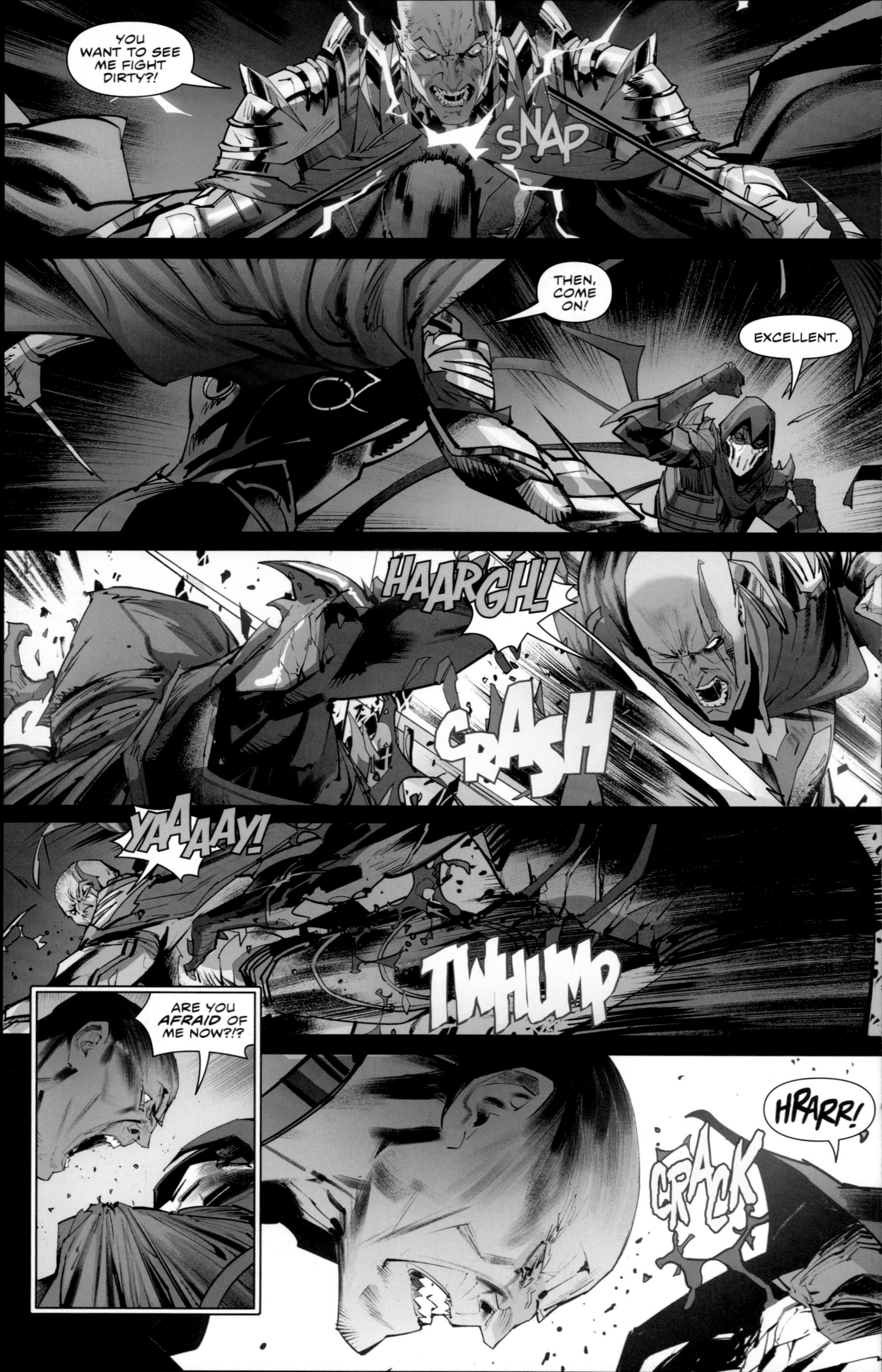
YOU WANT TO SEE ME FIGHT DIRTY?!
SNAP
THEN, COME ON!
EXCELLENT.
HAARGH!
CRASH
YAAAAY!
TWHUMP
ARE YOU *AFRAID* OF ME NOW?!?
HRARR!
CRACK

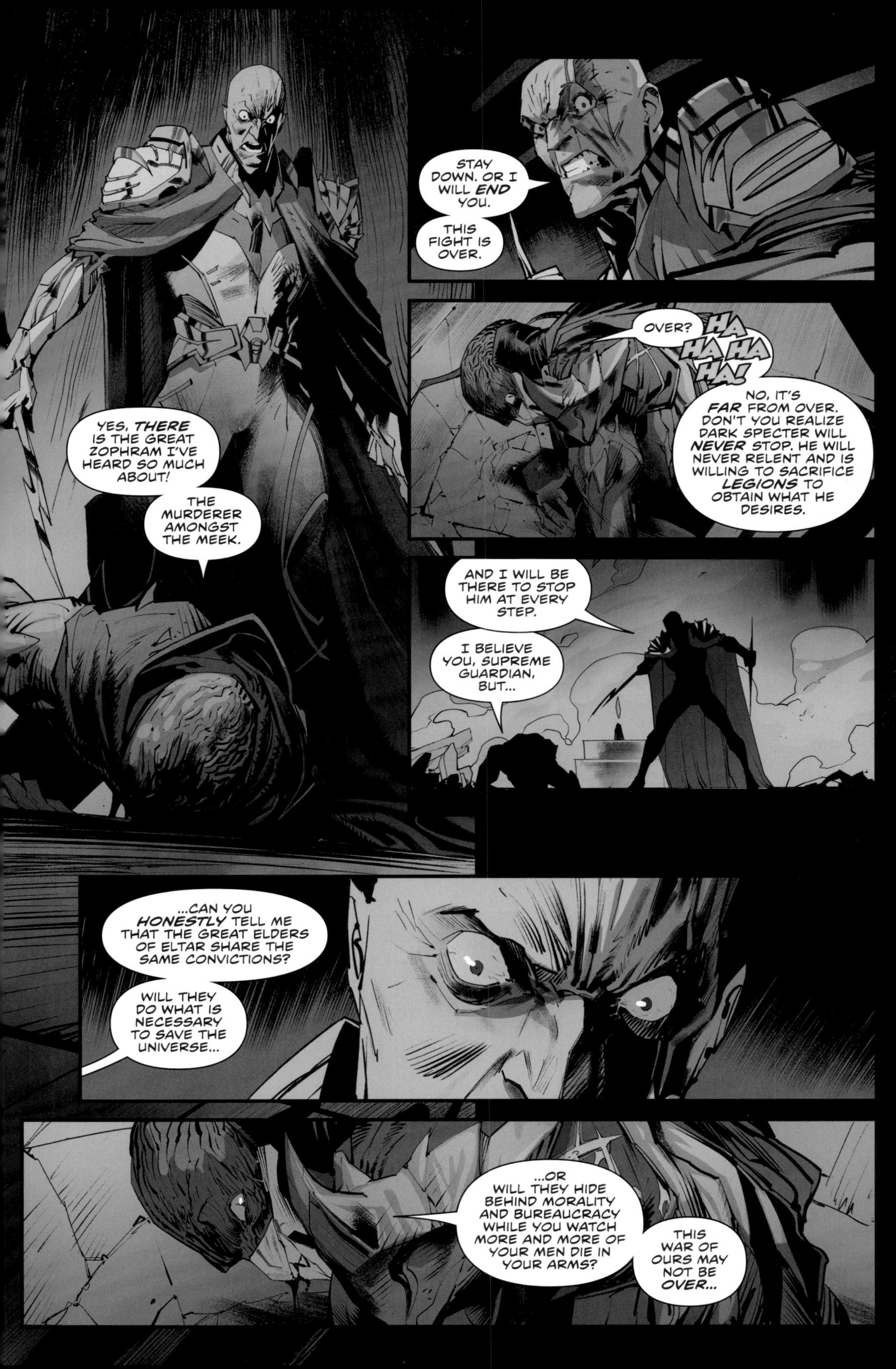
STAY DOWN. OR I WILL END YOU.
THIS FIGHT IS OVER.
YES, THERE IS THE GREAT ZOPHRAM I'VE HEARD SO MUCH ABOUT!
THE MURDERER AMONGST THE MEEK.
OVER?
HA HA HA HA HA!
NO, IT'S FAR FROM OVER. DON'T YOU REALIZE DARK SPECTER WILL NEVER STOP. HE WILL NEVER RELENT AND IS WILLING TO SACRIFICE LEGIONS TO OBTAIN WHAT HE DESIRES.
AND I WILL BE THERE TO STOP HIM AT EVERY STEP.
I BELIEVE YOU, SUPREME GUARDIAN, BUT...
...CAN YOU HONESTLY TELL ME THAT THE GREAT ELDERS OF ELTAR SHARE THE SAME CONVICTIONS?
WILL THEY DO WHAT IS NECESSARY TO SAVE THE UNIVERSE...
...OR WILL THEY HIDE BEHIND MORALITY AND BUREAUCRACY WHILE YOU WATCH MORE AND MORE OF YOUR MEN DIE IN YOUR ARMS?
THIS WAR OF OURS MAY NOT BE OVER...

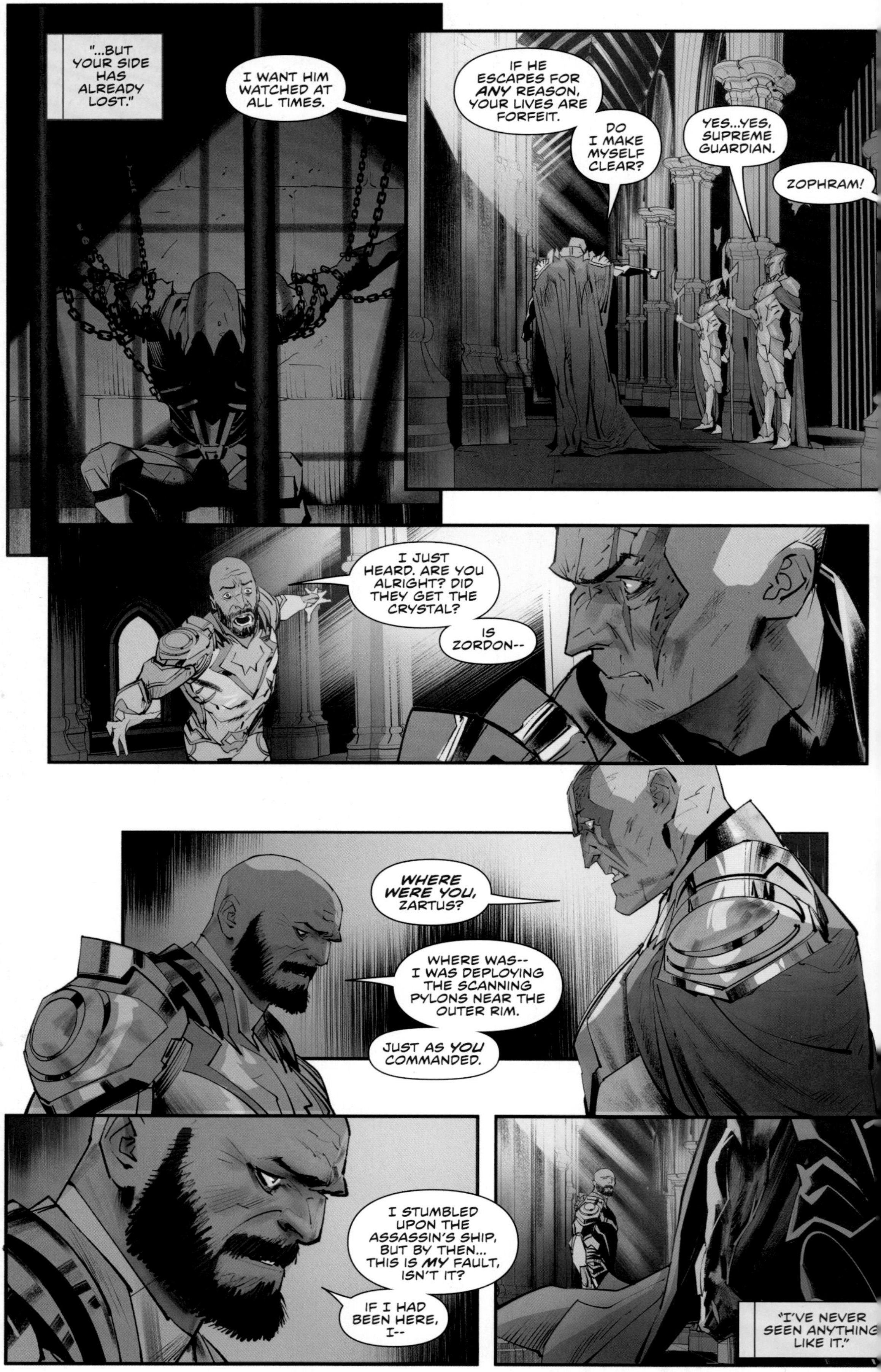
"...BUT YOUR SIDE HAS ALREADY LOST."
I WANT HIM WATCHED AT ALL TIMES.
IF HE ESCAPES FOR *ANY* REASON, YOUR LIVES ARE FORFEIT.
DO I MAKE MYSELF CLEAR?
YES...YES, SUPREME GUARDIAN.
ZOPHRAM!
I JUST HEARD. ARE YOU ALRIGHT? DID THEY GET THE CRYSTAL?
IS ZORDON--
WHERE WERE YOU, ZARTUS?
WHERE WAS-- I WAS DEPLOYING THE SCANNING PYLONS NEAR THE OUTER RIM.
JUST AS *YOU* COMMANDED.
I STUMBLED UPON THE ASSASSIN'S SHIP, BUT BY THEN... THIS IS *MY* FAULT, ISN'T IT?
IF I HAD BEEN HERE, I--
"I'VE NEVER SEEN ANYTHING LIKE IT."

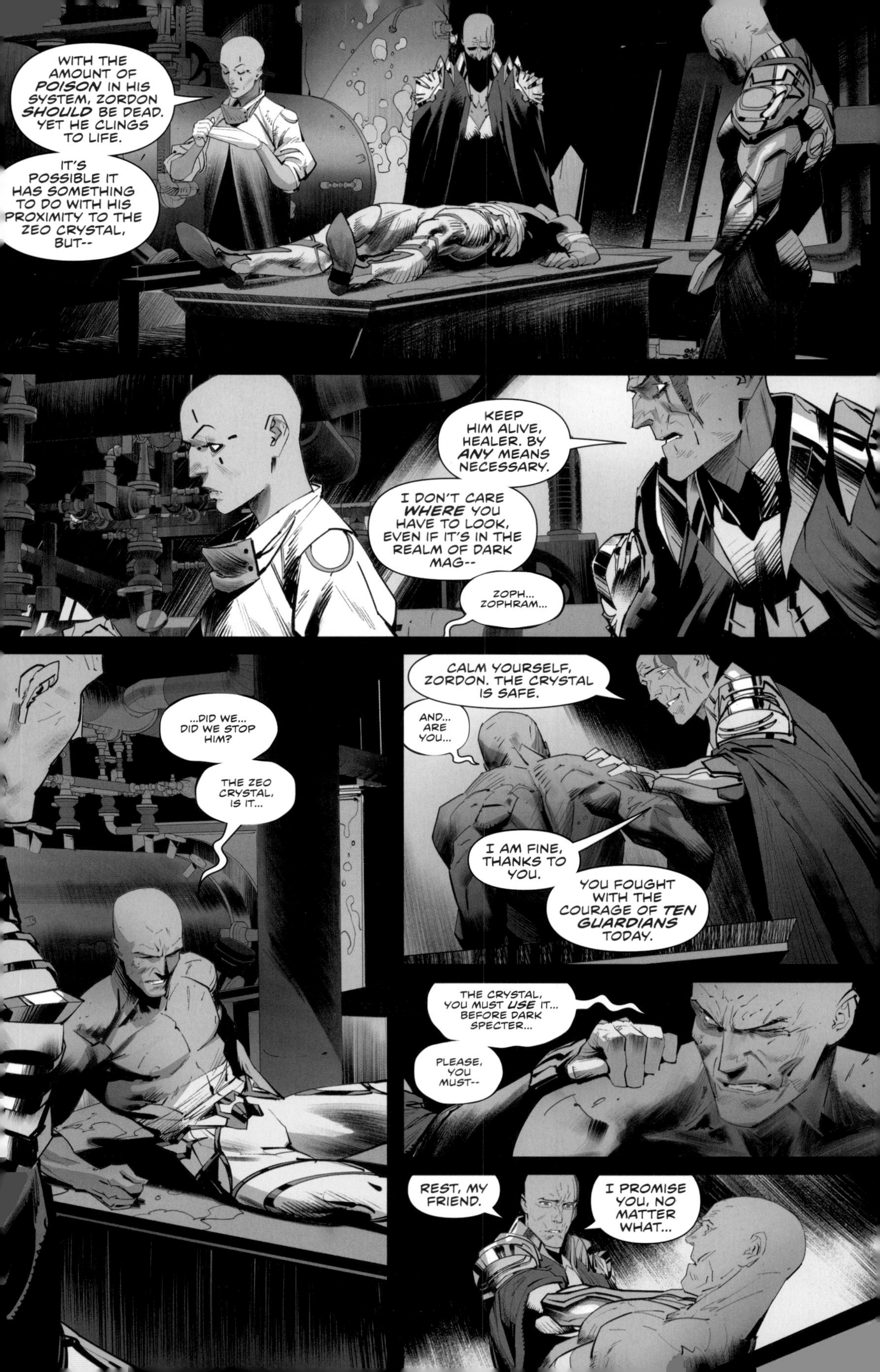
WITH THE AMOUNT OF *POISON* IN HIS SYSTEM, ZORDON *SHOULD* BE DEAD. YET HE CLINGS TO LIFE.
IT'S POSSIBLE IT HAS SOMETHING TO DO WITH HIS PROXIMITY TO THE ZEO CRYSTAL, BUT--
KEEP HIM ALIVE, HEALER. BY *ANY* MEANS NECESSARY.
I DON'T CARE *WHERE* YOU HAVE TO LOOK, EVEN IF IT'S IN THE REALM OF DARK MAG--
ZOPH... ZOPHRAM...
...DID WE... DID WE STOP HIM?
THE ZEO CRYSTAL, IS IT...
CALM YOURSELF, ZORDON. THE CRYSTAL IS SAFE.
AND... ARE YOU...
I AM FINE, THANKS TO YOU.
YOU FOUGHT WITH THE COURAGE OF *TEN GUARDIANS* TODAY.
THE CRYSTAL, YOU MUST *USE* IT... BEFORE DARK SPECTER...
PLEASE, YOU MUST--
REST, MY FRIEND.
I PROMISE YOU, NO MATTER WHAT...

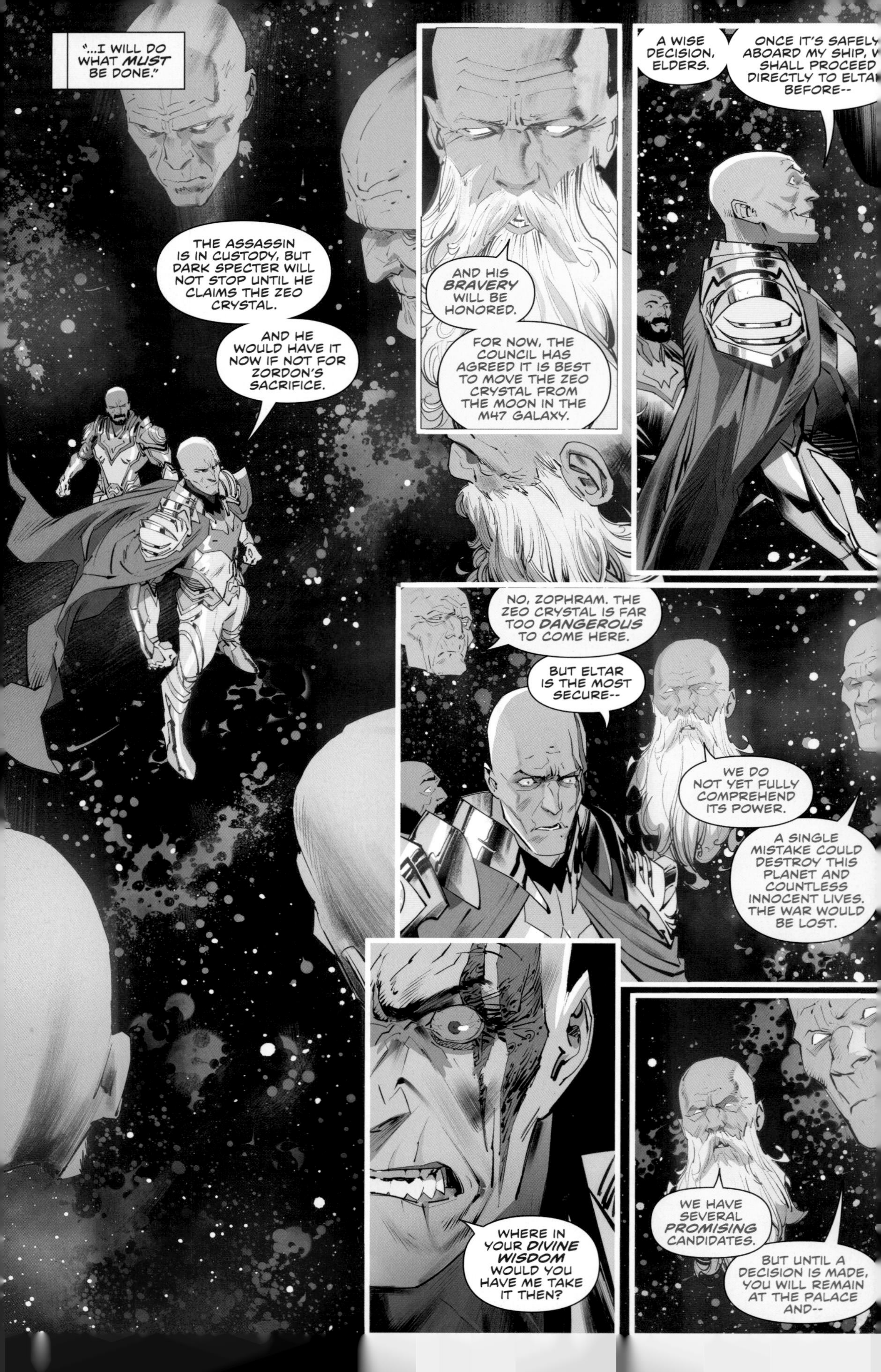
"...I WILL DO WHAT MUST BE DONE."
THE ASSASSIN IS IN CUSTODY, BUT DARK SPECTER WILL NOT STOP UNTIL HE CLAIMS THE ZEO CRYSTAL.
AND HE WOULD HAVE IT NOW IF NOT FOR ZORDON'S SACRIFICE.
AND HIS BRAVERY WILL BE HONORED.
FOR NOW, THE COUNCIL HAS AGREED IT IS BEST TO MOVE THE ZEO CRYSTAL FROM THE MOON IN THE M47 GALAXY.
A WISE DECISION, ELDERS.
ONCE IT'S SAFELY ABOARD MY SHIP, W SHALL PROCEED DIRECTLY TO ELTA BEFORE--
NO, ZOPHRAM. THE ZEO CRYSTAL IS FAR TOO DANGEROUS TO COME HERE.
BUT ELTAR IS THE MOST SECURE--
WE DO NOT YET FULLY COMPREHEND ITS POWER.
A SINGLE MISTAKE COULD DESTROY THIS PLANET AND COUNTLESS INNOCENT LIVES. THE WAR WOULD BE LOST.
WHERE IN YOUR DIVINE WISDOM WOULD YOU HAVE ME TAKE IT THEN?
WE HAVE SEVERAL PROMISING CANDIDATES.
BUT UNTIL A DECISION IS MADE, YOU WILL REMAIN AT THE PALACE AND--

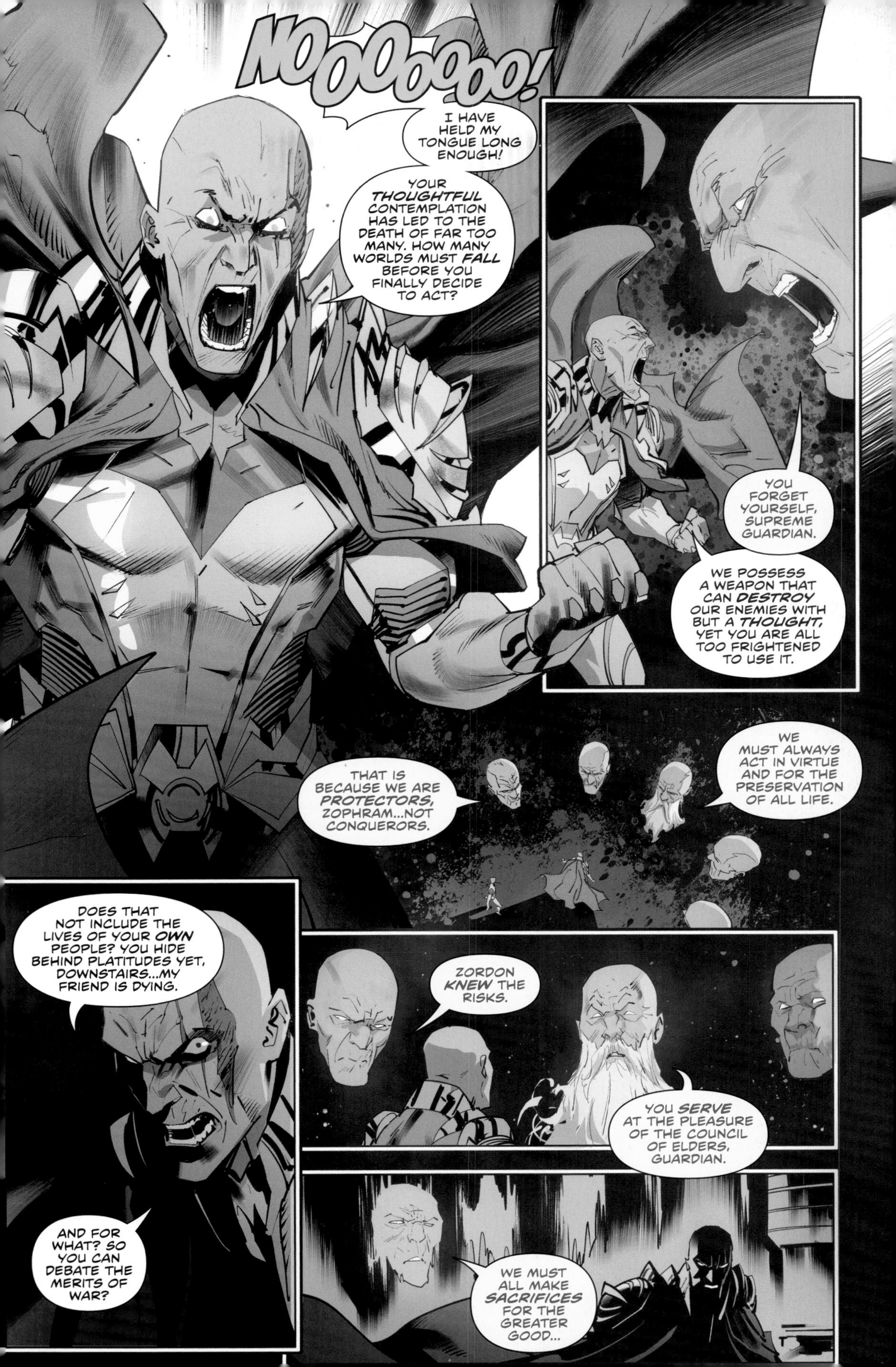
NOOOOOOOO!
I HAVE HELD MY TONGUE LONG ENOUGH!
YOUR THOUGHTFUL CONTEMPLATION HAS LED TO THE DEATH OF FAR TOO MANY. HOW MANY WORLDS MUST FALL BEFORE YOU FINALLY DECIDE TO ACT?
YOU FORGET YOURSELF, SUPREME GUARDIAN.
WE POSSESS A WEAPON THAT CAN DESTROY OUR ENEMIES WITH BUT A THOUGHT, YET YOU ARE ALL TOO FRIGHTENED TO USE IT.
THAT IS BECAUSE WE ARE PROTECTORS, ZOPHRAM...NOT CONQUERORS.
WE MUST ALWAYS ACT IN VIRTUE AND FOR THE PRESERVATION OF ALL LIFE.
DOES THAT NOT INCLUDE THE LIVES OF YOUR OWN PEOPLE? YOU HIDE BEHIND PLATITUDES YET, DOWNSTAIRS...MY FRIEND IS DYING.
ZORDON KNEW THE RISKS.
YOU SERVE AT THE PLEASURE OF THE COUNCIL OF ELDERS, GUARDIAN.
AND FOR WHAT? SO YOU CAN DEBATE THE MERITS OF WAR?
WE MUST ALL MAKE SACRIFICES FOR THE GREATER GOOD...

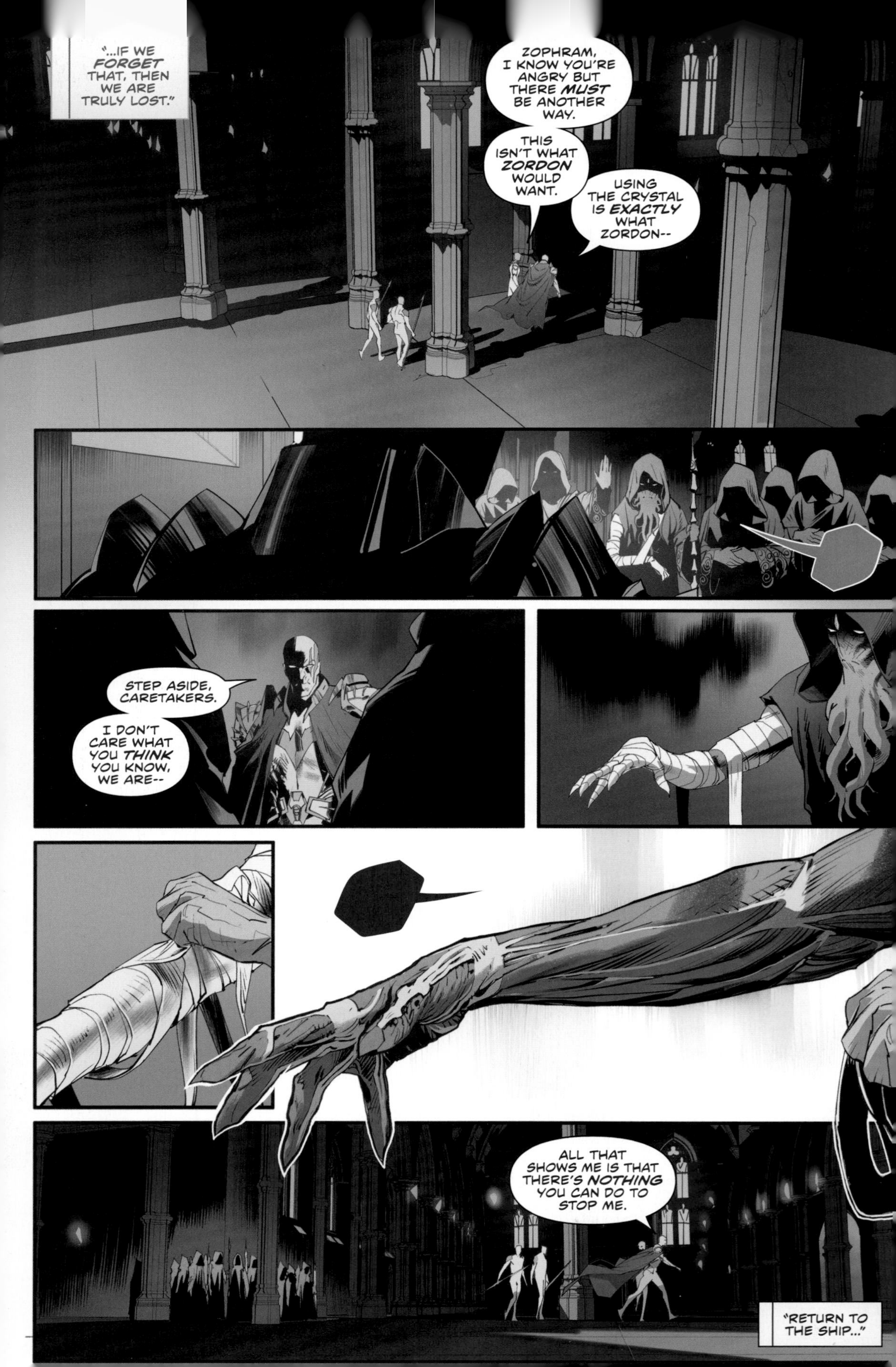
"...IF WE FORGET THAT, THEN WE ARE TRULY LOST."
ZOPHRAM, I KNOW YOU'RE ANGRY BUT THERE MUST BE ANOTHER WAY.
THIS ISN'T WHAT ZORDON WOULD WANT.
USING THE CRYSTAL IS EXACTLY WHAT ZORDON--
STEP ASIDE, CARETAKERS.
I DON'T CARE WHAT YOU THINK YOU KNOW, WE ARE--
ALL THAT SHOWS ME IS THAT THERE'S NOTHING YOU CAN DO TO STOP ME.
"RETURN TO THE SHIP..."

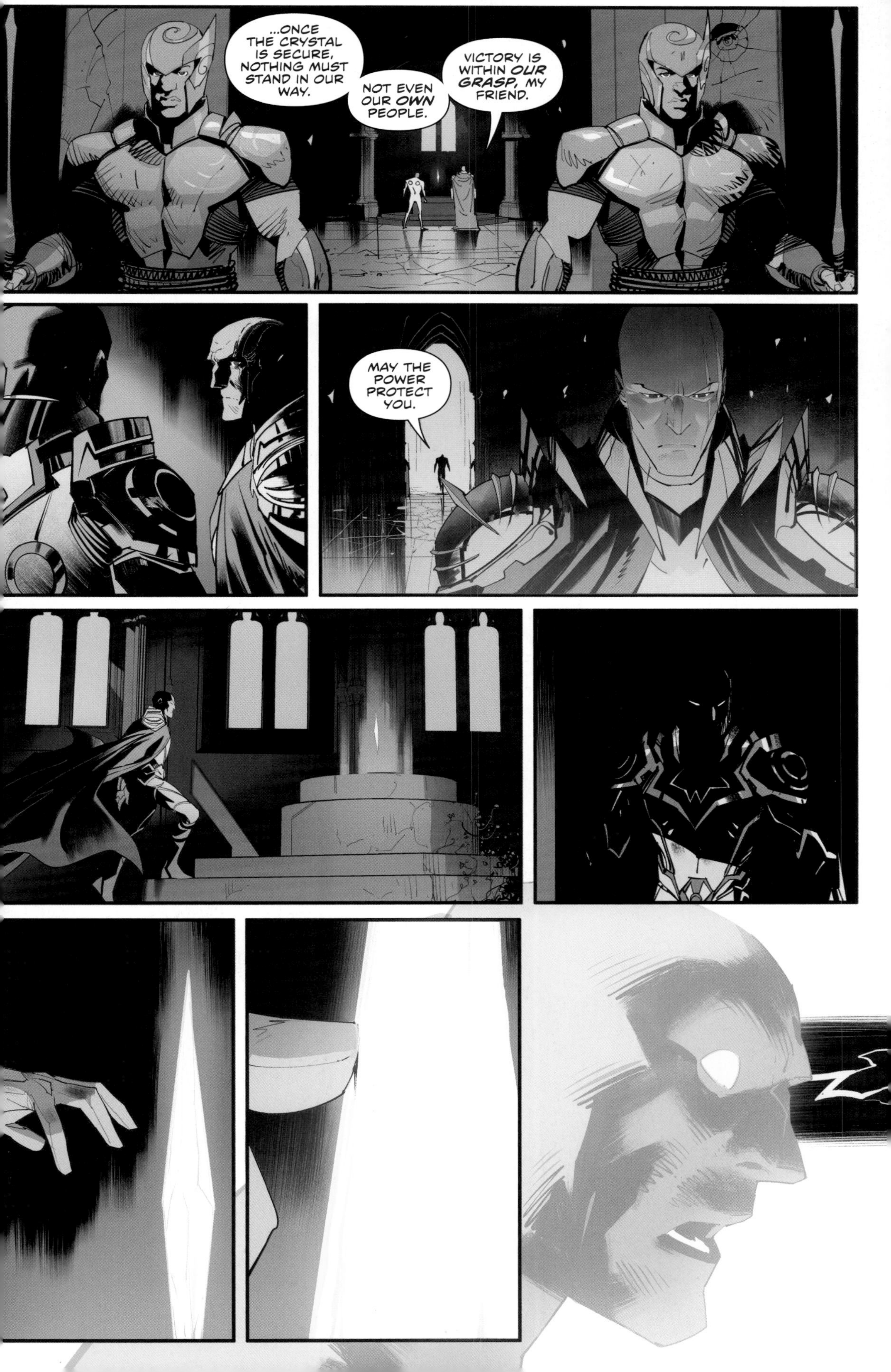
...ONCE THE CRYSTAL IS SECURE, NOTHING MUST STAND IN OUR WAY.
NOT EVEN OUR OWN PEOPLE.
VICTORY IS WITHIN OUR GRASP, MY FRIEND.
MAY THE POWER PROTECT YOU.

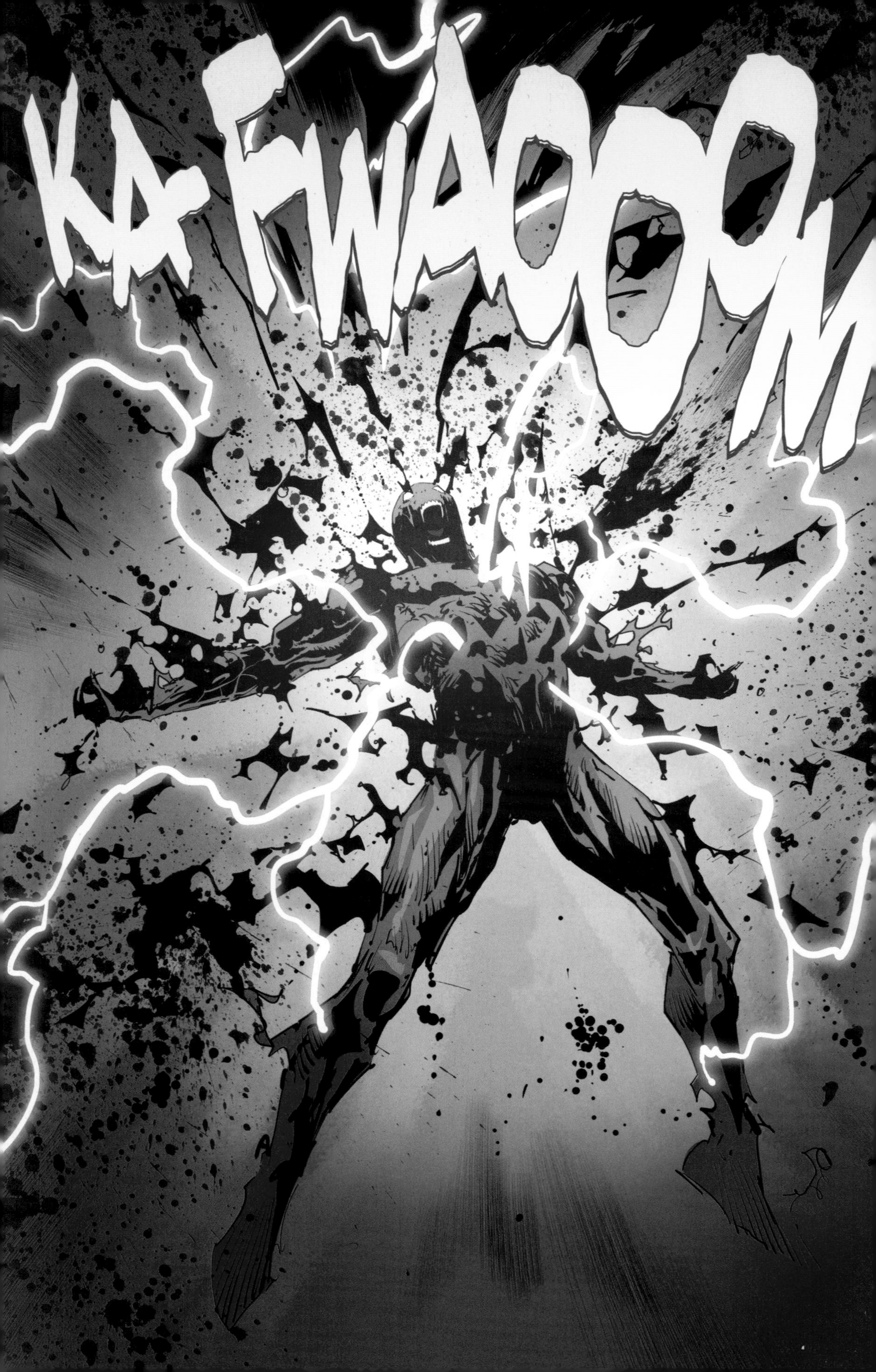
KA-FWAOOOM

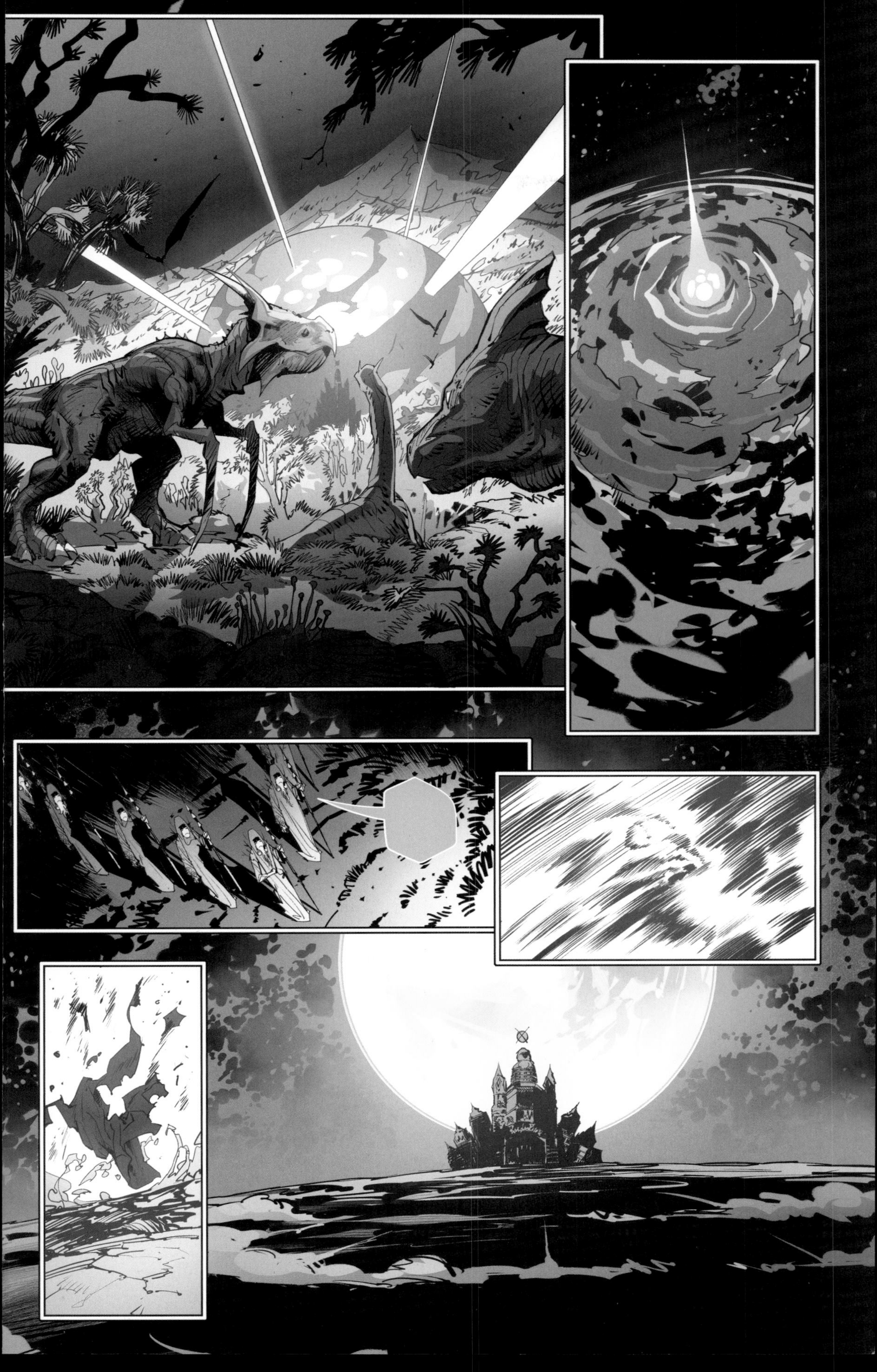

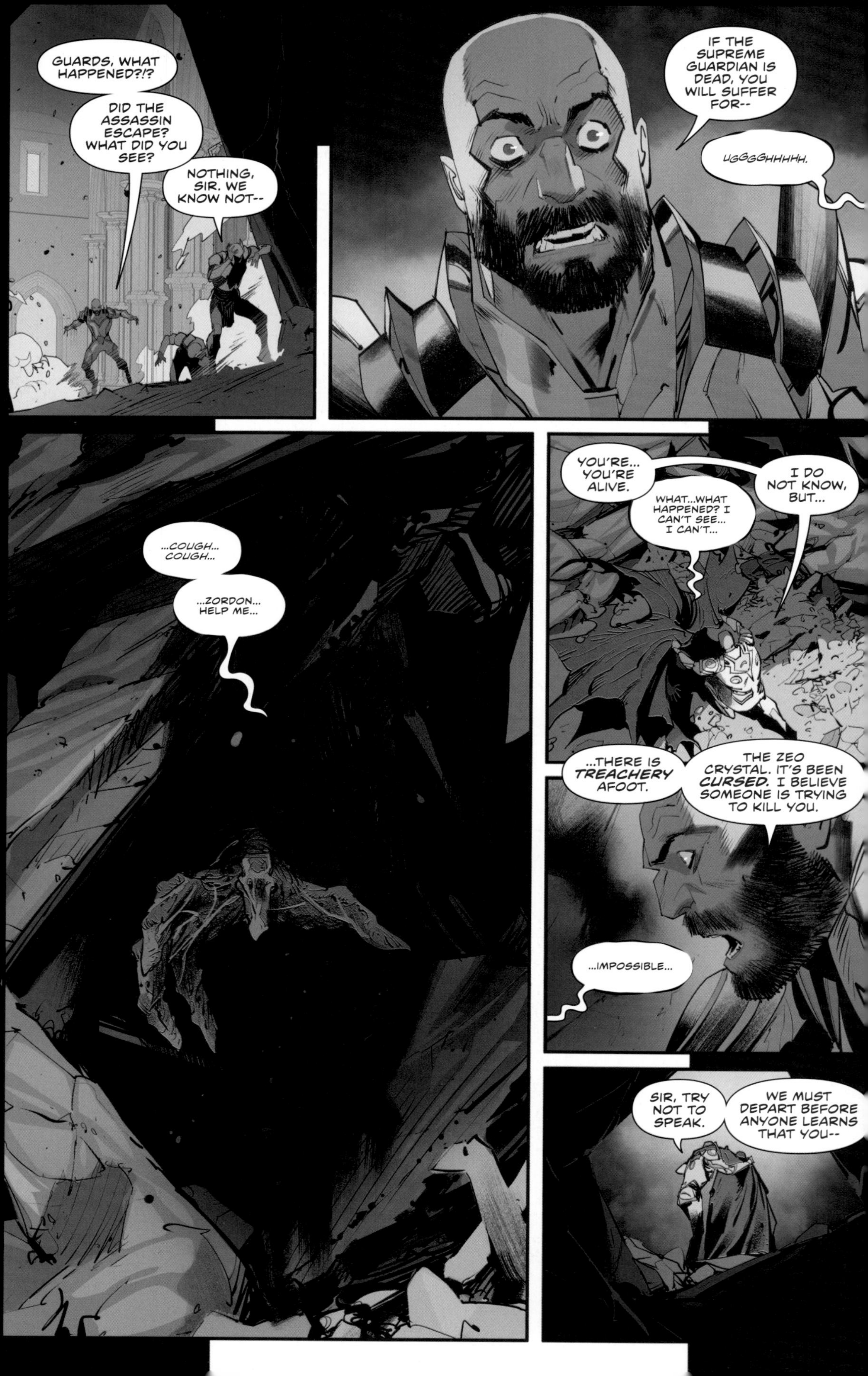
GUARDS, WHAT HAPPENED?!?
DID THE ASSASSIN ESCAPE? WHAT DID YOU SEE?
NOTHING, SIR. WE KNOW NOT--
IF THE SUPREME GUARDIAN IS DEAD, YOU WILL SUFFER FOR--
UGGGGHHHHH.
...COUGH... COUGH...
...ZORDON... HELP ME...
YOU'RE... YOU'RE ALIVE.
WHAT...WHAT HAPPENED? I CAN'T SEE... I CAN'T...
I DO NOT KNOW, BUT...
...THERE IS TREACHERY AFOOT.
THE ZEO CRYSTAL. IT'S BEEN CURSED. I BELIEVE SOMEONE IS TRYING TO KILL YOU.
...IMPOSSIBLE...
SIR, TRY NOT TO SPEAK.
WE MUST DEPART BEFORE ANYONE LEARNS THAT YOU--

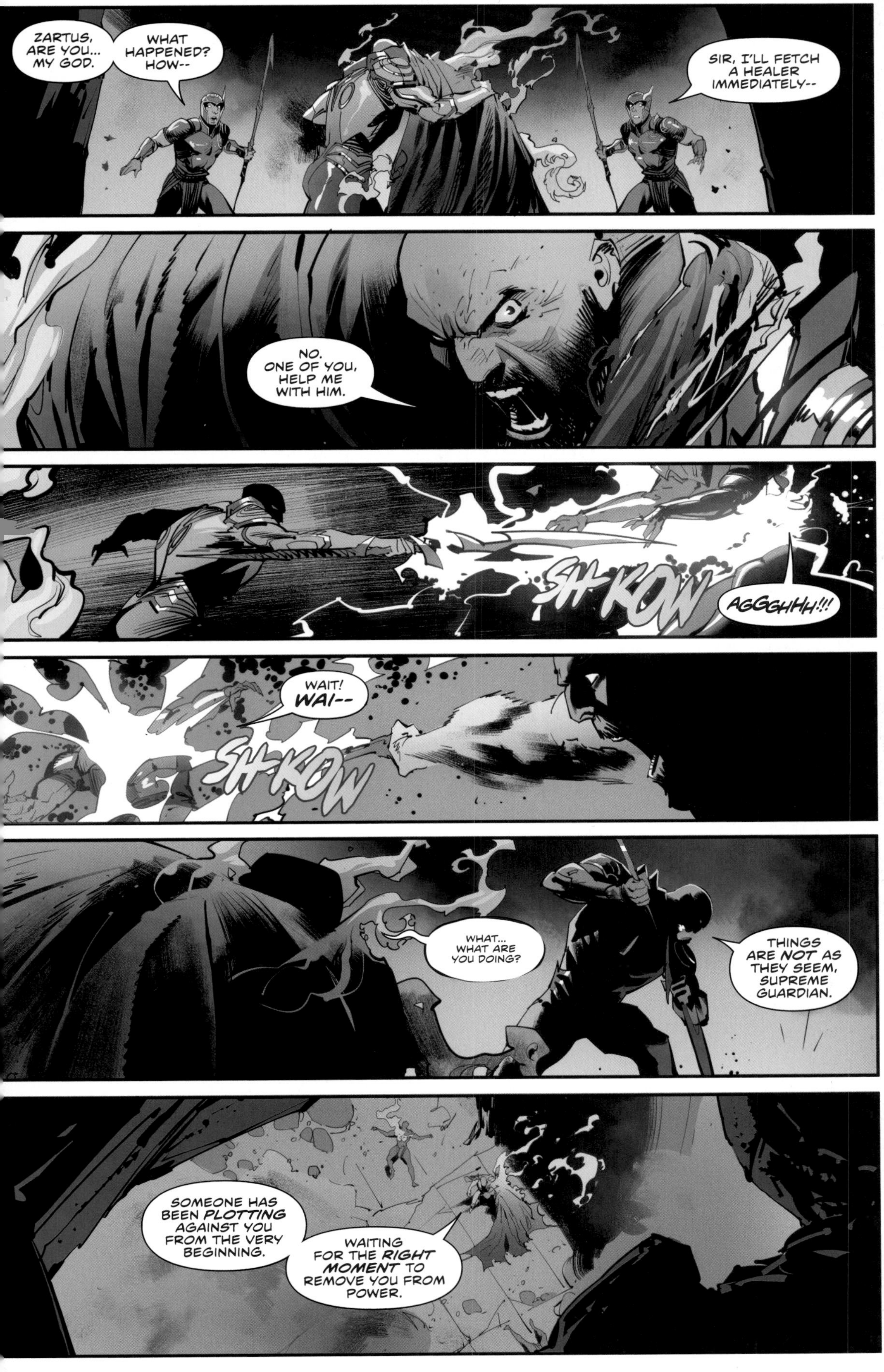

ZARTUS, ARE YOU... MY GOD.
WHAT HAPPENED? HOW--
SIR, I'LL FETCH A HEALER IMMEDIATELY--
NO. ONE OF YOU, HELP ME WITH HIM.
SH-KOW
AGGGHHH!!!
WAIT! WAI--
SH-KOW
WHAT... WHAT ARE YOU DOING?
THINGS ARE NOT AS THEY SEEM, SUPREME GUARDIAN.
SOMEONE HAS BEEN PLOTTING AGAINST YOU FROM THE VERY BEGINNING.
WAITING FOR THE RIGHT MOMENT TO REMOVE YOU FROM POWER.

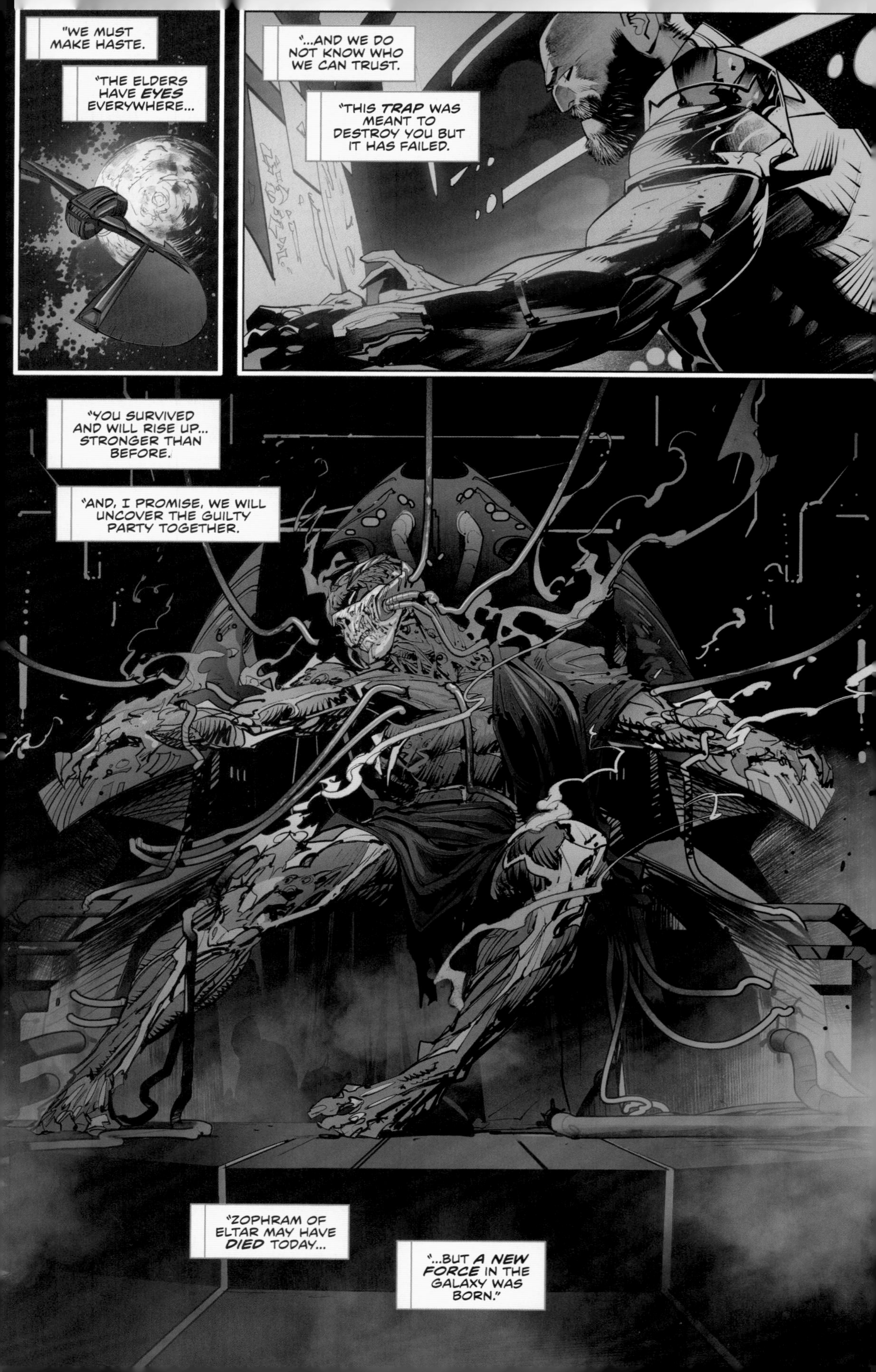
"WE MUST MAKE HASTE.
"THE ELDERS HAVE EYES EVERYWHERE...
"...AND WE DO NOT KNOW WHO WE CAN TRUST.
"THIS TRAP WAS MEANT TO DESTROY YOU BUT IT HAS FAILED.
"YOU SURVIVED AND WILL RISE UP... STRONGER THAN BEFORE.
"AND, I PROMISE, WE WILL UNCOVER THE GUILTY PARTY TOGETHER.
"ZOPHRAM OF ELTAR MAY HAVE DIED TODAY...
"...BUT A NEW FORCE IN THE GALAXY WAS BORN."

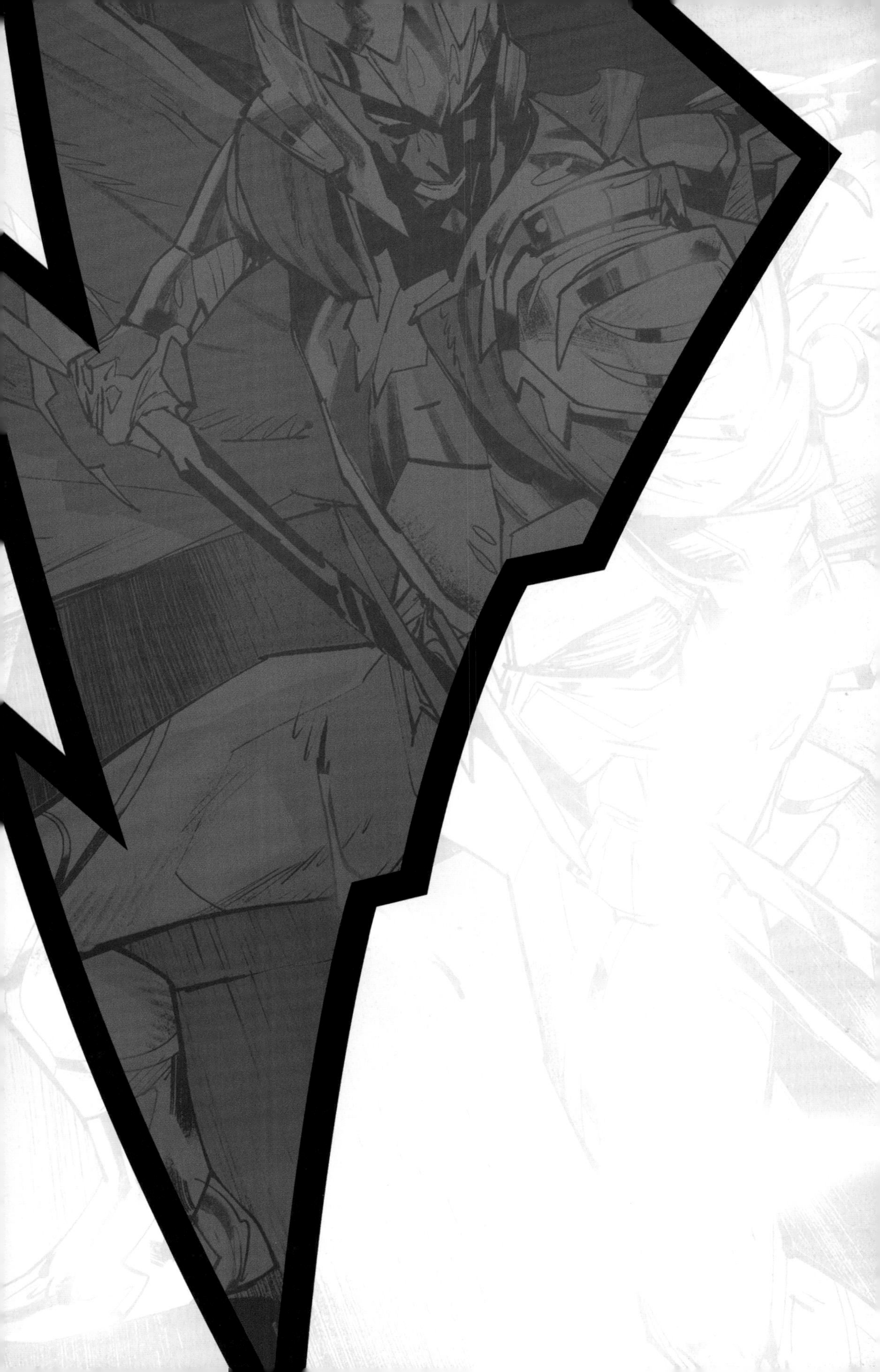

CHAPTER ELEVEN

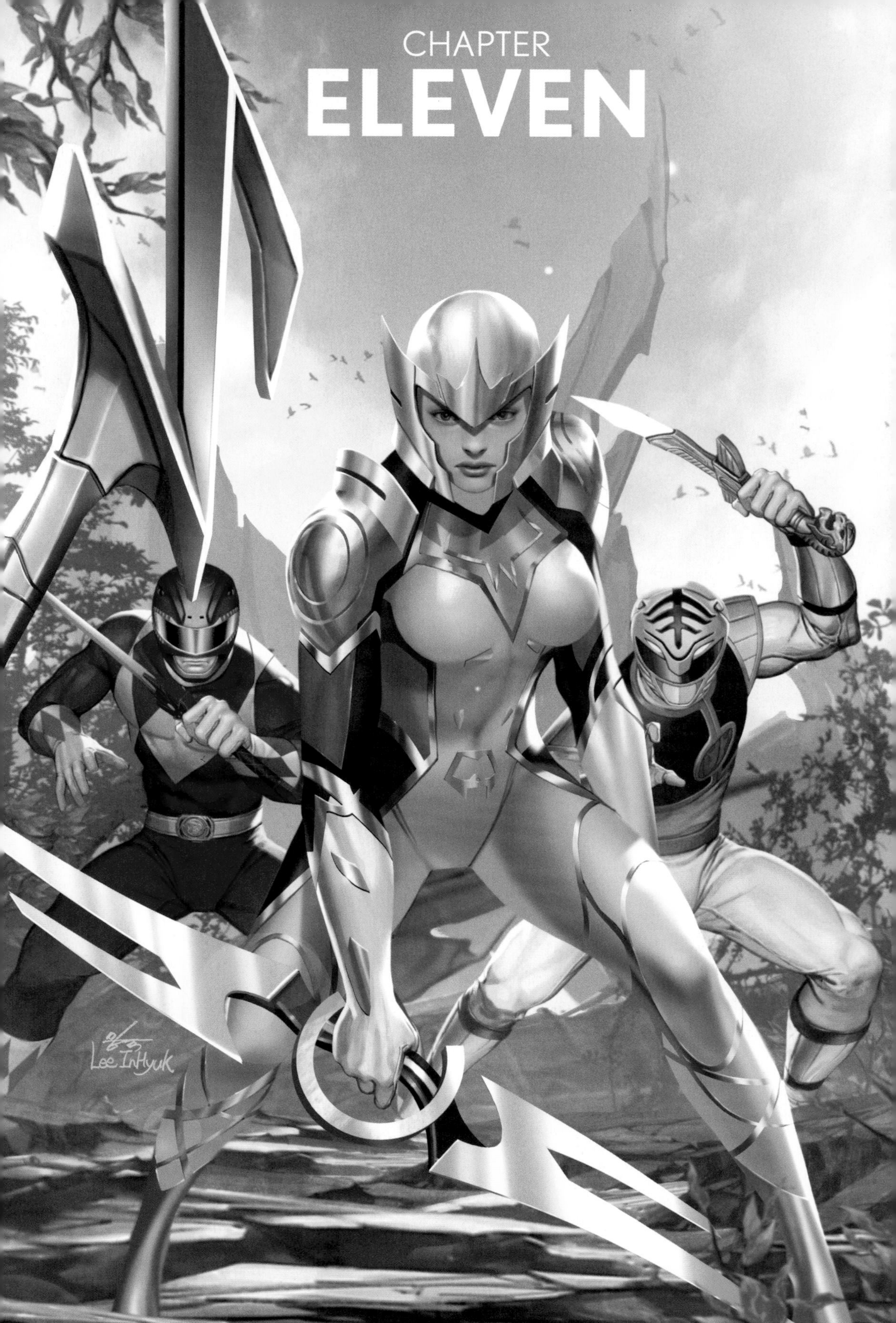
Lee InHyuk

INHYUK LEE | ISSUE ELEVEN COVER

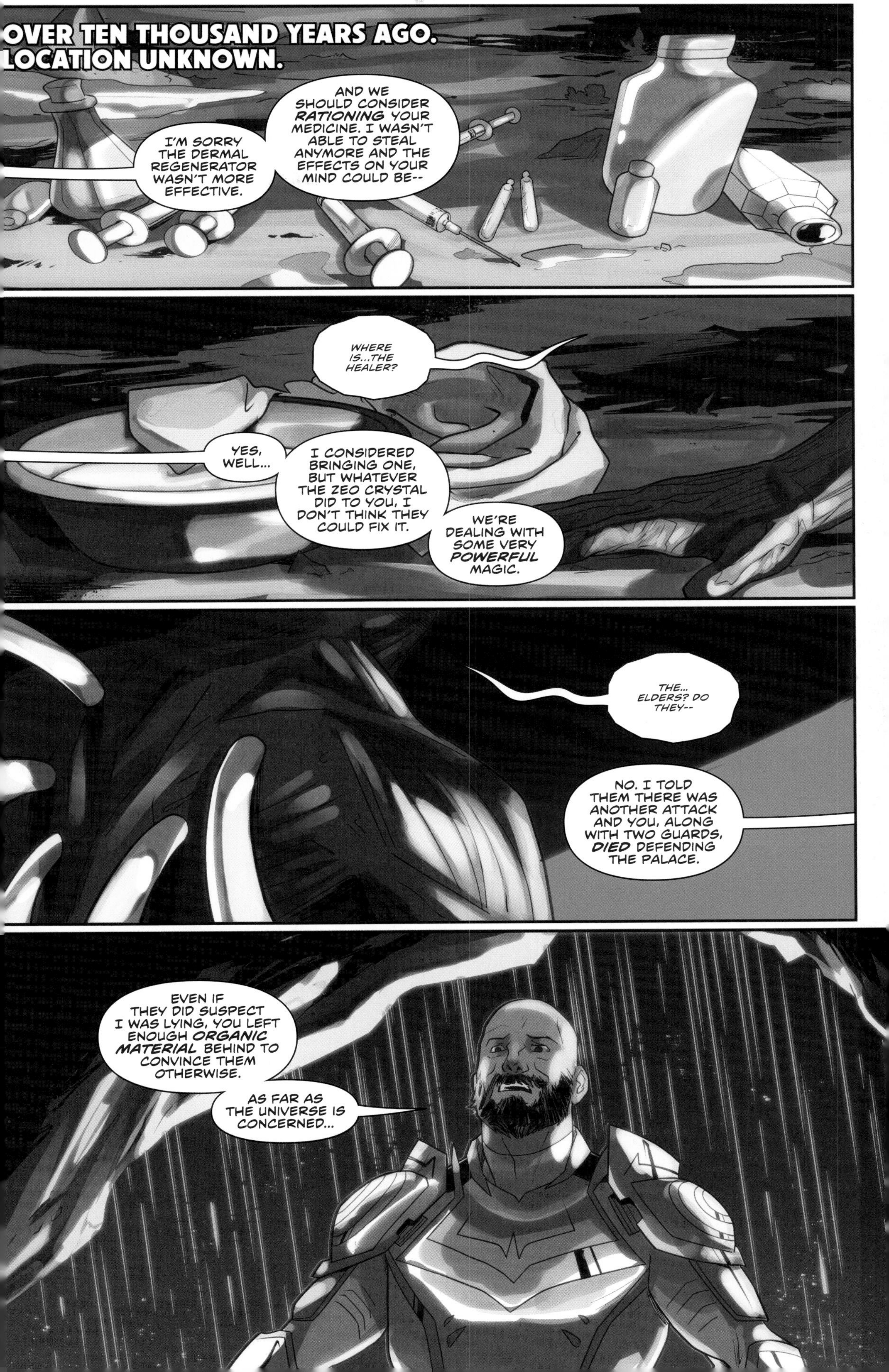
OVER TEN THOUSAND YEARS AGO. LOCATION UNKNOWN.
I'M SORRY THE DERMAL REGENERATOR WASN'T MORE EFFECTIVE.
AND WE SHOULD CONSIDER RATIONING YOUR MEDICINE. I WASN'T ABLE TO STEAL ANYMORE AND THE EFFECTS ON YOUR MIND COULD BE--
WHERE IS...THE HEALER?
YES, WELL...
I CONSIDERED BRINGING ONE, BUT WHATEVER THE ZEO CRYSTAL DID TO YOU, I DON'T THINK THEY COULD FIX IT.
WE'RE DEALING WITH SOME VERY POWERFUL MAGIC.
THE... ELDERS? DO THEY--
NO. I TOLD THEM THERE WAS ANOTHER ATTACK AND YOU, ALONG WITH TWO GUARDS, DIED DEFENDING THE PALACE.
EVEN IF THEY DID SUSPECT I WAS LYING, YOU LEFT ENOUGH ORGANIC MATERIAL BEHIND TO CONVINCE THEM OTHERWISE.
AS FAR AS THE UNIVERSE IS CONCERNED...

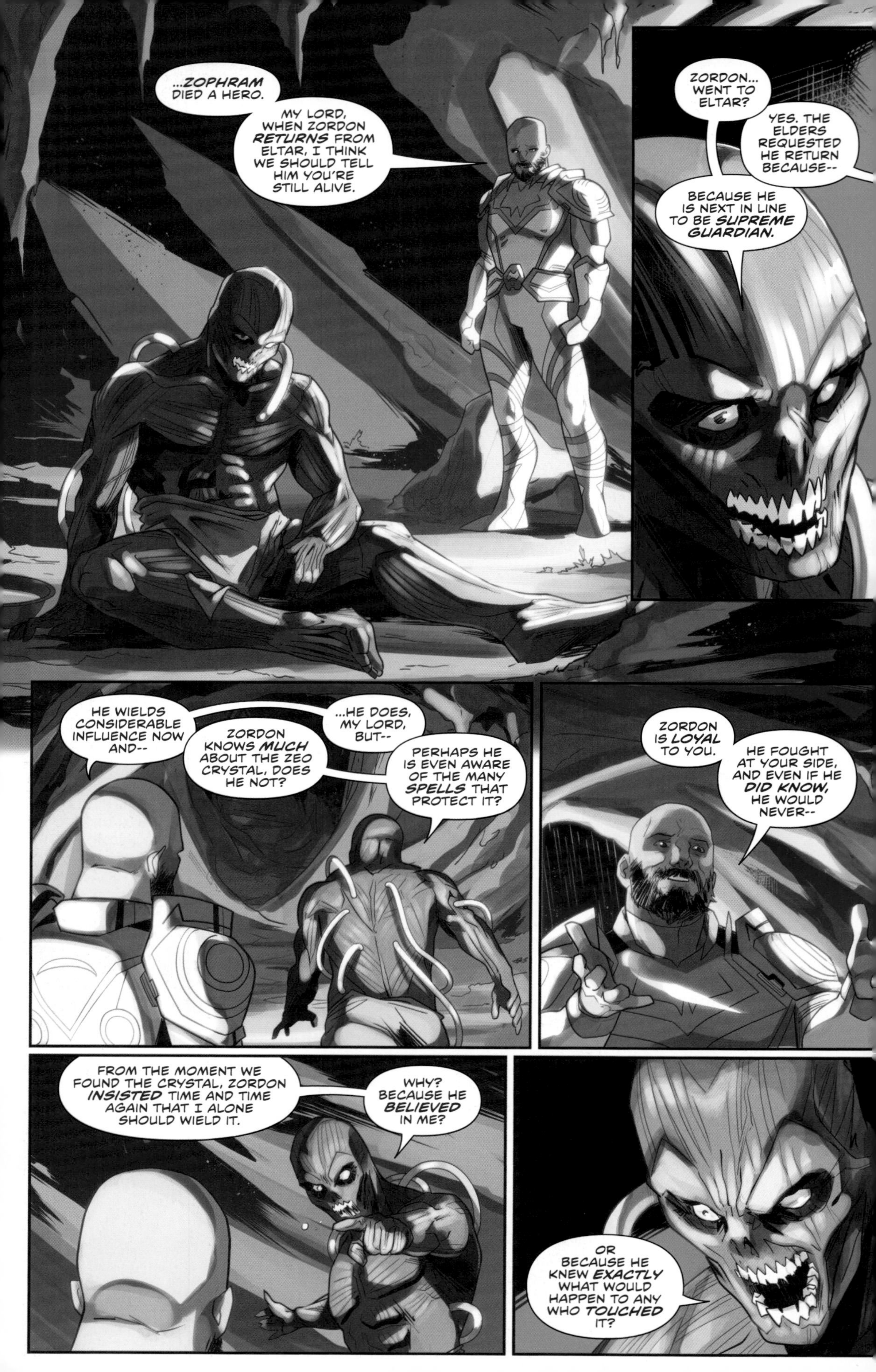
...ZOPHRAM DIED A HERO.
MY LORD, WHEN ZORDON RETURNS FROM ELTAR, I THINK WE SHOULD TELL HIM YOU'RE STILL ALIVE.
ZORDON... WENT TO ELTAR?
YES. THE ELDERS REQUESTED HE RETURN BECAUSE--
BECAUSE HE IS NEXT IN LINE TO BE SUPREME GUARDIAN.
HE WIELDS CONSIDERABLE INFLUENCE NOW AND--
...HE DOES, MY LORD, BUT--
ZORDON KNOWS MUCH ABOUT THE ZEO CRYSTAL, DOES HE NOT?
PERHAPS HE IS EVEN AWARE OF THE MANY SPELLS THAT PROTECT IT?
ZORDON IS LOYAL TO YOU.
HE FOUGHT AT YOUR SIDE, AND EVEN IF HE DID KNOW, HE WOULD NEVER--
FROM THE MOMENT WE FOUND THE CRYSTAL, ZORDON INSISTED TIME AND TIME AGAIN THAT I ALONE SHOULD WIELD IT.
WHY? BECAUSE HE BELIEVED IN ME?
OR BECAUSE HE KNEW EXACTLY WHAT WOULD HAPPEN TO ANY WHO TOUCHED IT?

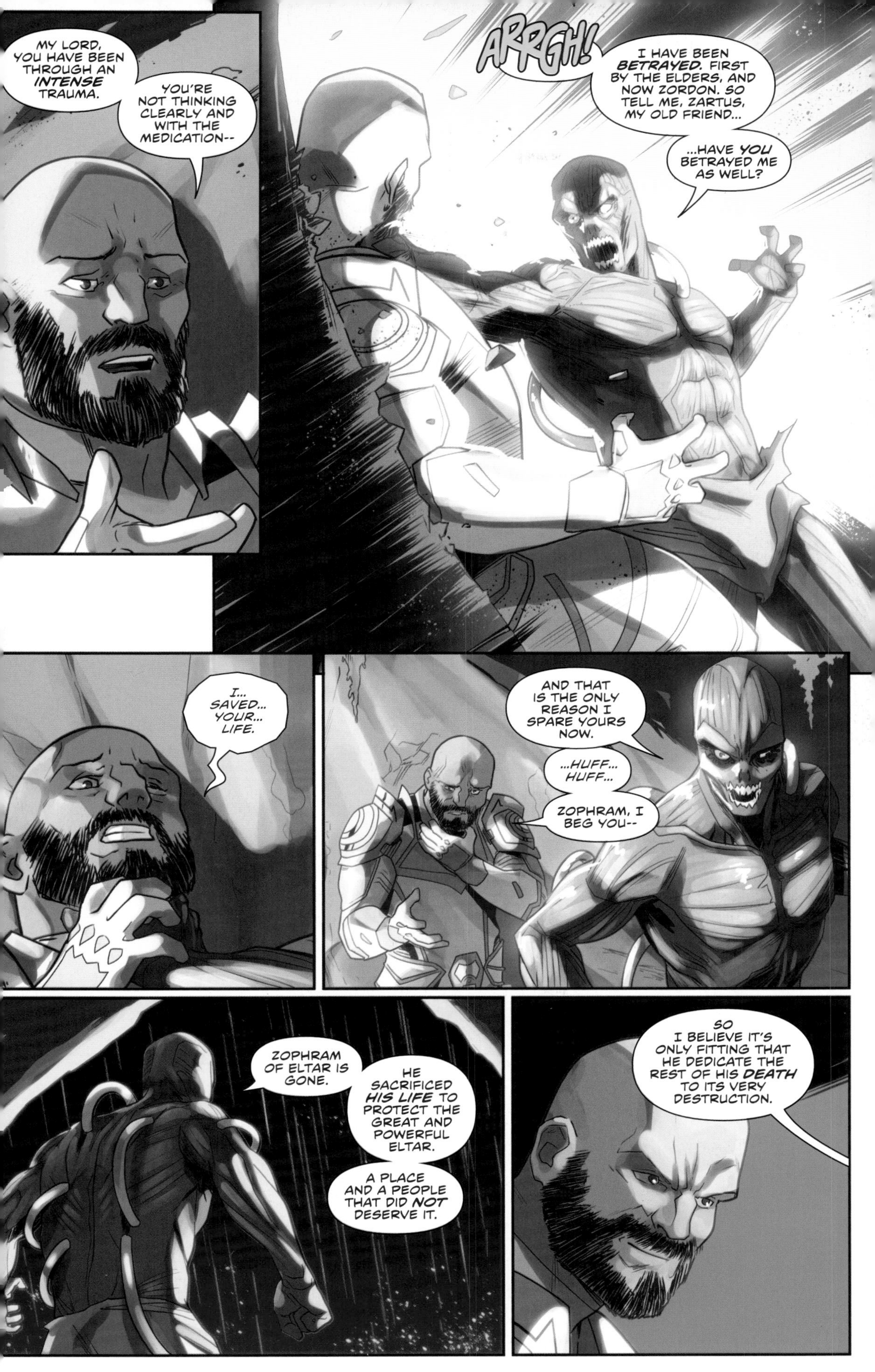
MY LORD, YOU HAVE BEEN THROUGH AN INTENSE TRAUMA.
YOU'RE NOT THINKING CLEARLY AND WITH THE MEDICATION--
ARRGH!
I HAVE BEEN BETRAYED. FIRST BY THE ELDERS, AND NOW ZORDON. SO TELL ME, ZARTUS, MY OLD FRIEND...
...HAVE YOU BETRAYED ME AS WELL?
I... SAVED... YOUR... LIFE.
AND THAT IS THE ONLY REASON I SPARE YOURS NOW.
...HUFF... HUFF...
ZOPHRAM, I BEG YOU--
ZOPHRAM OF ELTAR IS GONE.
HE SACRIFICED HIS LIFE TO PROTECT THE GREAT AND POWERFUL ELTAR.
A PLACE AND A PEOPLE THAT DID NOT DESERVE IT.
SO I BELIEVE IT'S ONLY FITTING THAT HE DEDICATE THE REST OF HIS DEATH TO ITS VERY DESTRUCTION.

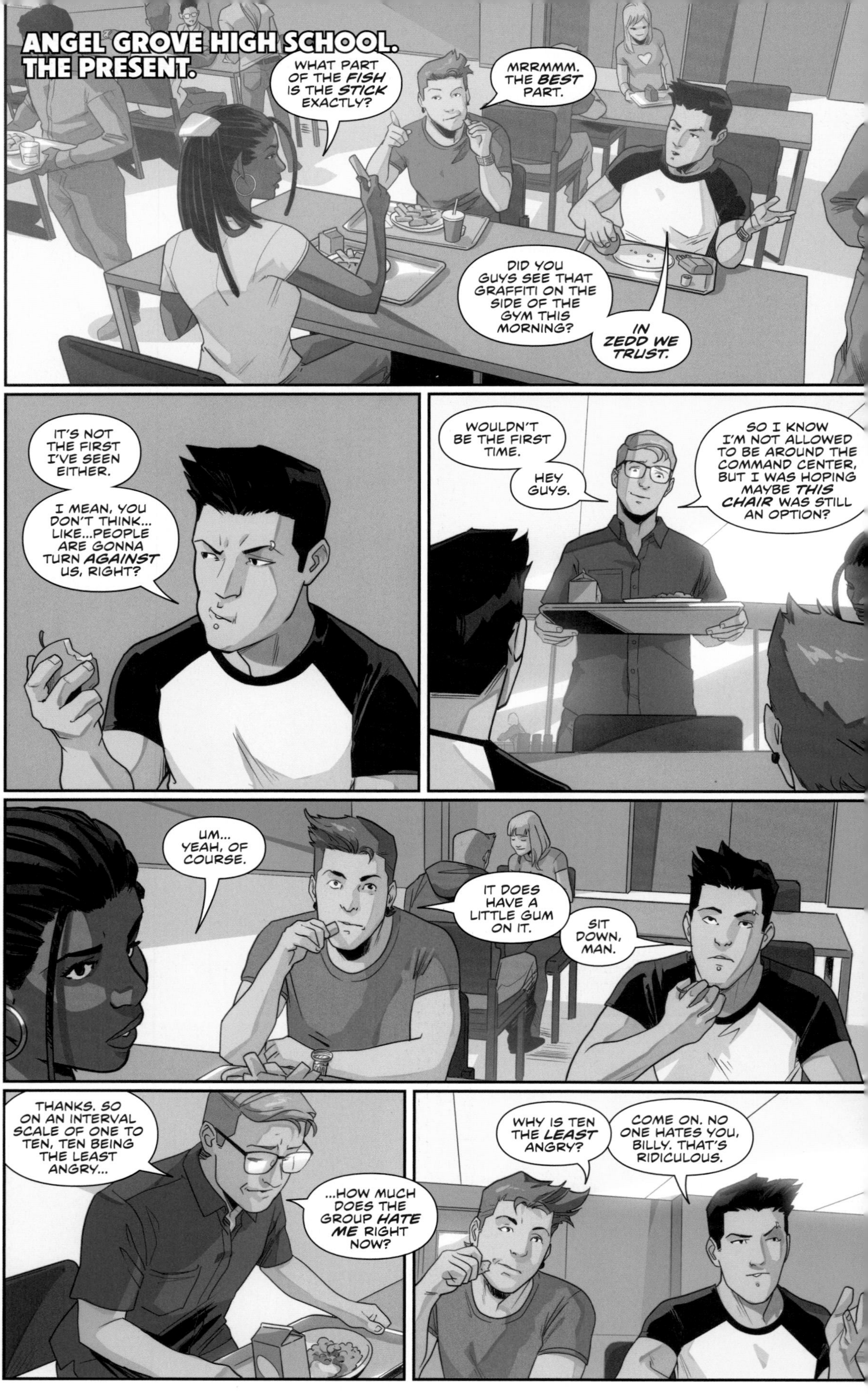
ANGEL GROVE HIGH SCHOOL. THE PRESENT.
WHAT PART OF THE FISH IS THE STICK EXACTLY?
MRRMMM. THE BEST PART.
DID YOU GUYS SEE THAT GRAFFITI ON THE SIDE OF THE GYM THIS MORNING?
IN ZEDD WE TRUST.
IT'S NOT THE FIRST I'VE SEEN EITHER.
I MEAN, YOU DON'T THINK... LIKE...PEOPLE ARE GONNA TURN AGAINST US, RIGHT?
WOULDN'T BE THE FIRST TIME.
HEY GUYS.
SO I KNOW I'M NOT ALLOWED TO BE AROUND THE COMMAND CENTER, BUT I WAS HOPING MAYBE THIS CHAIR WAS STILL AN OPTION?
UM... YEAH, OF COURSE.
IT DOES HAVE A LITTLE GUM ON IT.
SIT DOWN, MAN.
THANKS. SO ON AN INTERVAL SCALE OF ONE TO TEN, TEN BEING THE LEAST ANGRY...
...HOW MUCH DOES THE GROUP HATE ME RIGHT NOW?
WHY IS TEN THE LEAST ANGRY?
COME ON. NO ONE HATES YOU, BILLY. THAT'S RIDICULOUS.

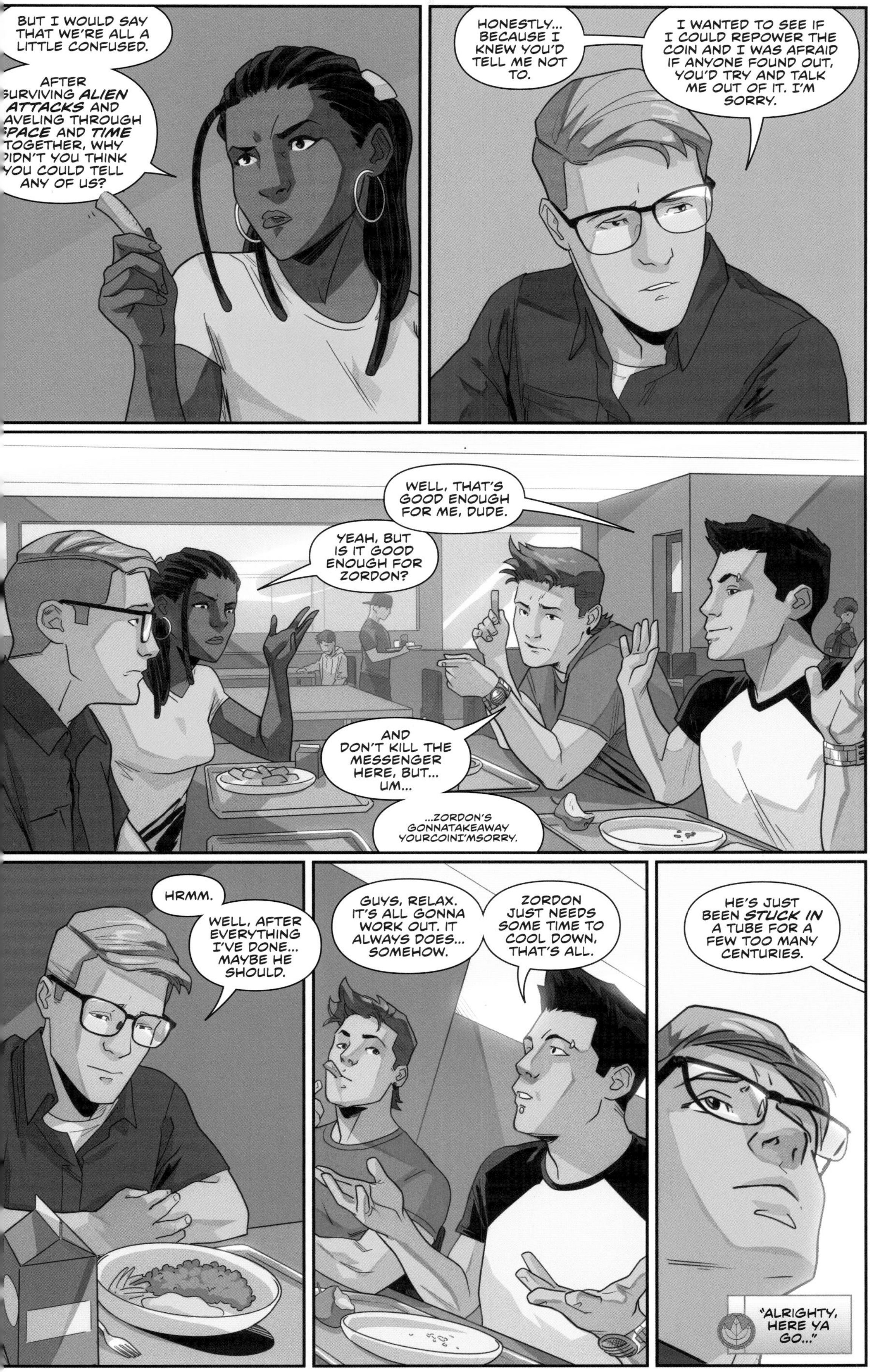
BUT I WOULD SAY THAT WE'RE ALL A LITTLE CONFUSED.
AFTER SURVIVING ALIEN ATTACKS AND TRAVELING THROUGH SPACE AND TIME TOGETHER, WHY DIDN'T YOU THINK YOU COULD TELL ANY OF US?
HONESTLY... BECAUSE I KNEW YOU'D TELL ME NOT TO.
I WANTED TO SEE IF I COULD REPOWER THE COIN AND I WAS AFRAID IF ANYONE FOUND OUT, YOU'D TRY AND TALK ME OUT OF IT. I'M SORRY.
WELL, THAT'S GOOD ENOUGH FOR ME, DUDE.
YEAH, BUT IS IT GOOD ENOUGH FOR ZORDON?
AND DON'T KILL THE MESSENGER HERE, BUT... UM...
...ZORDON'S GONNATAKEAWAY YOURCOINI'MSORRY.
HRMM.
WELL, AFTER EVERYTHING I'VE DONE... MAYBE HE SHOULD.
GUYS, RELAX. IT'S ALL GONNA WORK OUT. IT ALWAYS DOES... SOMEHOW.
ZORDON JUST NEEDS SOME TIME TO COOL DOWN, THAT'S ALL.
HE'S JUST BEEN STUCK IN A TUBE FOR A FEW TOO MANY CENTURIES.
"ALRIGHTY, HERE YA GO..."

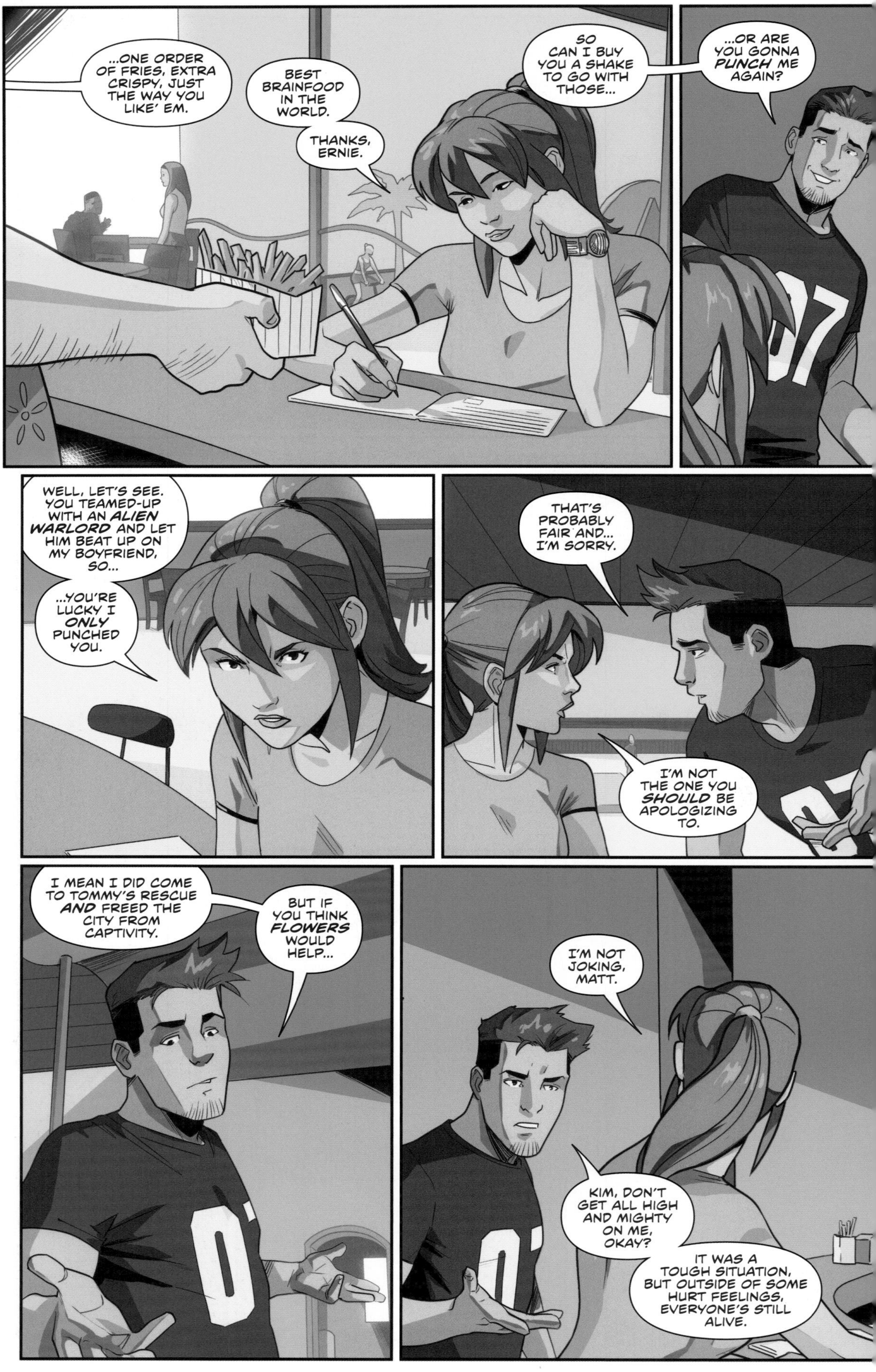
...ONE ORDER OF FRIES, EXTRA CRISPY, JUST THE WAY YOU LIKE' EM.
BEST BRAINFOOD IN THE WORLD.
THANKS, ERNIE.
SO CAN I BUY YOU A SHAKE TO GO WITH THOSE...
...OR ARE YOU GONNA PUNCH ME AGAIN?
WELL, LET'S SEE. YOU TEAMED-UP WITH AN ALIEN WARLORD AND LET HIM BEAT UP ON MY BOYFRIEND, SO...
...YOU'RE LUCKY I ONLY PUNCHED YOU.
THAT'S PROBABLY FAIR AND... I'M SORRY.
I'M NOT THE ONE YOU SHOULD BE APOLOGIZING TO.
I MEAN I DID COME TO TOMMY'S RESCUE AND FREED THE CITY FROM CAPTIVITY.
BUT IF YOU THINK FLOWERS WOULD HELP...
I'M NOT JOKING, MATT.
KIM, DON'T GET ALL HIGH AND MIGHTY ON ME, OKAY?
IT WAS A TOUGH SITUATION, BUT OUTSIDE OF SOME HURT FEELINGS, EVERYONE'S STILL ALIVE.

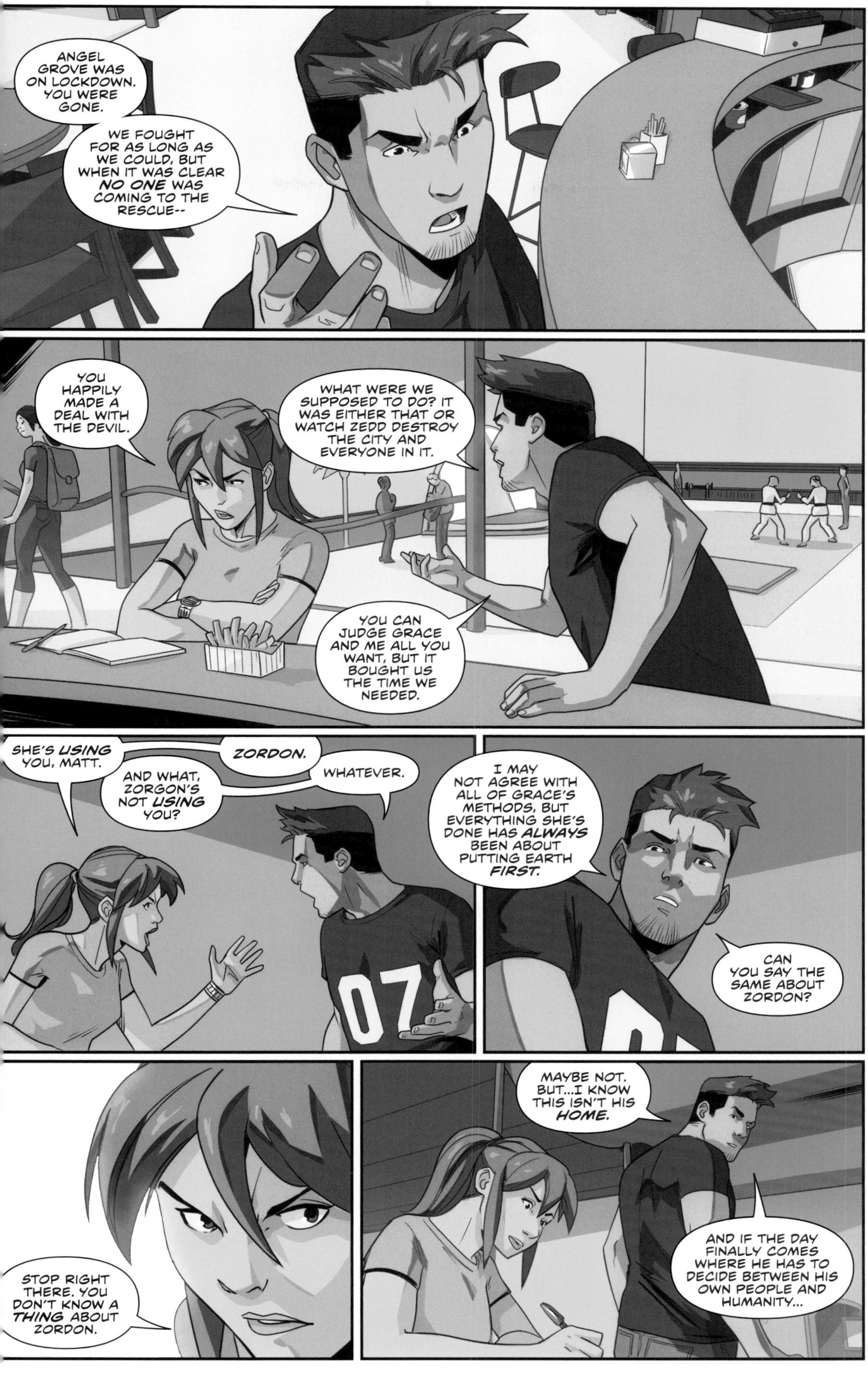
ANGEL GROVE WAS ON LOCKDOWN. YOU WERE GONE.
WE FOUGHT FOR AS LONG AS WE COULD, BUT WHEN IT WAS CLEAR ***NO ONE*** WAS COMING TO THE RESCUE--
YOU HAPPILY MADE A DEAL WITH THE DEVIL.
WHAT WERE WE SUPPOSED TO DO? IT WAS EITHER THAT OR WATCH ZEDD DESTROY THE CITY AND EVERYONE IN IT.
YOU CAN JUDGE GRACE AND ME ALL YOU WANT, BUT IT BOUGHT US THE TIME WE NEEDED.
SHE'S ***USING*** YOU, MATT.
AND WHAT, ZORGON'S NOT ***USING*** YOU?
ZORDON.
WHATEVER.
I MAY NOT AGREE WITH ALL OF GRACE'S METHODS, BUT EVERYTHING SHE'S DONE HAS ***ALWAYS*** BEEN ABOUT PUTTING EARTH ***FIRST.***
CAN YOU SAY THE SAME ABOUT ZORDON?
STOP RIGHT THERE. YOU DON'T KNOW A ***THING*** ABOUT ZORDON.
MAYBE NOT. BUT...I KNOW THIS ISN'T HIS ***HOME.***
AND IF THE DAY FINALLY COMES WHERE HE HAS TO DECIDE BETWEEN HIS OWN PEOPLE AND HUMANITY...

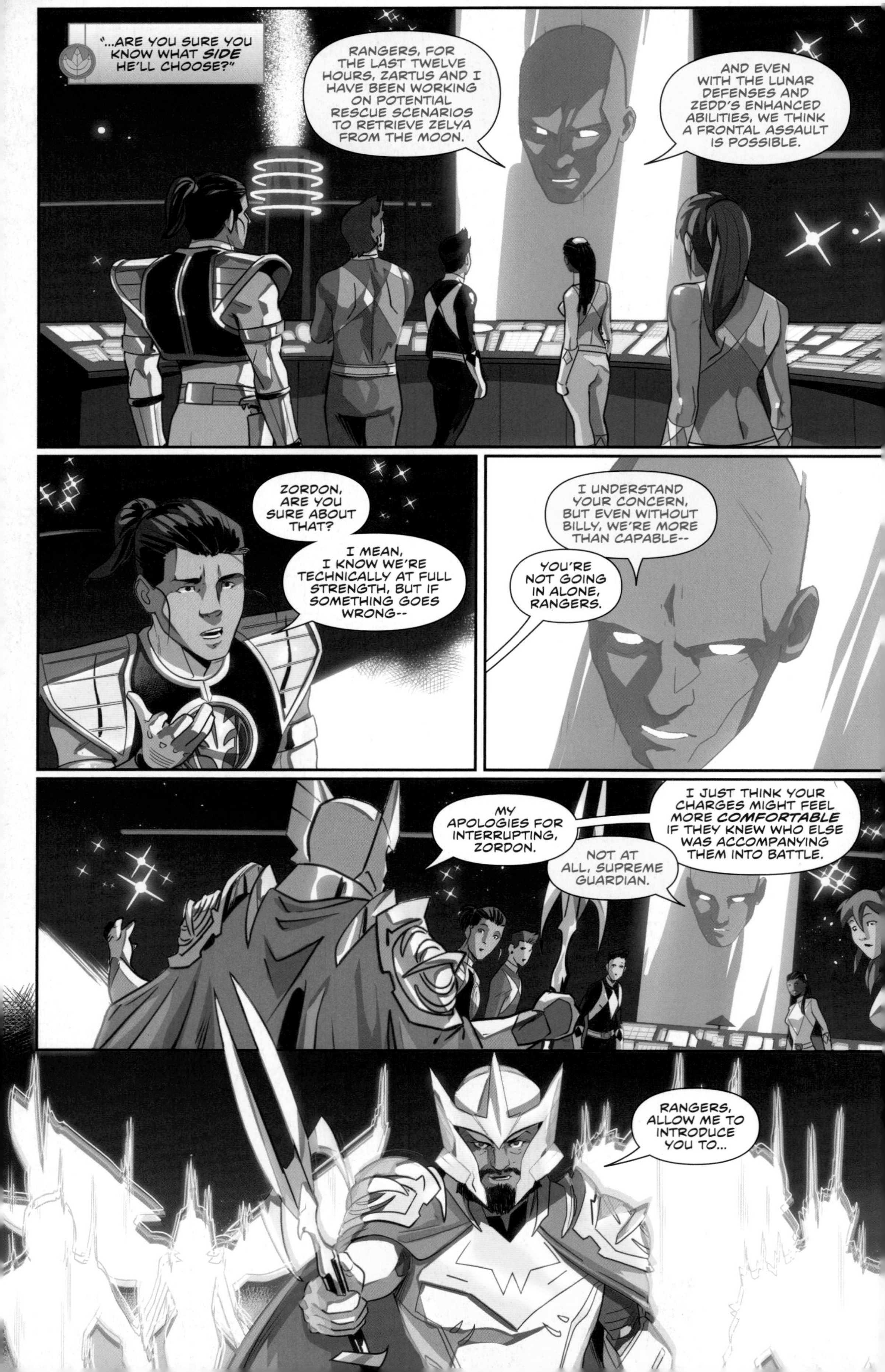
"...ARE YOU SURE YOU KNOW WHAT *SIDE* HE'LL CHOOSE?"
RANGERS, FOR THE LAST TWELVE HOURS, ZARTUS AND I HAVE BEEN WORKING ON POTENTIAL RESCUE SCENARIOS TO RETRIEVE ZELYA FROM THE MOON.
AND EVEN WITH THE LUNAR DEFENSES AND ZEDD'S ENHANCED ABILITIES, WE THINK A FRONTAL ASSAULT IS POSSIBLE.
ZORDON, ARE YOU SURE ABOUT THAT?
I MEAN, I KNOW WE'RE TECHNICALLY AT FULL STRENGTH, BUT IF SOMETHING GOES WRONG--
I UNDERSTAND YOUR CONCERN, BUT EVEN WITHOUT BILLY, WE'RE MORE THAN CAPABLE--
YOU'RE NOT GOING IN ALONE, RANGERS.
MY APOLOGIES FOR INTERRUPTING, ZORDON.
NOT AT ALL, SUPREME GUARDIAN.
I JUST THINK YOUR CHARGES MIGHT FEEL MORE *COMFORTABLE* IF THEY KNEW WHO ELSE WAS ACCOMPANYING THEM INTO BATTLE.
RANGERS, ALLOW ME TO INTRODUCE YOU TO...

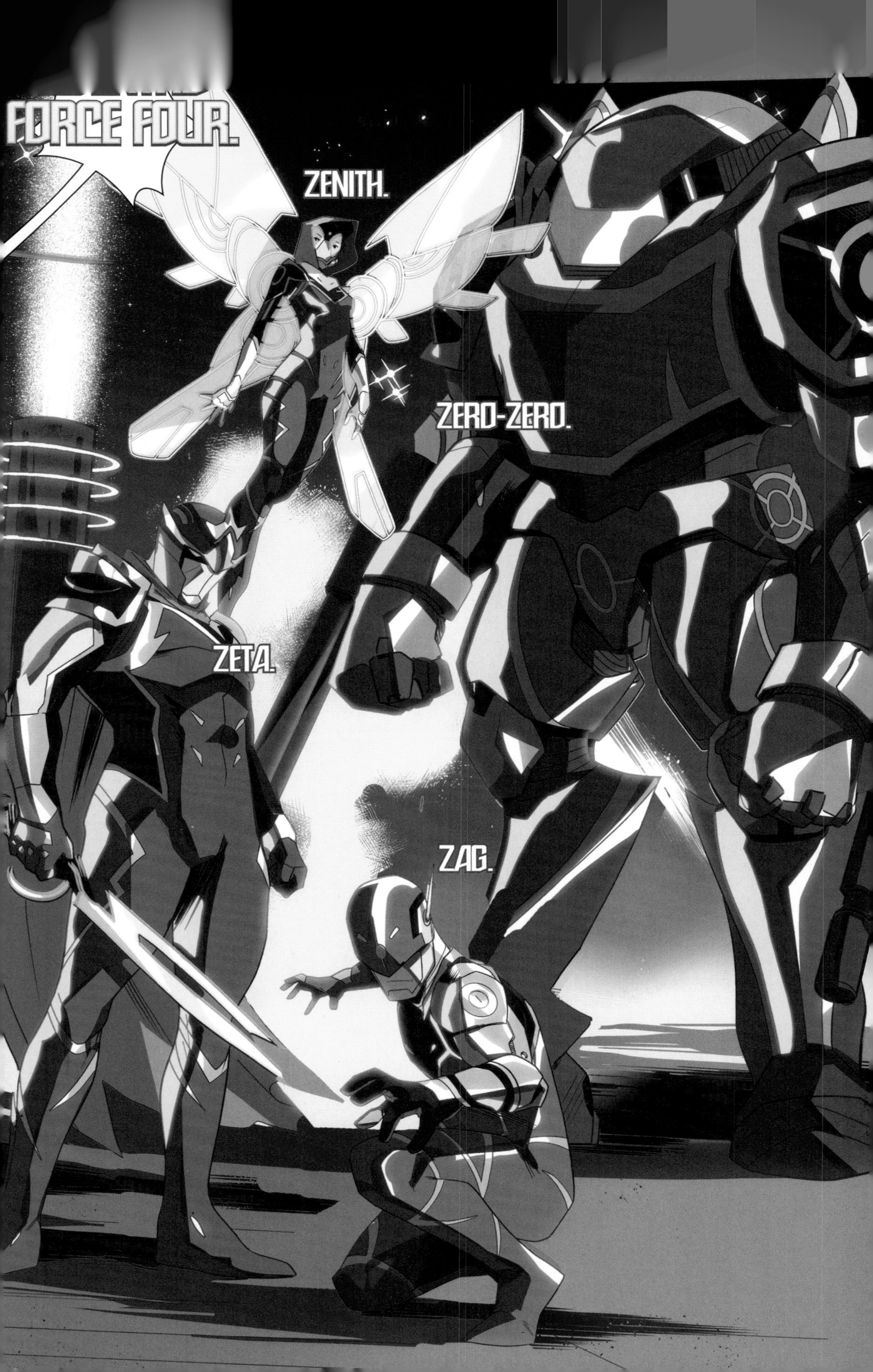
FORCE FOUR.
ZENITH.
ZERO-ZERO.
ZETA.
ZAG.

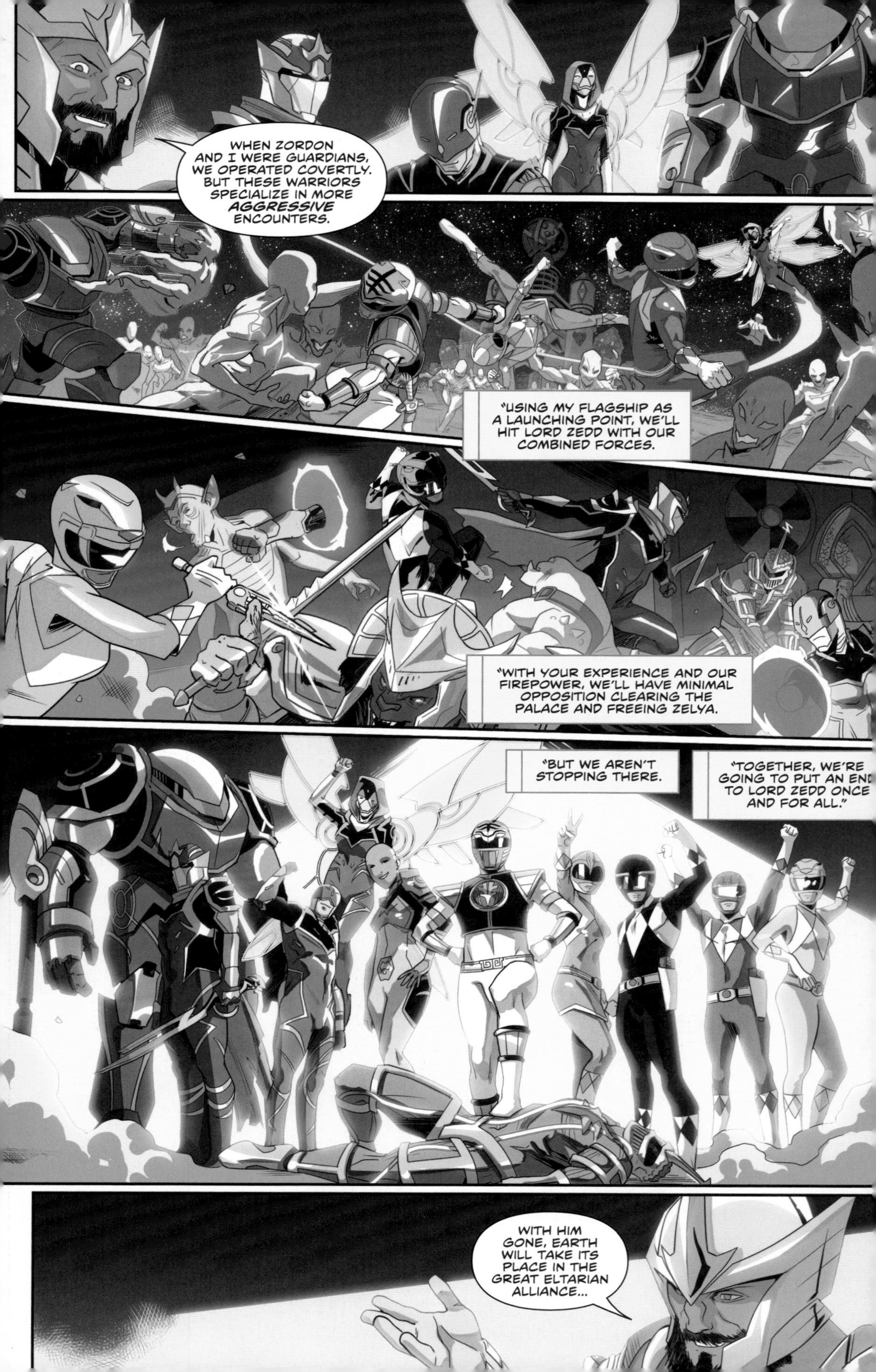

WHEN ZORDON AND I WERE GUARDIANS, WE OPERATED COVERTLY. BUT THESE WARRIORS SPECIALIZE IN MORE AGGRESSIVE ENCOUNTERS.
"USING MY FLAGSHIP AS A LAUNCHING POINT, WE'LL HIT LORD ZEDD WITH OUR COMBINED FORCES.
"WITH YOUR EXPERIENCE AND OUR FIREPOWER, WE'LL HAVE MINIMAL OPPOSITION CLEARING THE PALACE AND FREEING ZELYA.
"BUT WE AREN'T STOPPING THERE.
"TOGETHER, WE'RE GOING TO PUT AN END TO LORD ZEDD ONCE AND FOR ALL."
WITH HIM GONE, EARTH WILL TAKE ITS PLACE IN THE GREAT ELTARIAN ALLIANCE...

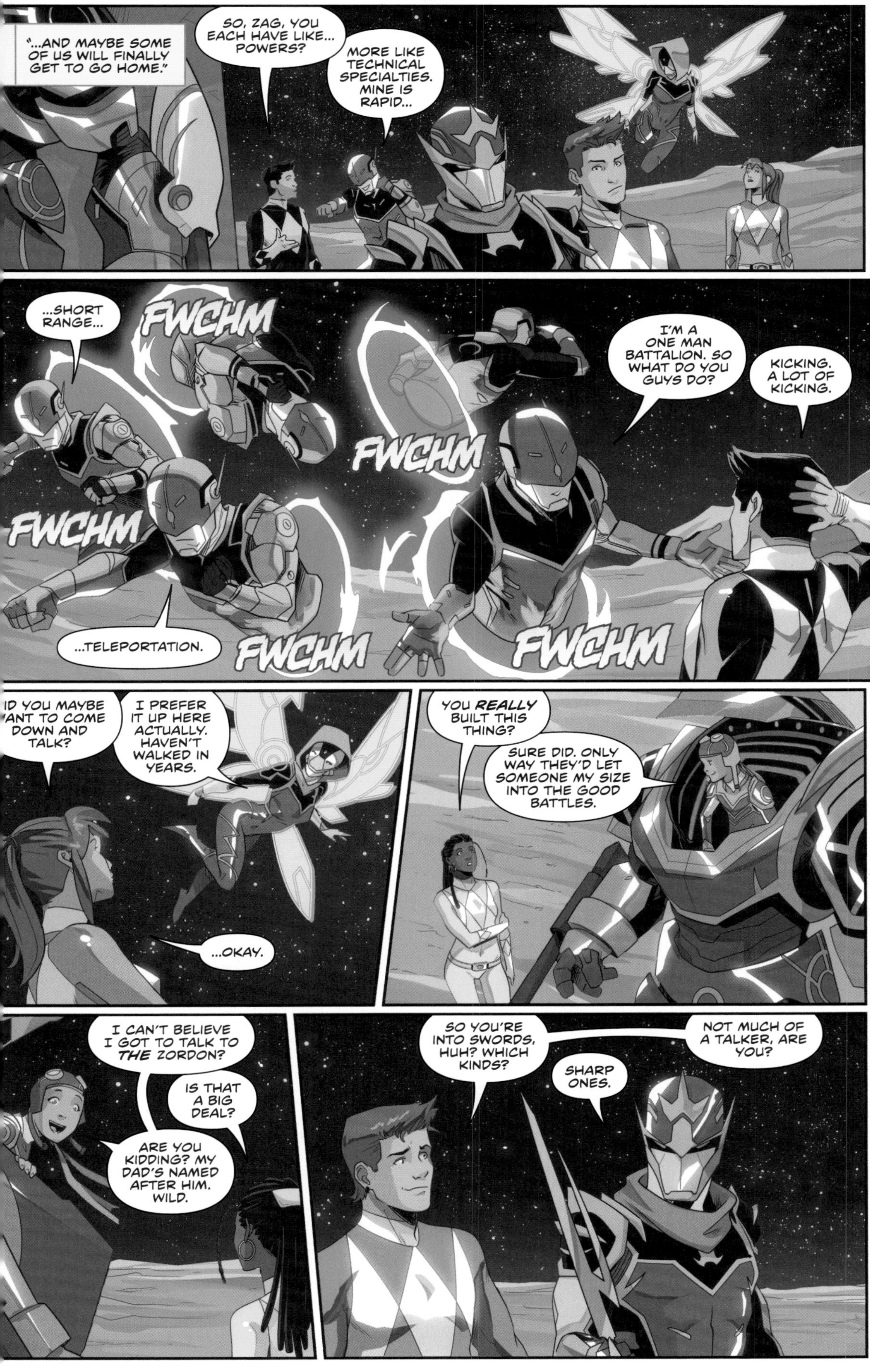
"...AND MAYBE SOME OF US WILL FINALLY GET TO GO HOME."
SO, ZAG, YOU EACH HAVE LIKE... POWERS?
MORE LIKE TECHNICAL SPECIALTIES. MINE IS RAPID...
...SHORT RANGE...
FWCHM
FWCHM
FWCHM
...TELEPORTATION.
FWCHM
FWCHM
I'M A ONE MAN BATTALION. SO WHAT DO YOU GUYS DO?
KICKING. A LOT OF KICKING.
ID YOU MAYBE ANT TO COME DOWN AND TALK?
I PREFER IT UP HERE ACTUALLY. HAVEN'T WALKED IN YEARS.
...OKAY.
YOU REALLY BUILT THIS THING?
SURE DID. ONLY WAY THEY'D LET SOMEONE MY SIZE INTO THE GOOD BATTLES.
I CAN'T BELIEVE I GOT TO TALK TO THE ZORDON?
IS THAT A BIG DEAL?
ARE YOU KIDDING? MY DAD'S NAMED AFTER HIM. WILD.
SO YOU'RE INTO SWORDS, HUH? WHICH KINDS?
SHARP ONES.
NOT MUCH OF A TALKER, ARE YOU?

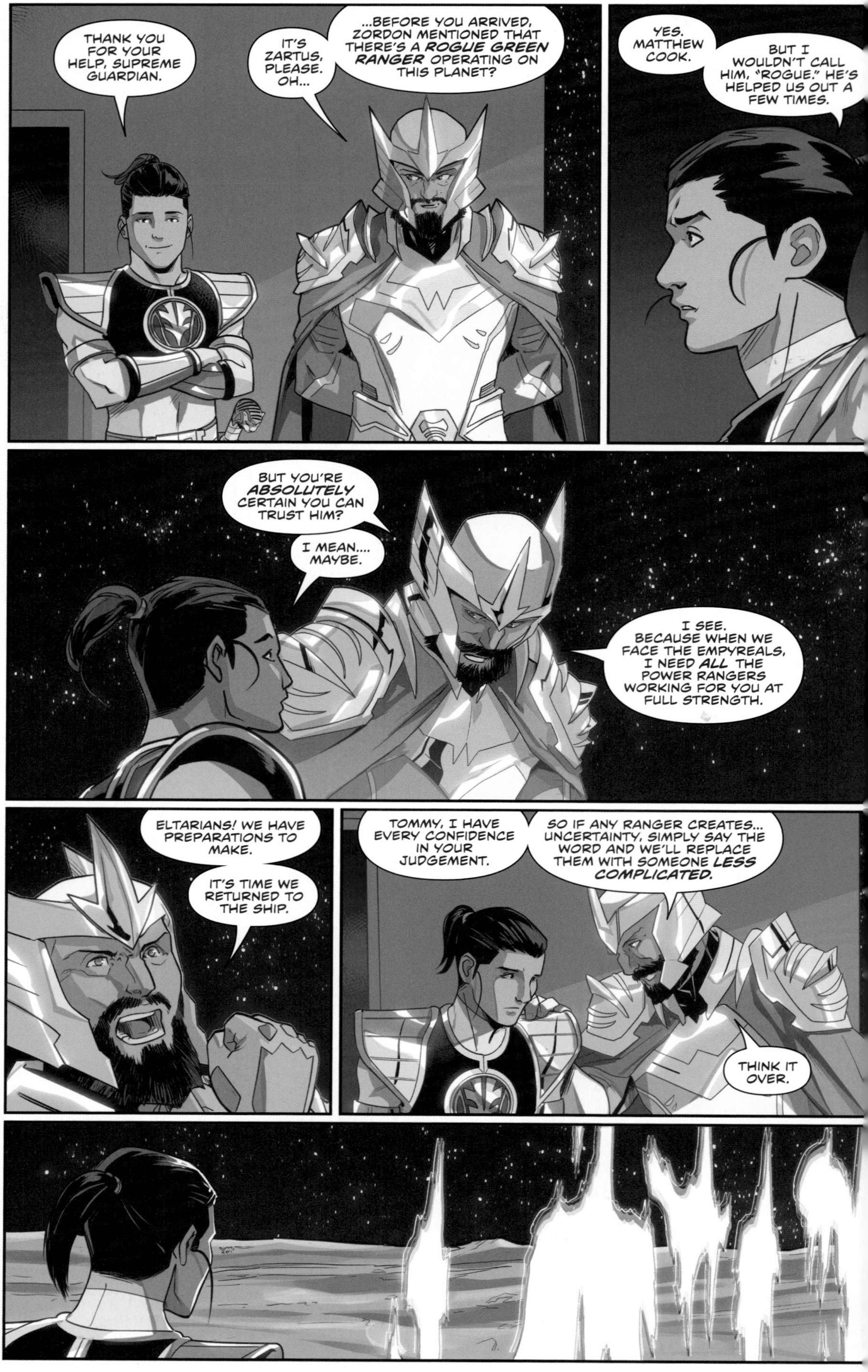
THANK YOU FOR YOUR HELP, SUPREME GUARDIAN.
IT'S ZARTUS, PLEASE. OH...
...BEFORE YOU ARRIVED, ZORDON MENTIONED THAT THERE'S A ROGUE GREEN RANGER OPERATING ON THIS PLANET?
YES. MATTHEW COOK.
BUT I WOULDN'T CALL HIM, "ROGUE." HE'S HELPED US OUT A FEW TIMES.
BUT YOU'RE ABSOLUTELY CERTAIN YOU CAN TRUST HIM?
I MEAN.... MAYBE.
I SEE. BECAUSE WHEN WE FACE THE EMPYREALS, I NEED ALL THE POWER RANGERS WORKING FOR YOU AT FULL STRENGTH.
ELTARIANS! WE HAVE PREPARATIONS TO MAKE.
IT'S TIME WE RETURNED TO THE SHIP.
TOMMY, I HAVE EVERY CONFIDENCE IN YOUR JUDGEMENT.
SO IF ANY RANGER CREATES... UNCERTAINTY, SIMPLY SAY THE WORD AND WE'LL REPLACE THEM WITH SOMEONE LESS COMPLICATED.
THINK IT OVER.

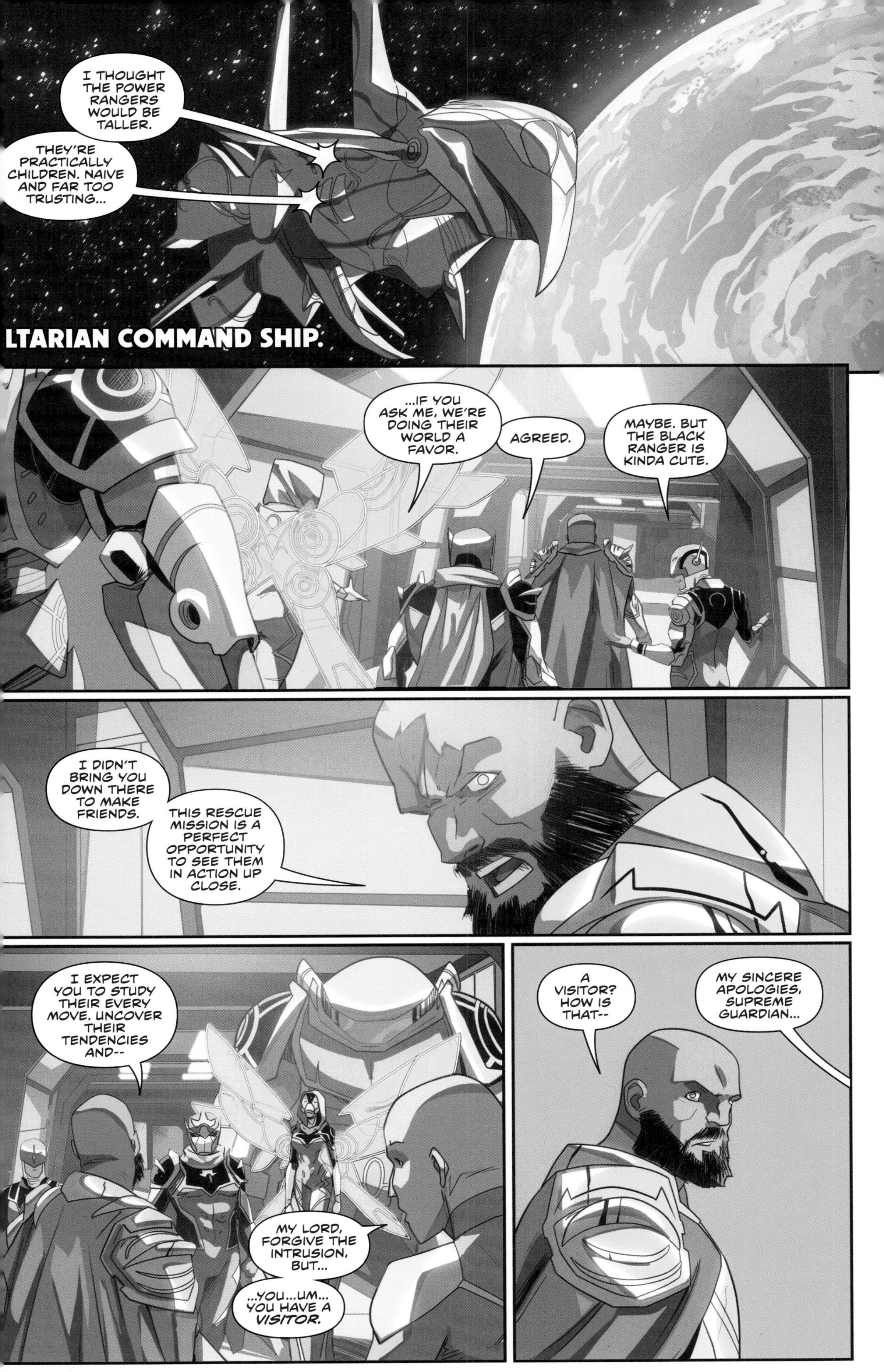
I THOUGHT THE POWER RANGERS WOULD BE TALLER.
THEY'RE PRACTICALLY CHILDREN. NAIVE AND FAR TOO TRUSTING...
LTARIAN COMMAND SHIP.
...IF YOU ASK ME, WE'RE DOING THEIR WORLD A FAVOR.
AGREED.
MAYBE. BUT THE BLACK RANGER IS KINDA CUTE.
I DIDN'T BRING YOU DOWN THERE TO MAKE FRIENDS.
THIS RESCUE MISSION IS A PERFECT OPPORTUNITY TO SEE THEM IN ACTION UP CLOSE.
I EXPECT YOU TO STUDY THEIR EVERY MOVE. UNCOVER THEIR TENDENCIES AND--
MY LORD, FORGIVE THE INTRUSION, BUT...
...YOU...UM... YOU HAVE A *VISITOR*.
A VISITOR? HOW IS THAT--
MY SINCERE APOLOGIES, SUPREME GUARDIAN...

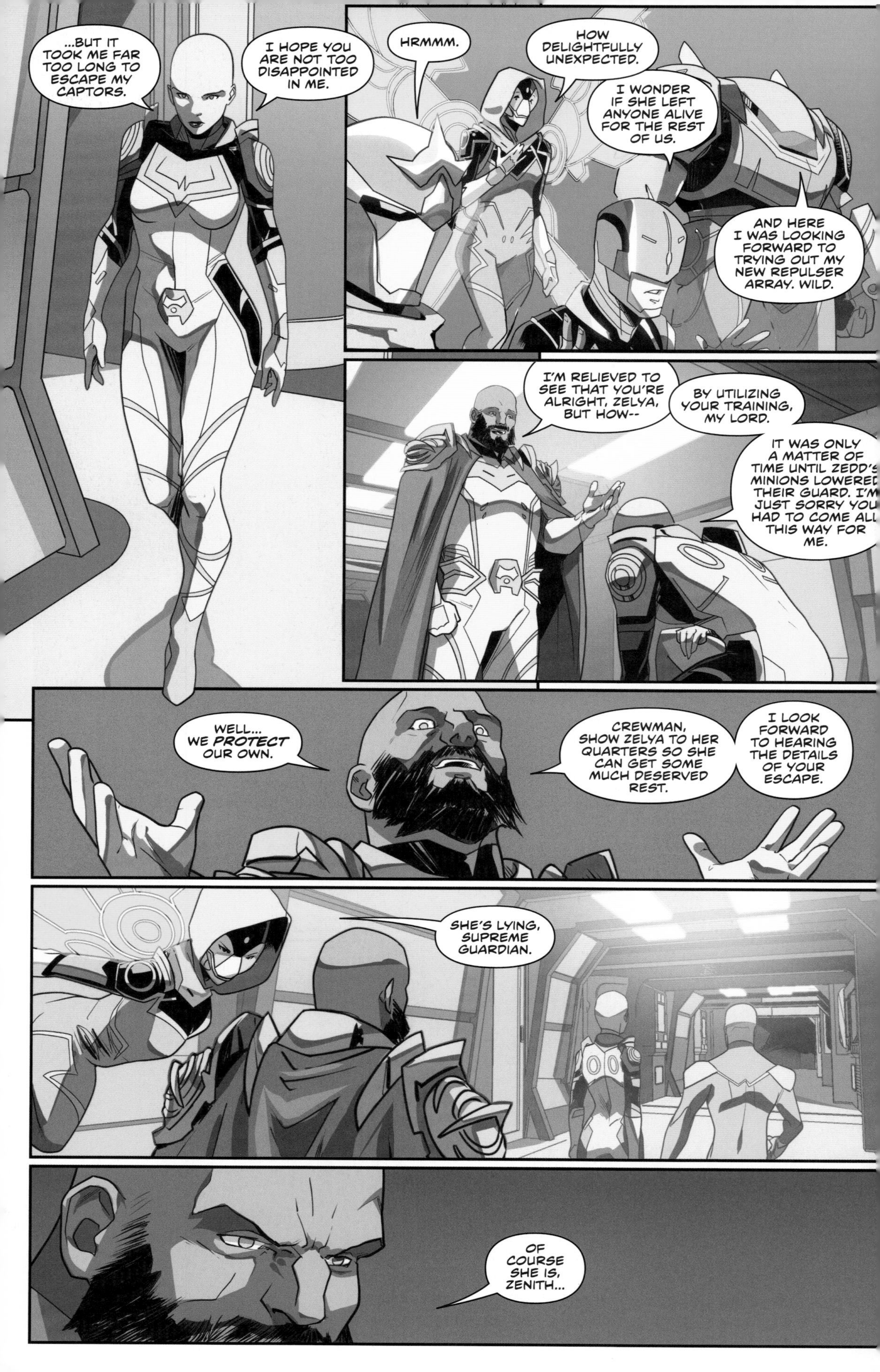
...BUT IT TOOK ME FAR TOO LONG TO ESCAPE MY CAPTORS.
I HOPE YOU ARE NOT TOO DISAPPOINTED IN ME.
HRMMM.
HOW DELIGHTFULLY UNEXPECTED.
I WONDER IF SHE LEFT ANYONE ALIVE FOR THE REST OF US.
AND HERE I WAS LOOKING FORWARD TO TRYING OUT MY NEW REPULSER ARRAY. WILD.
I'M RELIEVED TO SEE THAT YOU'RE ALRIGHT, ZELYA, BUT HOW--
BY UTILIZING YOUR TRAINING, MY LORD.
IT WAS ONLY A MATTER OF TIME UNTIL ZEDD'S MINIONS LOWERED THEIR GUARD. I'M JUST SORRY YOU HAD TO COME ALL THIS WAY FOR ME.
WELL... WE *PROTECT* OUR OWN.
CREWMAN, SHOW ZELYA TO HER QUARTERS SO SHE CAN GET SOME MUCH DESERVED REST.
I LOOK FORWARD TO HEARING THE DETAILS OF YOUR ESCAPE.
SHE'S LYING, SUPREME GUARDIAN.
OF COURSE SHE IS, ZENITH...

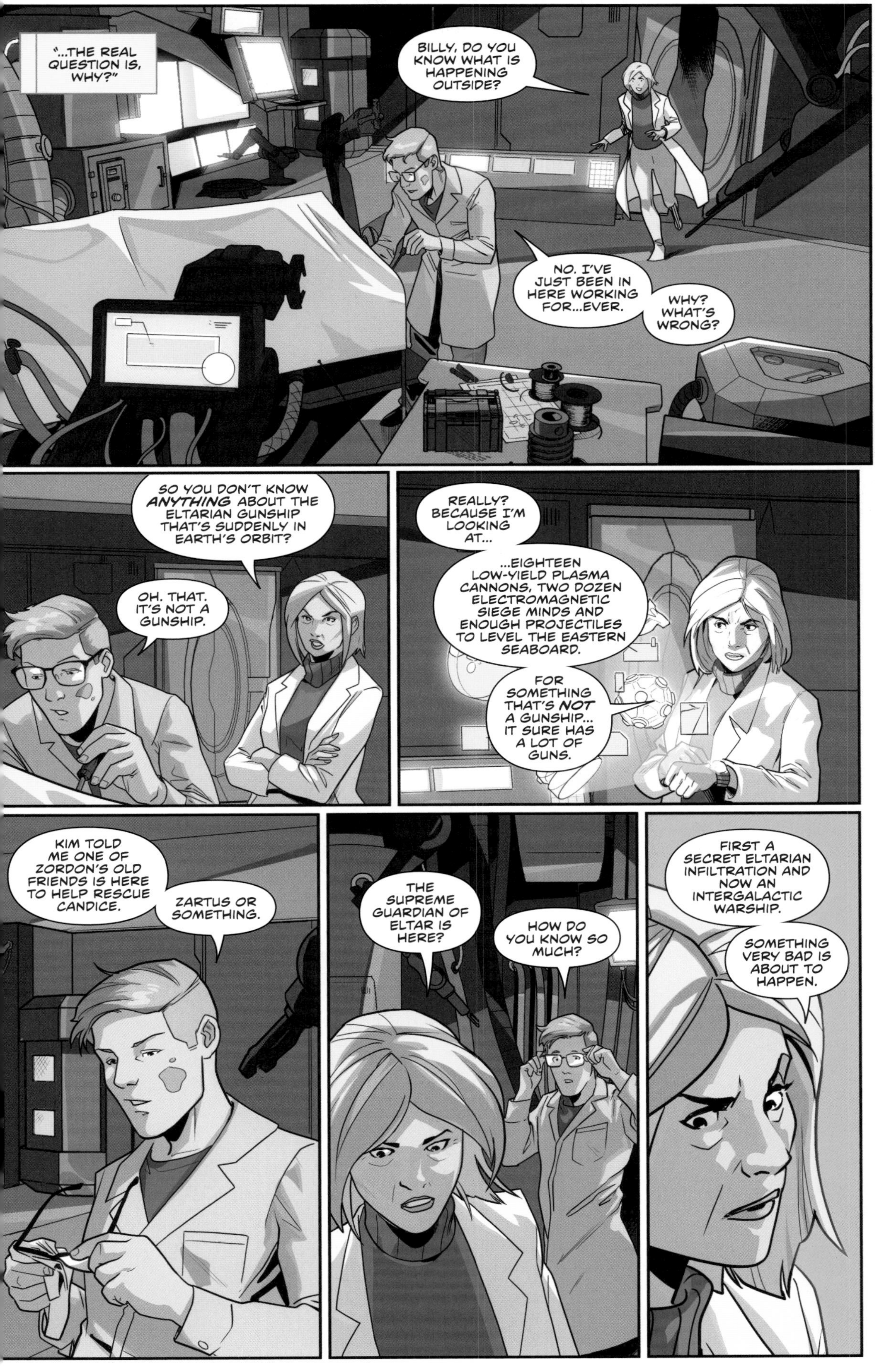
"...THE REAL QUESTION IS, WHY?"
BILLY, DO YOU KNOW WHAT IS HAPPENING OUTSIDE?
NO. I'VE JUST BEEN IN HERE WORKING FOR...EVER.
WHY? WHAT'S WRONG?
SO YOU DON'T KNOW ANYTHING ABOUT THE ELTARIAN GUNSHIP THAT'S SUDDENLY IN EARTH'S ORBIT?
OH. THAT. IT'S NOT A GUNSHIP.
REALLY? BECAUSE I'M LOOKING AT...
...EIGHTEEN LOW-YIELD PLASMA CANNONS, TWO DOZEN ELECTROMAGNETIC SIEGE MINDS AND ENOUGH PROJECTILES TO LEVEL THE EASTERN SEABOARD.
FOR SOMETHING THAT'S NOT A GUNSHIP... IT SURE HAS A LOT OF GUNS.
KIM TOLD ME ONE OF ZORDON'S OLD FRIENDS IS HERE TO HELP RESCUE CANDICE.
ZARTUS OR SOMETHING.
THE SUPREME GUARDIAN OF ELTAR IS HERE?
HOW DO YOU KNOW SO MUCH?
FIRST A SECRET ELTARIAN INFILTRATION AND NOW AN INTERGALACTIC WARSHIP.
SOMETHING VERY BAD IS ABOUT TO HAPPEN.

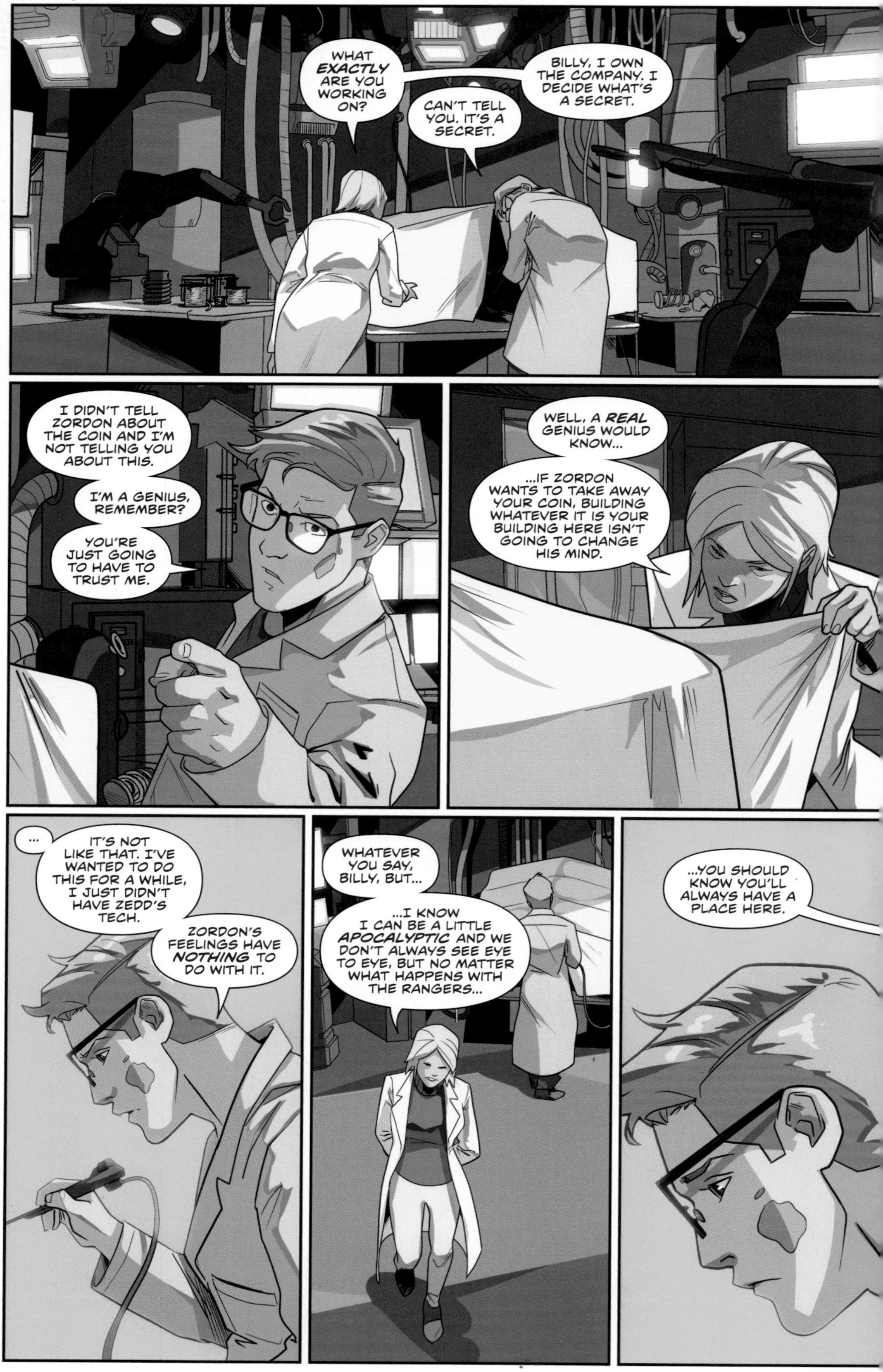
WHAT EXACTLY ARE YOU WORKING ON?
CAN'T TELL YOU. IT'S A SECRET.
BILLY, I OWN THE COMPANY. I DECIDE WHAT'S A SECRET.
I DIDN'T TELL ZORDON ABOUT THE COIN AND I'M NOT TELLING YOU ABOUT THIS.
I'M A GENIUS, REMEMBER?
YOU'RE JUST GOING TO HAVE TO TRUST ME.
WELL, A REAL GENIUS WOULD KNOW...
...IF ZORDON WANTS TO TAKE AWAY YOUR COIN, BUILDING WHATEVER IT IS YOUR BUILDING HERE ISN'T GOING TO CHANGE HIS MIND.
...
IT'S NOT LIKE THAT. I'VE WANTED TO DO THIS FOR A WHILE, I JUST DIDN'T HAVE ZEDD'S TECH.
ZORDON'S FEELINGS HAVE NOTHING TO DO WITH IT.
WHATEVER YOU SAY, BILLY, BUT...
...I KNOW I CAN BE A LITTLE APOCALYPTIC AND WE DON'T ALWAYS SEE EYE TO EYE, BUT NO MATTER WHAT HAPPENS WITH THE RANGERS...
...YOU SHOULD KNOW YOU'LL ALWAYS HAVE A PLACE HERE.

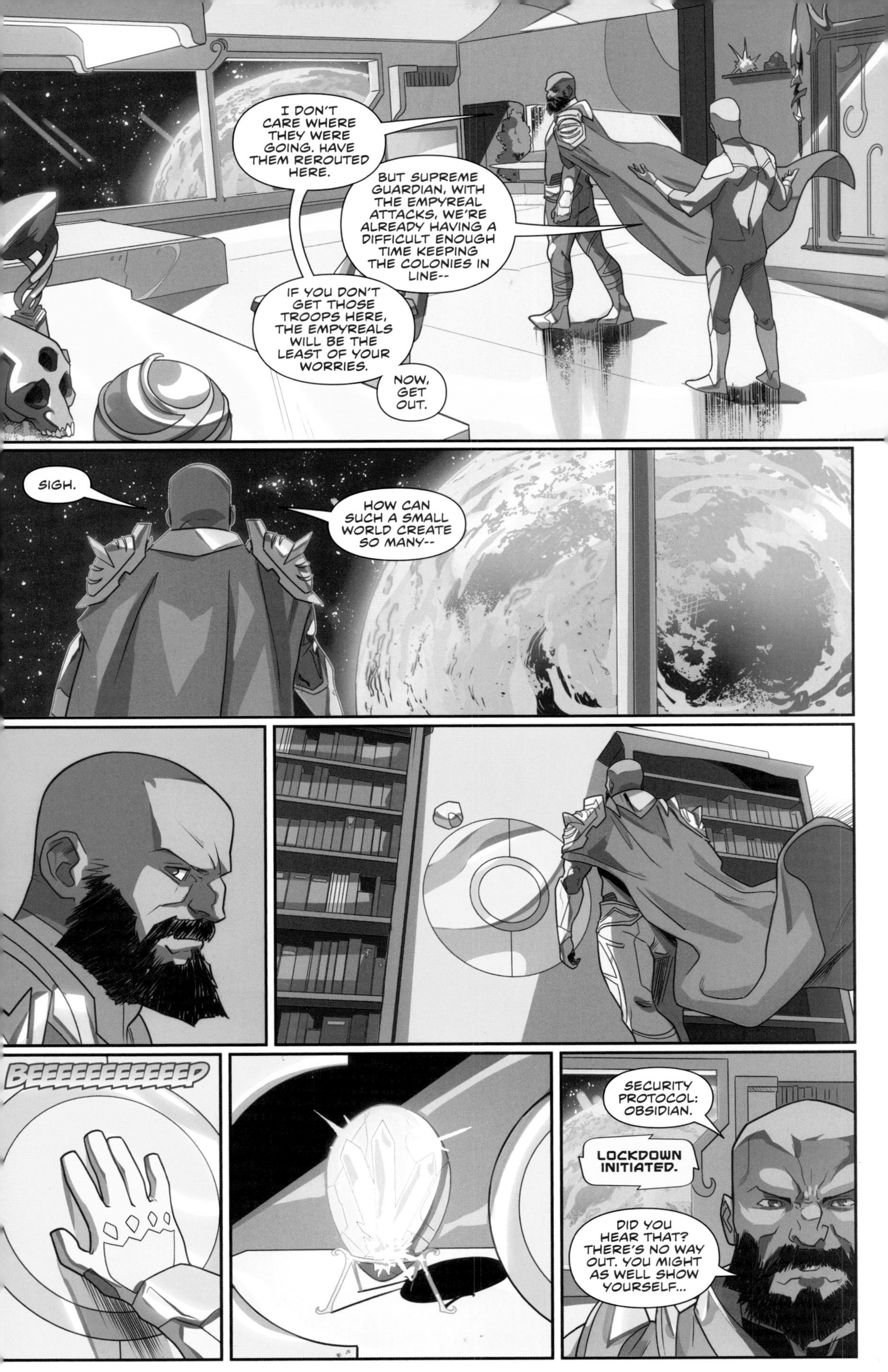
I DON'T CARE WHERE THEY WERE GOING. HAVE THEM REROUTED HERE.
BUT SUPREME GUARDIAN, WITH THE EMPYREAL ATTACKS, WE'RE ALREADY HAVING A DIFFICULT ENOUGH TIME KEEPING THE COLONIES IN LINE--
IF YOU DON'T GET THOSE TROOPS HERE, THE EMPYREALS WILL BE THE LEAST OF YOUR WORRIES.
NOW, GET OUT.
SIGH.
HOW CAN SUCH A SMALL WORLD CREATE SO MANY--
BEEEEEEEEEEEEP
SECURITY PROTOCOL: OBSIDIAN.
LOCKDOWN INITIATED.
DID YOU HEAR THAT? THERE'S NO WAY OUT. YOU MIGHT AS WELL SHOW YOURSELF...

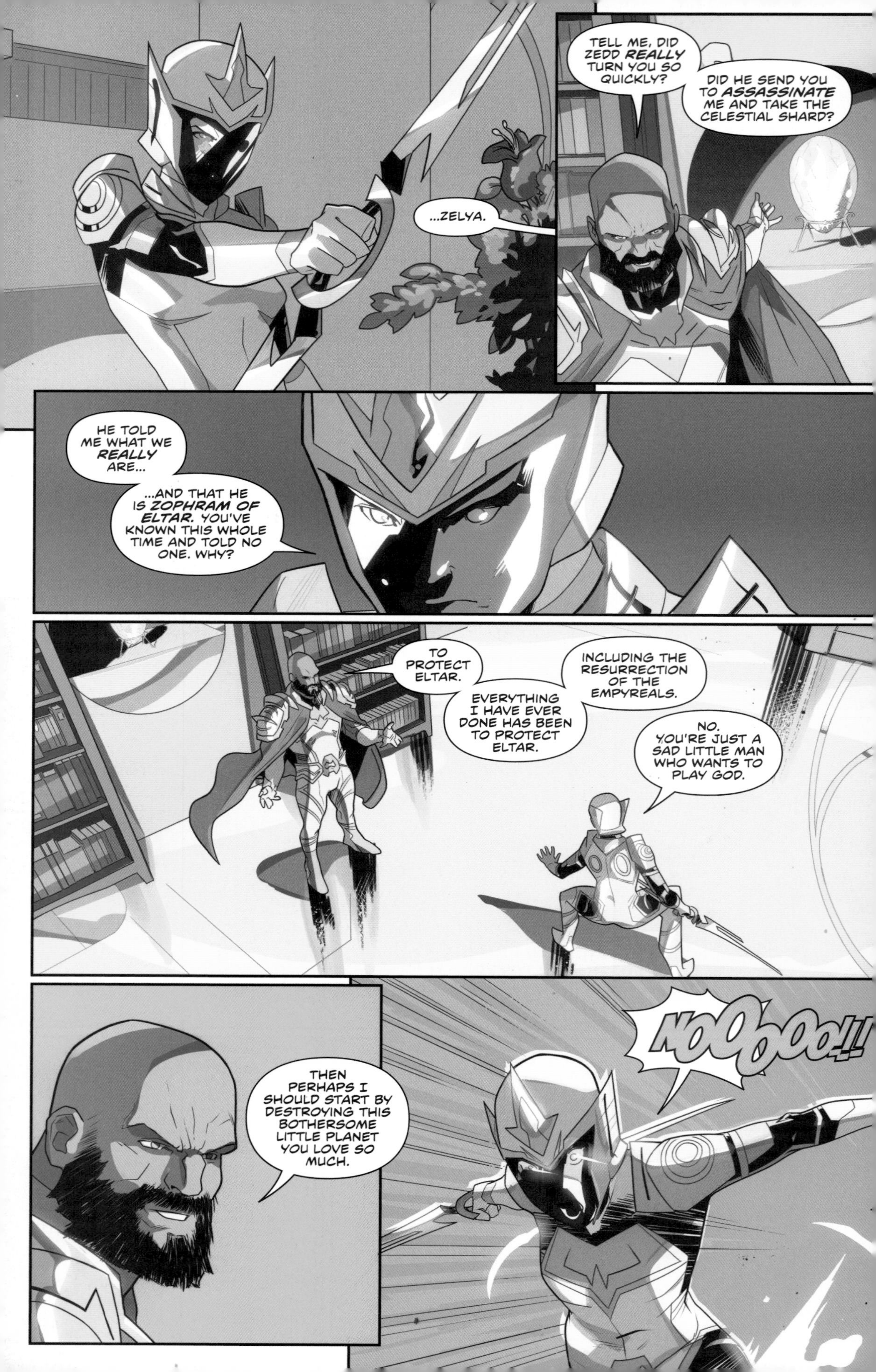
TELL ME, DID ZEDD REALLY TURN YOU SO QUICKLY?
DID HE SEND YOU TO ASSASSINATE ME AND TAKE THE CELESTIAL SHARD?
...ZELYA.
HE TOLD ME WHAT WE REALLY ARE...
...AND THAT HE IS ZOPHRAM OF ELTAR. YOU'VE KNOWN THIS WHOLE TIME AND TOLD NO ONE. WHY?
TO PROTECT ELTAR.
EVERYTHING I HAVE EVER DONE HAS BEEN TO PROTECT ELTAR.
INCLUDING THE RESURRECTION OF THE EMPYREALS.
NO. YOU'RE JUST A SAD LITTLE MAN WHO WANTS TO PLAY GOD.
THEN PERHAPS I SHOULD START BY DESTROYING THIS BOTHERSOME LITTLE PLANET YOU LOVE SO MUCH.
NOOOOOO!!

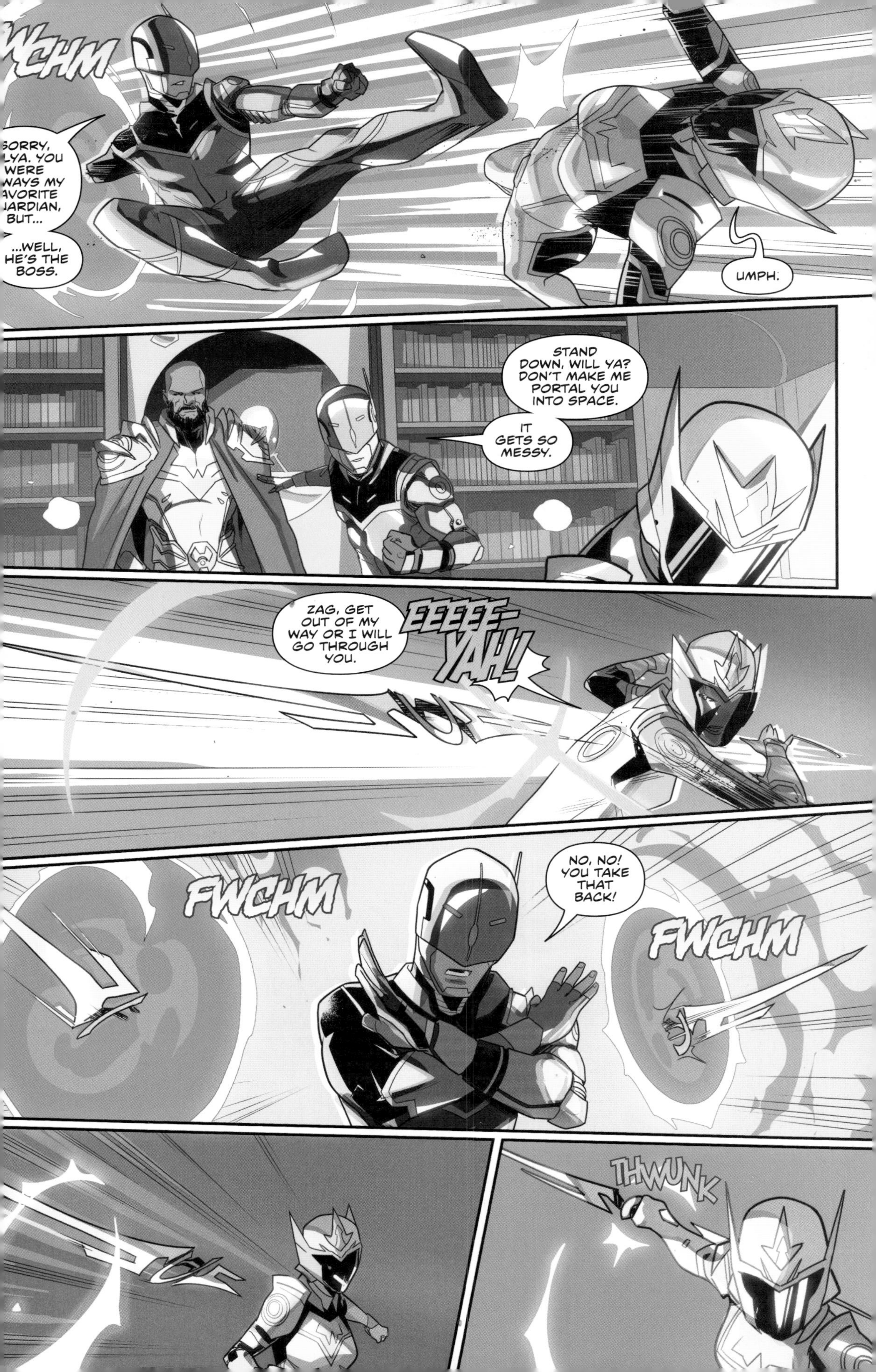

FWCHM
SORRY, LYA. YOU WERE WAYS MY AVORITE JARDIAN, BUT...
...WELL, HE'S THE BOSS.
UMPH.
STAND DOWN, WILL YA? DON'T MAKE ME PORTAL YOU INTO SPACE.
IT GETS SO MESSY.
ZAG, GET OUT OF MY WAY OR I WILL GO THROUGH YOU.
EEEEE-YAH!
FWCHM
NO, NO! YOU TAKE THAT BACK!
FWCHM
THWUNK

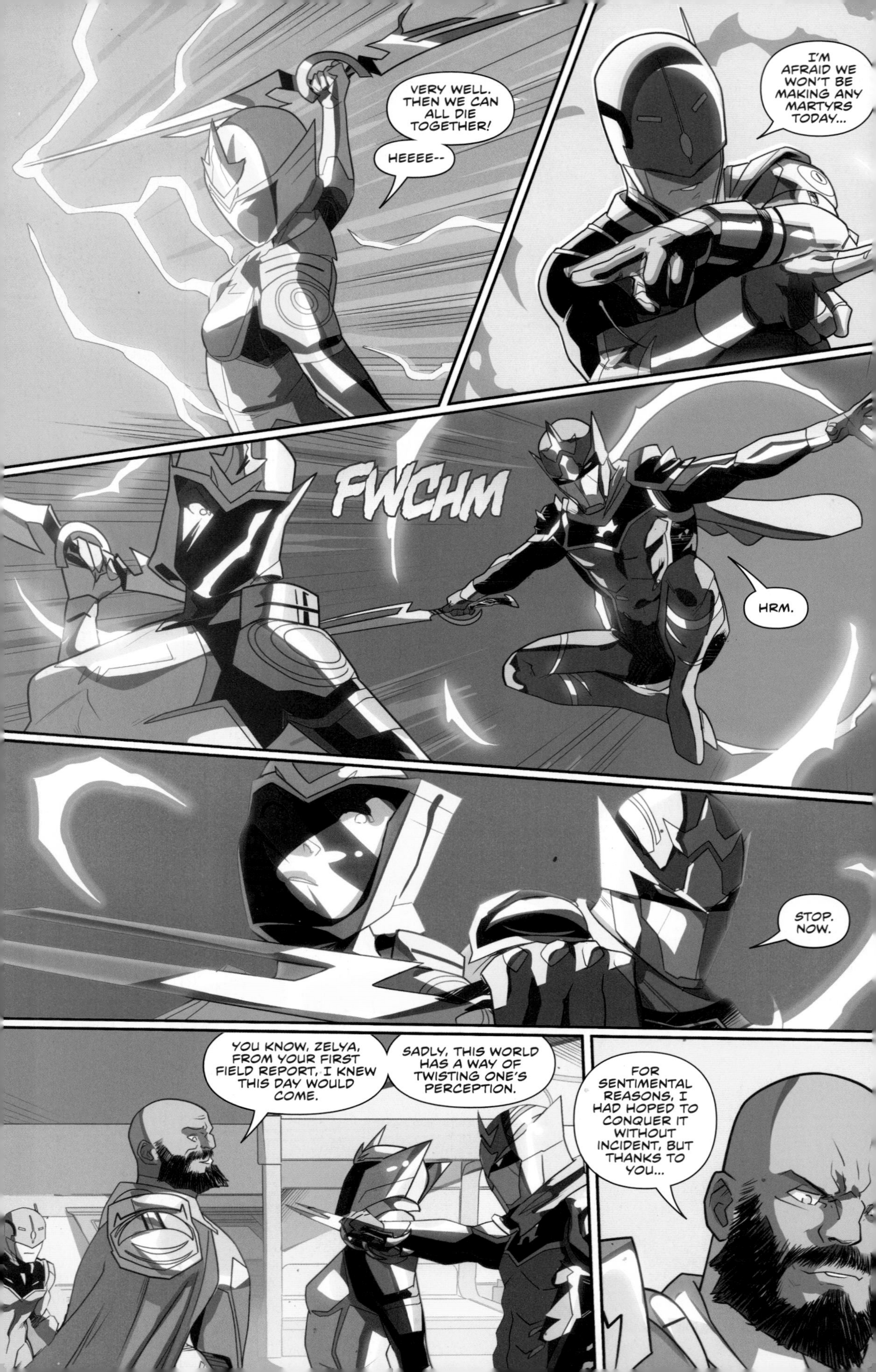
VERY WELL. THEN WE CAN ALL DIE TOGETHER!
HEEEE--
I'M AFRAID WE WON'T BE MAKING ANY MARTYRS TODAY...
FWCHM
HRM.
STOP. NOW.
YOU KNOW, ZELYA, FROM YOUR FIRST FIELD REPORT, I KNEW THIS DAY WOULD COME.
SADLY, THIS WORLD HAS A WAY OF TWISTING ONE'S PERCEPTION.
FOR SENTIMENTAL REASONS, I HAD HOPED TO CONQUER IT WITHOUT INCIDENT, BUT THANKS TO YOU...

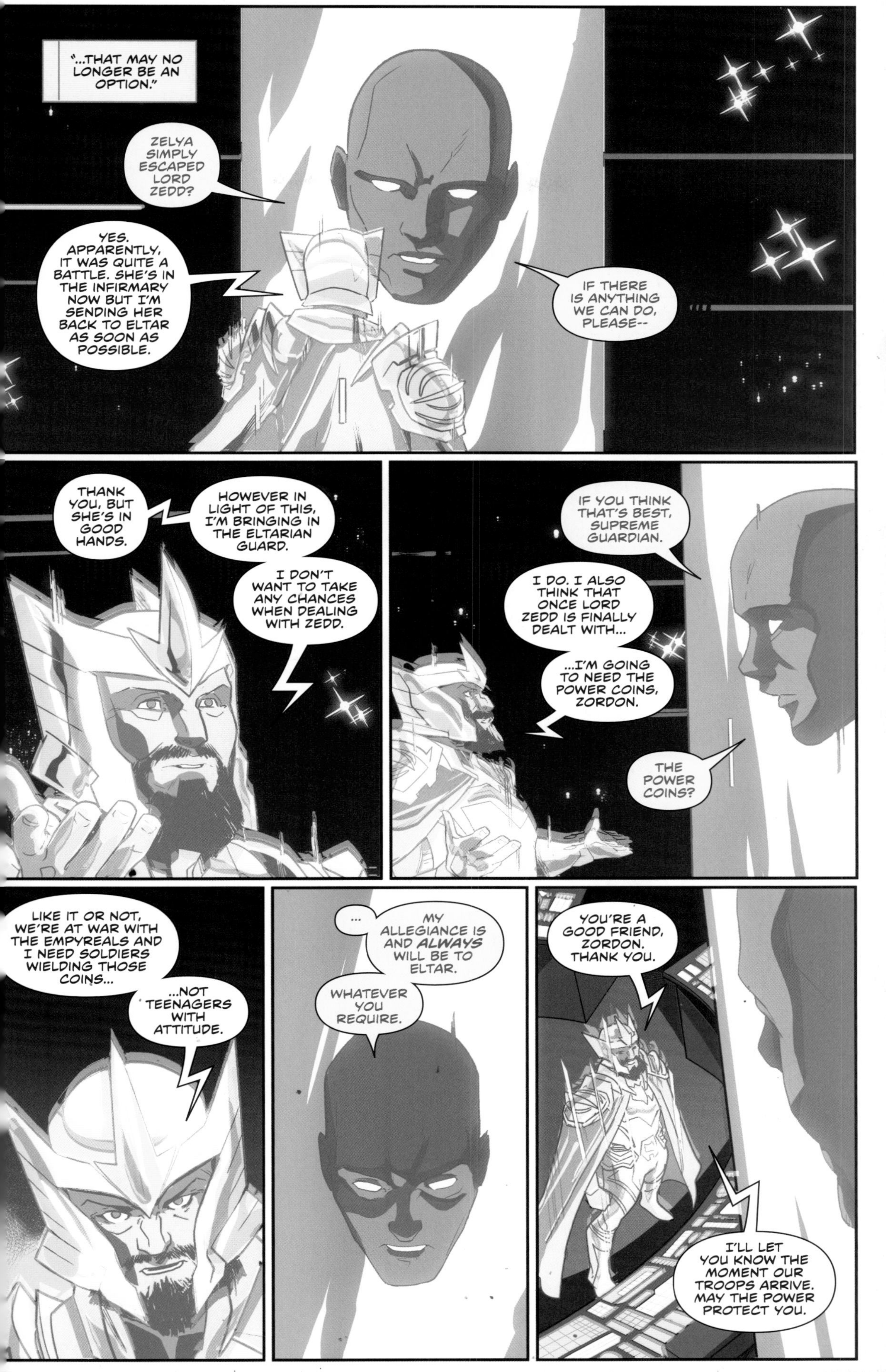
"...THAT MAY NO LONGER BE AN OPTION."
ZELYA SIMPLY ESCAPED LORD ZEDD?
YES. APPARENTLY, IT WAS QUITE A BATTLE. SHE'S IN THE INFIRMARY NOW BUT I'M SENDING HER BACK TO ELTAR AS SOON AS POSSIBLE.
IF THERE IS ANYTHING WE CAN DO, PLEASE--
THANK YOU, BUT SHE'S IN GOOD HANDS.
HOWEVER IN LIGHT OF THIS, I'M BRINGING IN THE ELTARIAN GUARD.
I DON'T WANT TO TAKE ANY CHANCES WHEN DEALING WITH ZEDD.
IF YOU THINK THAT'S BEST, SUPREME GUARDIAN.
I DO. I ALSO THINK THAT ONCE LORD ZEDD IS FINALLY DEALT WITH...
...I'M GOING TO NEED THE POWER COINS, ZORDON.
THE POWER COINS?
LIKE IT OR NOT, WE'RE AT WAR WITH THE EMPYREALS AND I NEED SOLDIERS WIELDING THOSE COINS...
...NOT TEENAGERS WITH ATTITUDE.
...
MY ALLEGIANCE IS AND ALWAYS WILL BE TO ELTAR.
WHATEVER YOU REQUIRE.
YOU'RE A GOOD FRIEND, ZORDON. THANK YOU.
I'LL LET YOU KNOW THE MOMENT OUR TROOPS ARRIVE. MAY THE POWER PROTECT YOU.

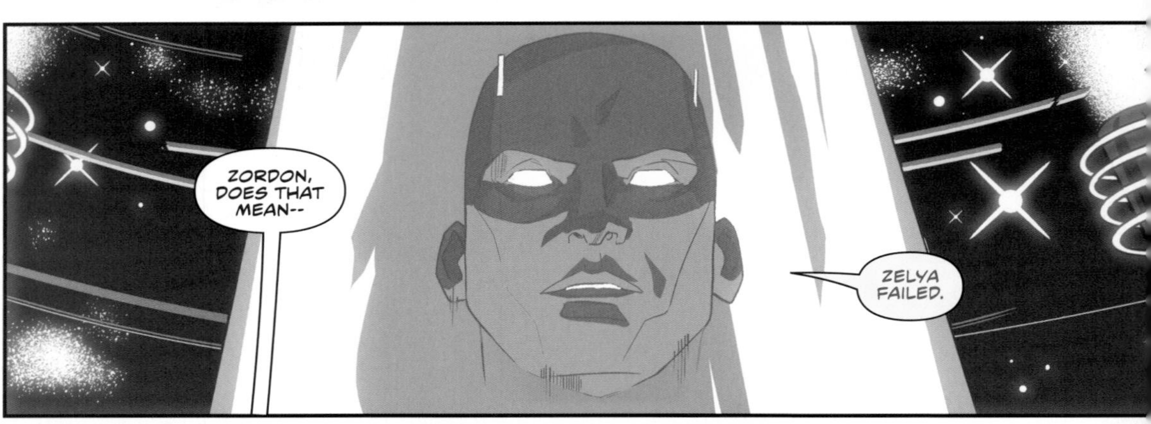
ZORDON, DOES THAT MEAN--
ZELYA FAILED.

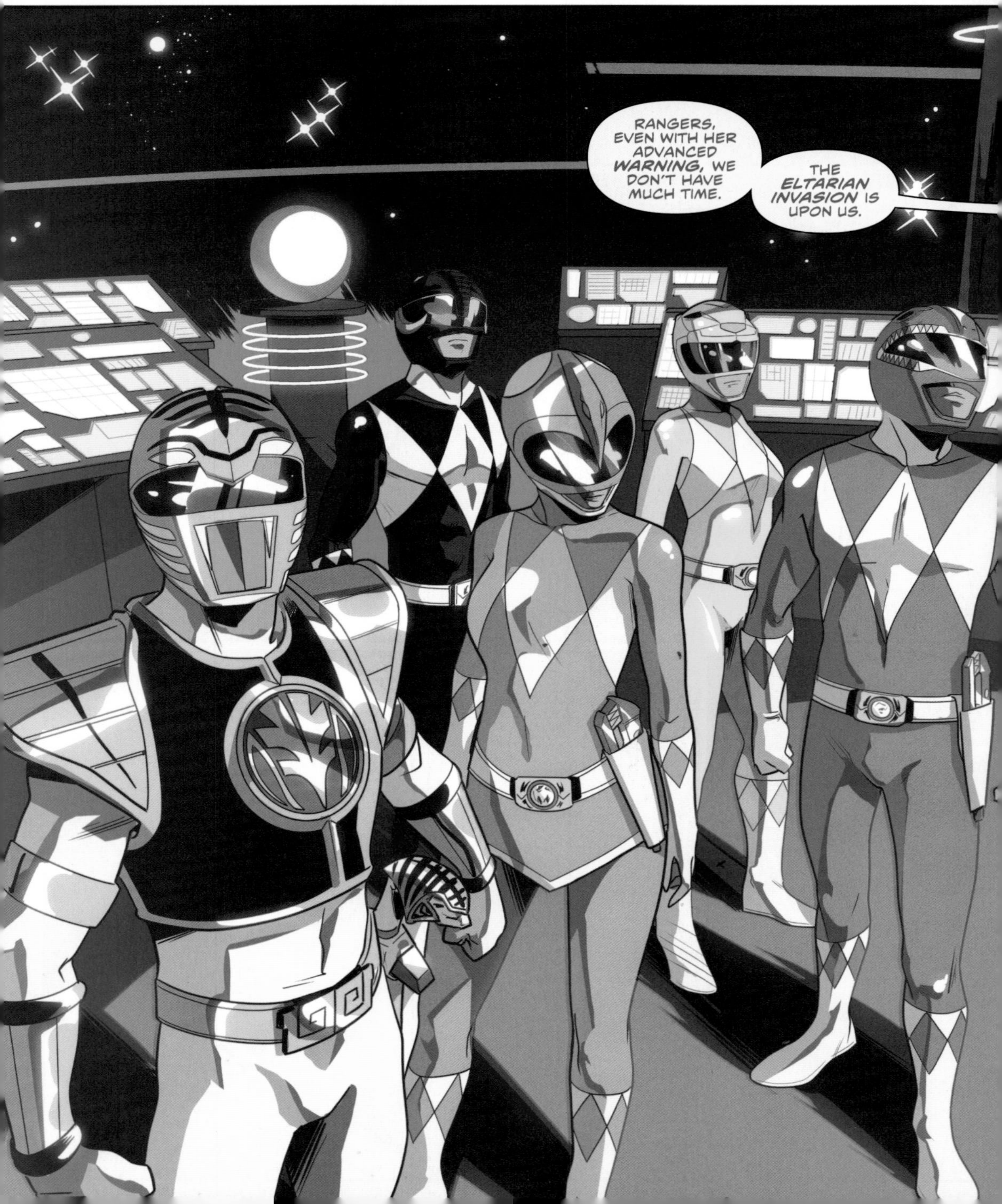
RANGERS, EVEN WITH HER ADVANCED WARNING, WE DON'T HAVE MUCH TIME.
THE ELTARIAN INVASION IS UPON US.

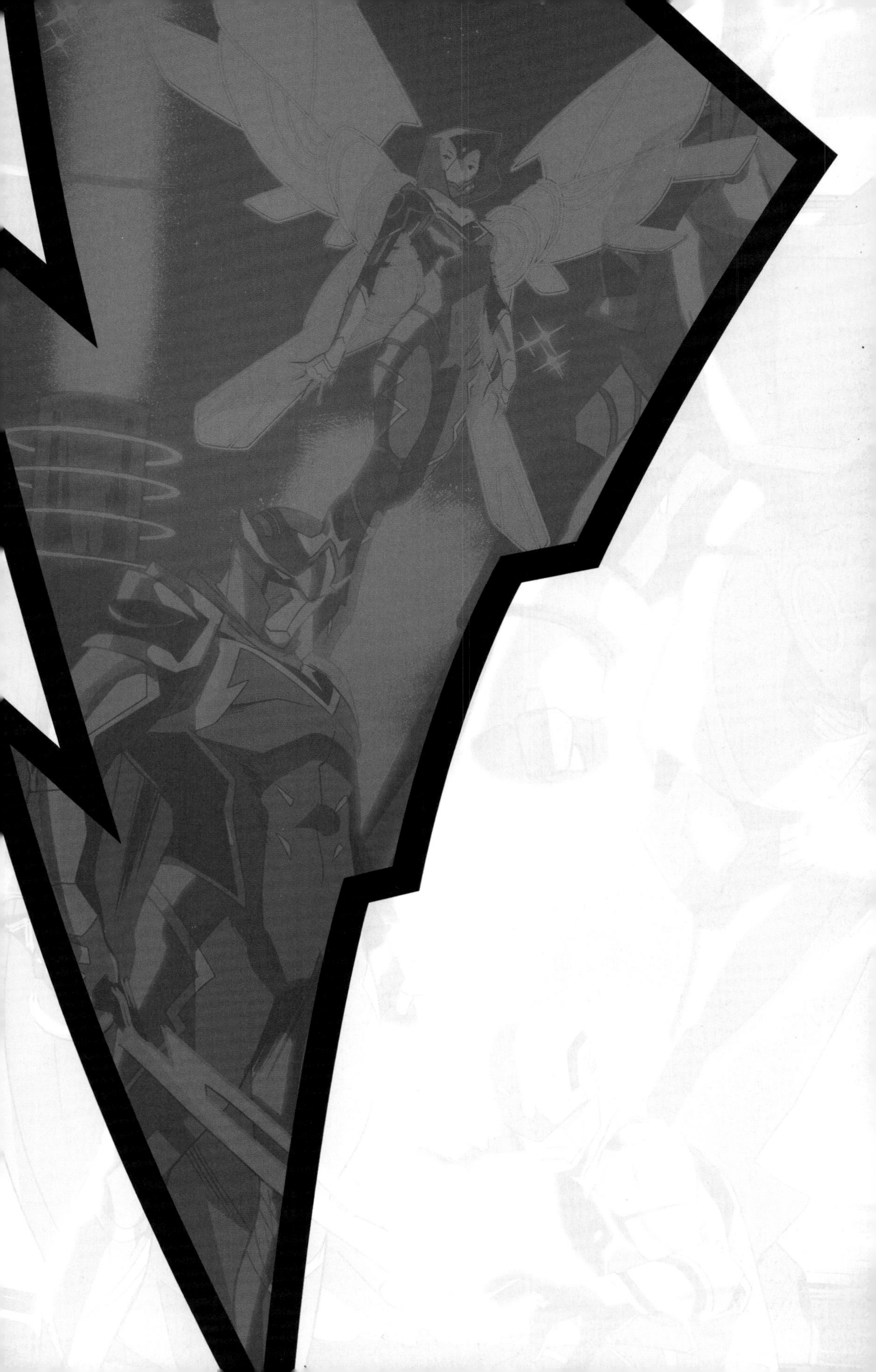

CHAPTER TWELVE

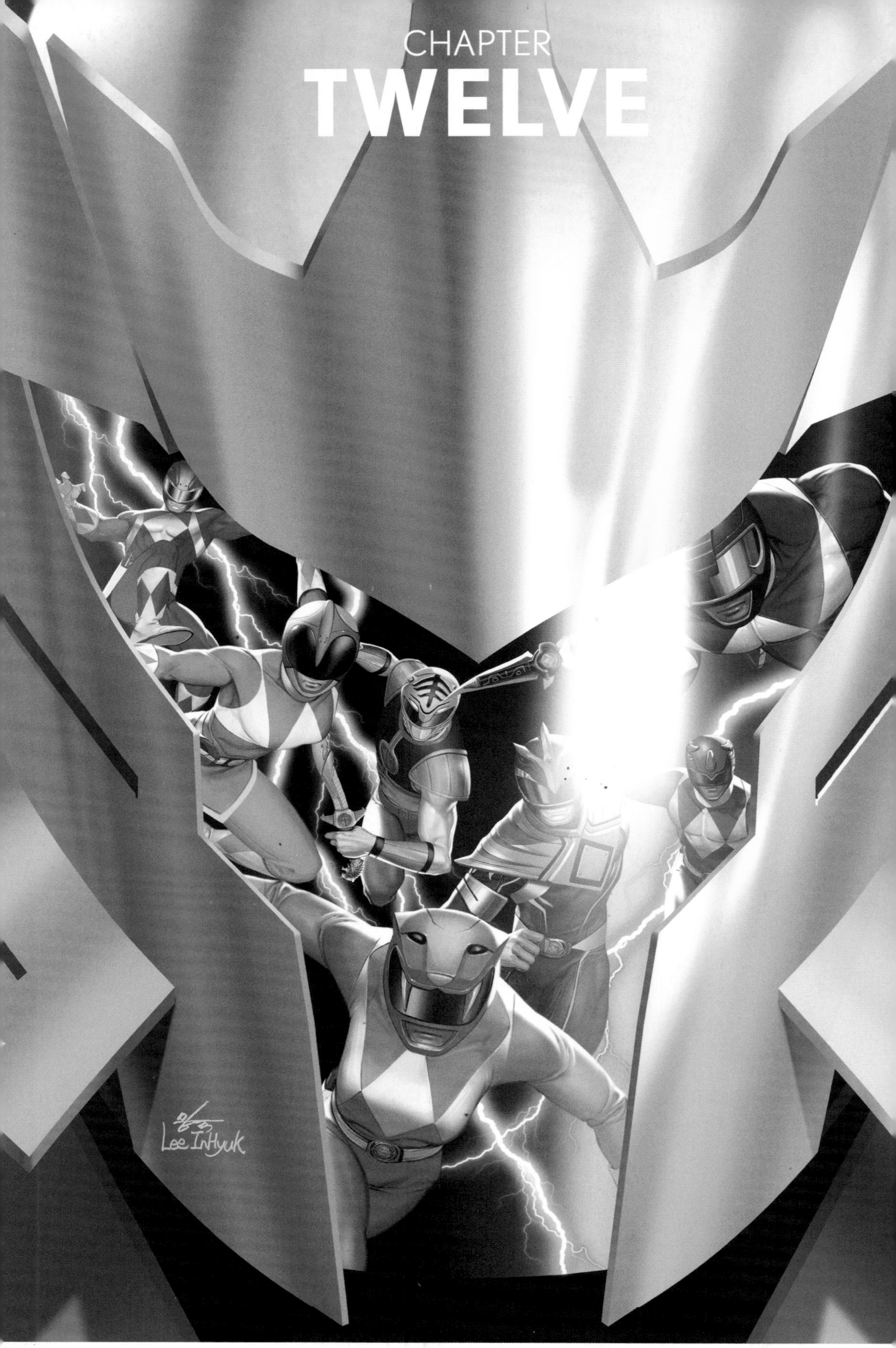
Lee InHyuk

INHYUK LEE | ISSUE TWELVE COVER

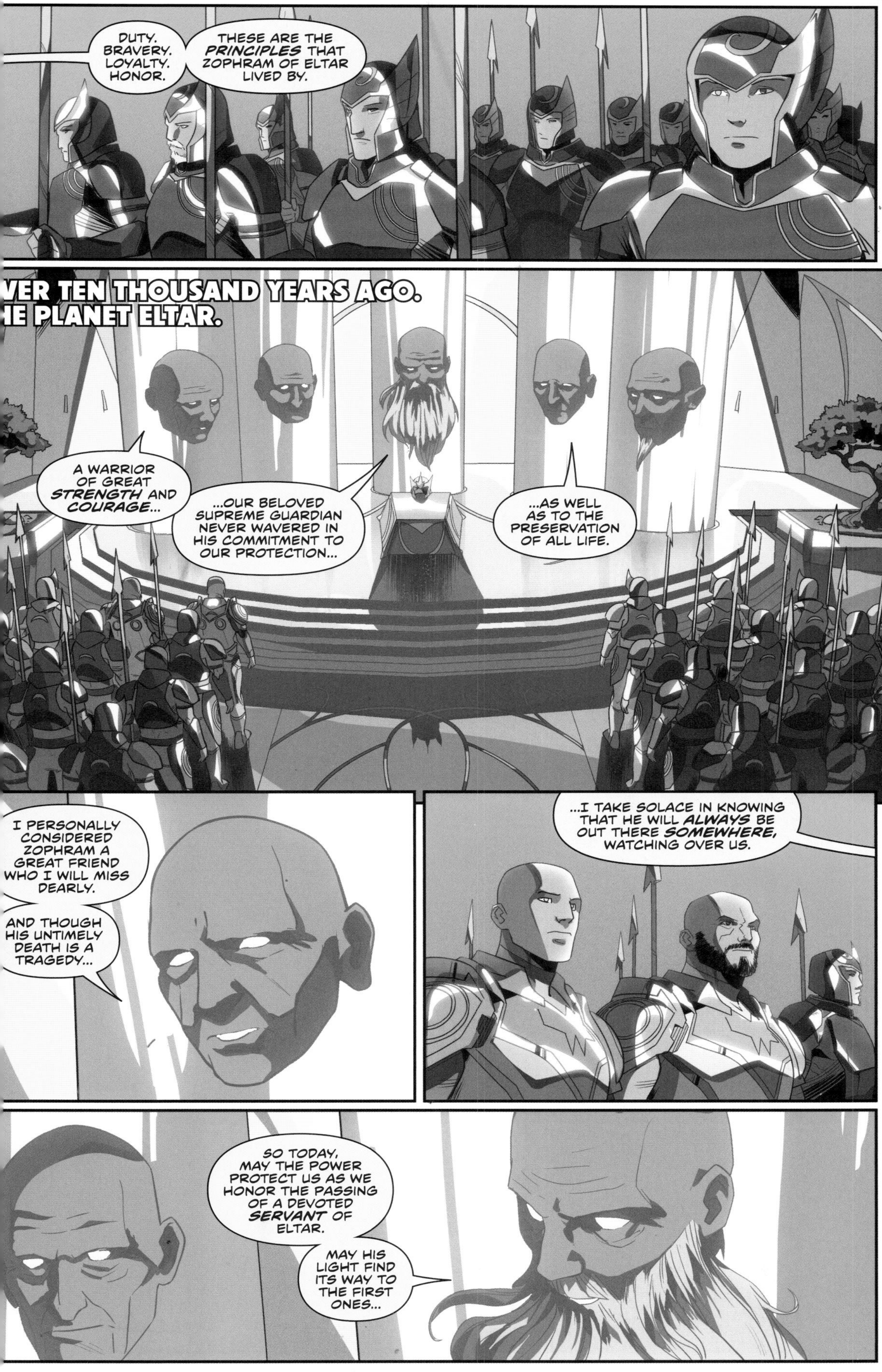
DUTY. BRAVERY. LOYALTY. HONOR.
THESE ARE THE PRINCIPLES THAT ZOPHRAM OF ELTAR LIVED BY.
VER TEN THOUSAND YEARS AGO. HE PLANET ELTAR.
A WARRIOR OF GREAT STRENGTH AND COURAGE...
...OUR BELOVED SUPREME GUARDIAN NEVER WAVERED IN HIS COMMITMENT TO OUR PROTECTION...
...AS WELL AS TO THE PRESERVATION OF ALL LIFE.
I PERSONALLY CONSIDERED ZOPHRAM A GREAT FRIEND WHO I WILL MISS DEARLY.
AND THOUGH HIS UNTIMELY DEATH IS A TRAGEDY...
...I TAKE SOLACE IN KNOWING THAT HE WILL ALWAYS BE OUT THERE SOMEWHERE, WATCHING OVER US.
SO TODAY, MAY THE POWER PROTECT US AS WE HONOR THE PASSING OF A DEVOTED SERVANT OF ELTAR.
MAY HIS LIGHT FIND ITS WAY TO THE FIRST ONES...

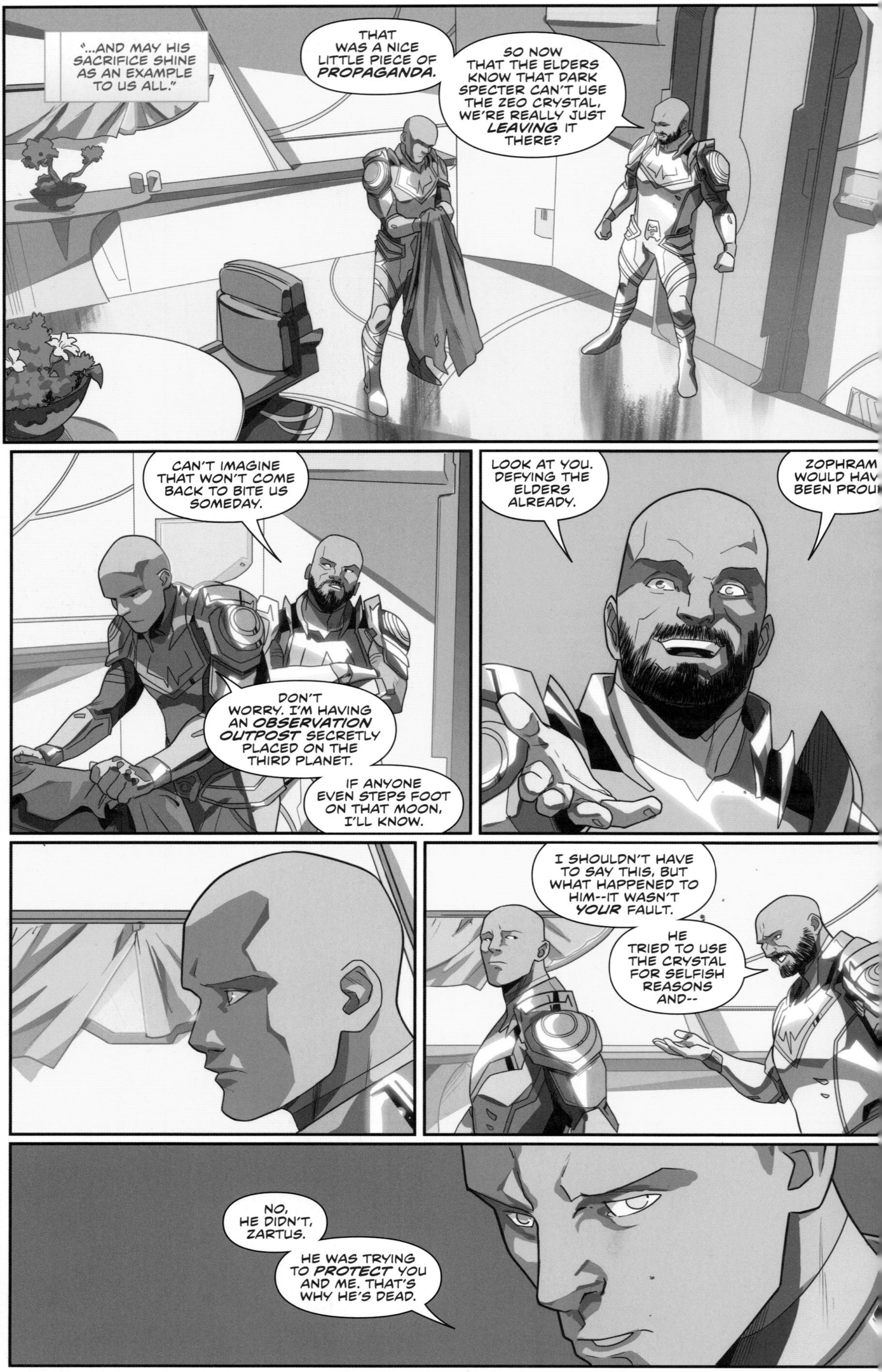
"...AND MAY HIS SACRIFICE SHINE AS AN EXAMPLE TO US ALL."
THAT WAS A NICE LITTLE PIECE OF PROPAGANDA.
SO NOW THAT THE ELDERS KNOW THAT DARK SPECTER CAN'T USE THE ZEO CRYSTAL, WE'RE REALLY JUST LEAVING IT THERE?
CAN'T IMAGINE THAT WON'T COME BACK TO BITE US SOMEDAY.
DON'T WORRY. I'M HAVING AN OBSERVATION OUTPOST SECRETLY PLACED ON THE THIRD PLANET.
IF ANYONE EVEN STEPS FOOT ON THAT MOON, I'LL KNOW.
LOOK AT YOU. DEFYING THE ELDERS ALREADY.
I SHOULDN'T HAVE TO SAY THIS, BUT WHAT HAPPENED TO HIM--IT WASN'T YOUR FAULT.
HE TRIED TO USE THE CRYSTAL FOR SELFISH REASONS AND--
NO, HE DIDN'T, ZARTUS.
HE WAS TRYING TO PROTECT YOU AND ME. THAT'S WHY HE'S DEAD.

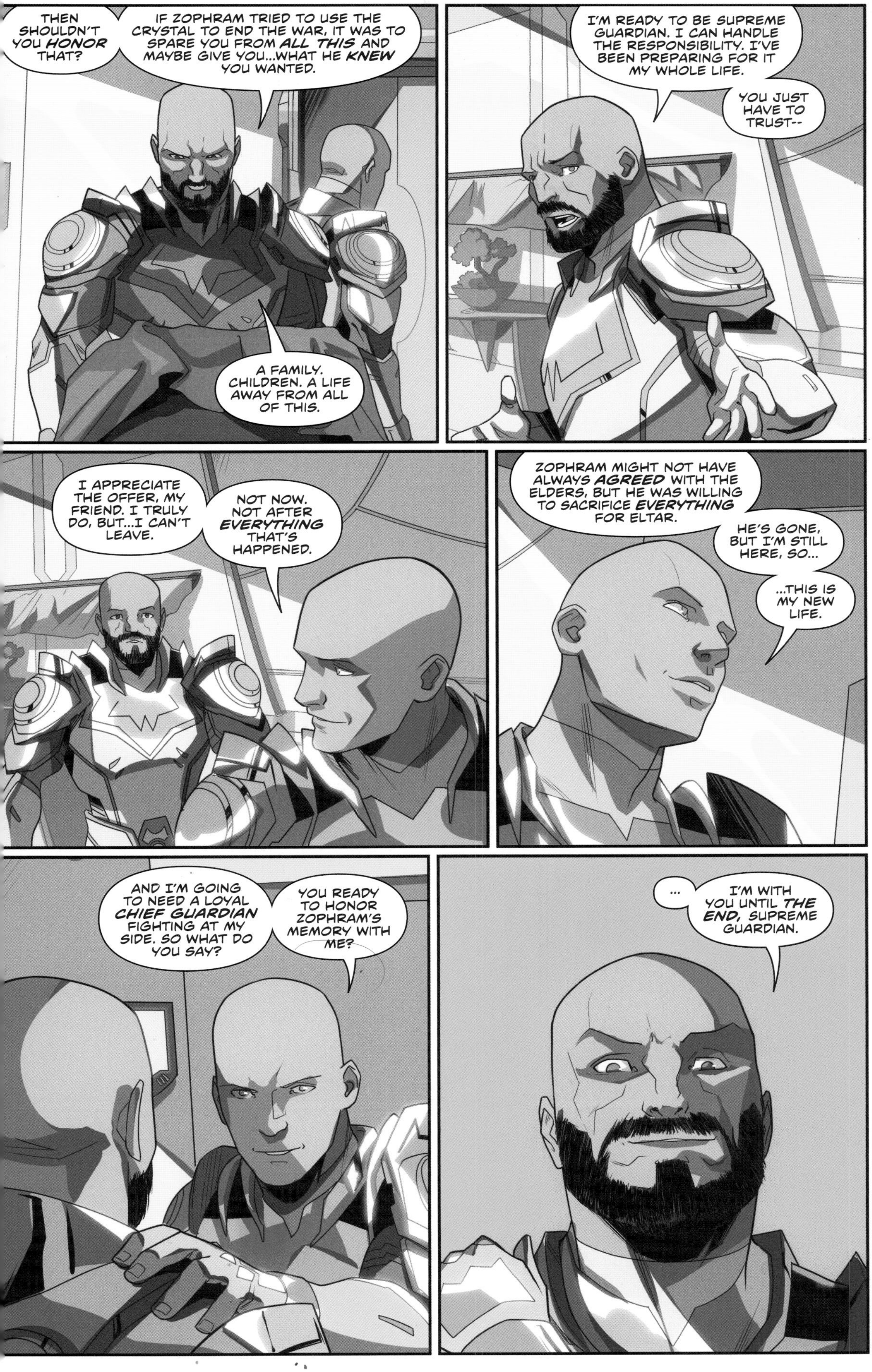
THEN SHOULDN'T YOU HONOR THAT?
IF ZOPHRAM TRIED TO USE THE CRYSTAL TO END THE WAR, IT WAS TO SPARE YOU FROM ALL THIS AND MAYBE GIVE YOU...WHAT HE KNEW YOU WANTED.
A FAMILY. CHILDREN. A LIFE AWAY FROM ALL OF THIS.
I'M READY TO BE SUPREME GUARDIAN. I CAN HANDLE THE RESPONSIBILITY. I'VE BEEN PREPARING FOR IT MY WHOLE LIFE.
YOU JUST HAVE TO TRUST--
I APPRECIATE THE OFFER, MY FRIEND. I TRULY DO, BUT...I CAN'T LEAVE.
NOT NOW. NOT AFTER EVERYTHING THAT'S HAPPENED.
ZOPHRAM MIGHT NOT HAVE ALWAYS AGREED WITH THE ELDERS, BUT HE WAS WILLING TO SACRIFICE EVERYTHING FOR ELTAR.
HE'S GONE, BUT I'M STILL HERE, SO...
...THIS IS MY NEW LIFE.
AND I'M GOING TO NEED A LOYAL CHIEF GUARDIAN FIGHTING AT MY SIDE. SO WHAT DO YOU SAY?
YOU READY TO HONOR ZOPHRAM'S MEMORY WITH ME?
...
I'M WITH YOU UNTIL THE END, SUPREME GUARDIAN.

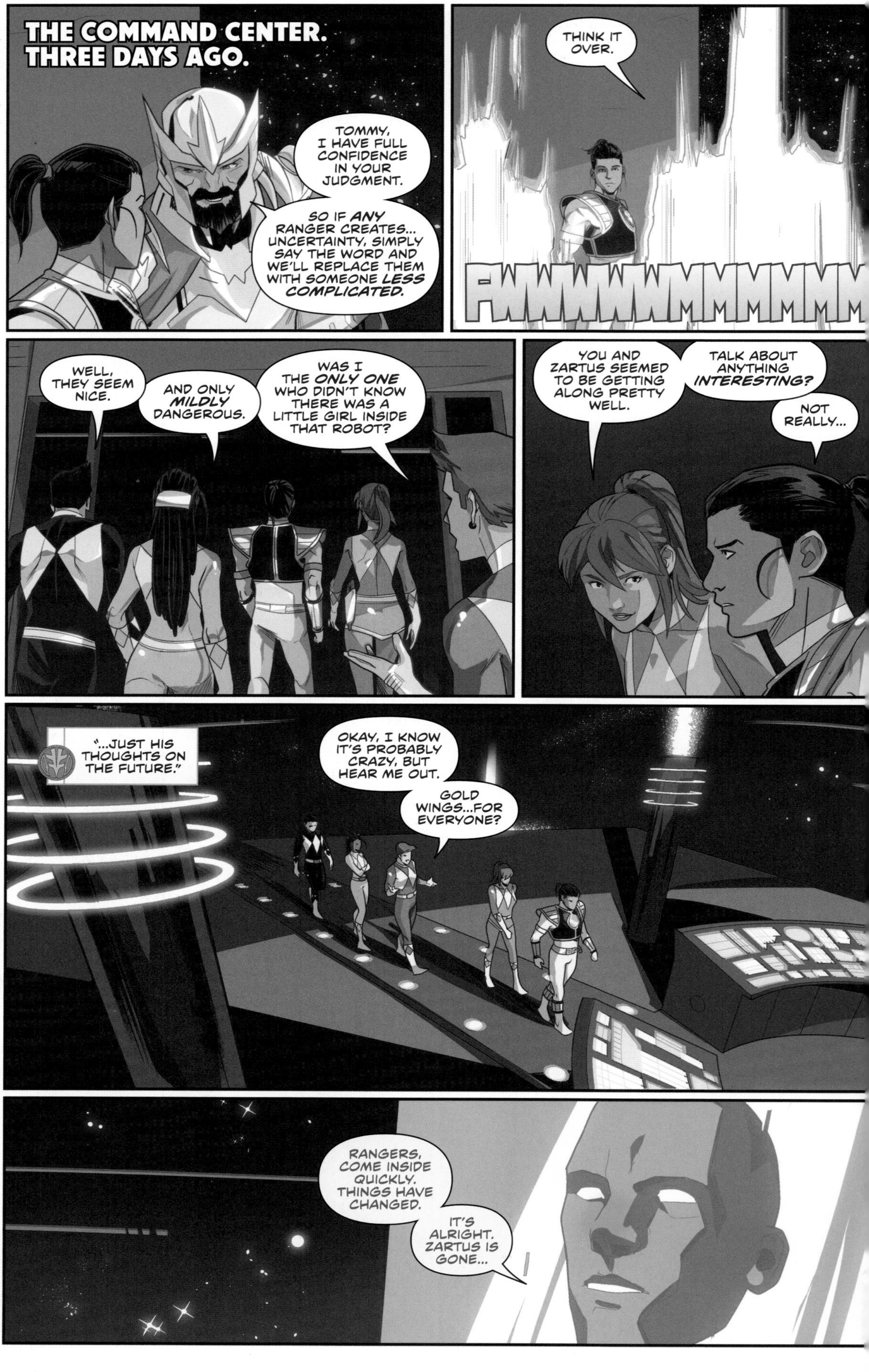

THE COMMAND CENTER. THREE DAYS AGO.
TOMMY, I HAVE FULL CONFIDENCE IN YOUR JUDGMENT.
SO IF *ANY* RANGER CREATES... UNCERTAINTY, SIMPLY SAY THE WORD AND WE'LL REPLACE THEM WITH SOMEONE *LESS COMPLICATED.*
THINK IT OVER.
FWWWWWWMMMMMMM
WELL, THEY SEEM NICE.
AND ONLY *MILDLY* DANGEROUS.
WAS I THE *ONLY ONE* WHO DIDN'T KNOW THERE WAS A LITTLE GIRL INSIDE THAT ROBOT?
YOU AND ZARTUS SEEMED TO BE GETTING ALONG PRETTY WELL.
TALK ABOUT ANYTHING *INTERESTING?*
NOT REALLY...
"...JUST HIS THOUGHTS ON THE FUTURE."
OKAY, I KNOW IT'S PROBABLY CRAZY, BUT HEAR ME OUT.
GOLD WINGS...FOR EVERYONE?
RANGERS, COME INSIDE QUICKLY. THINGS HAVE CHANGED.
IT'S ALRIGHT. ZARTUS IS GONE...

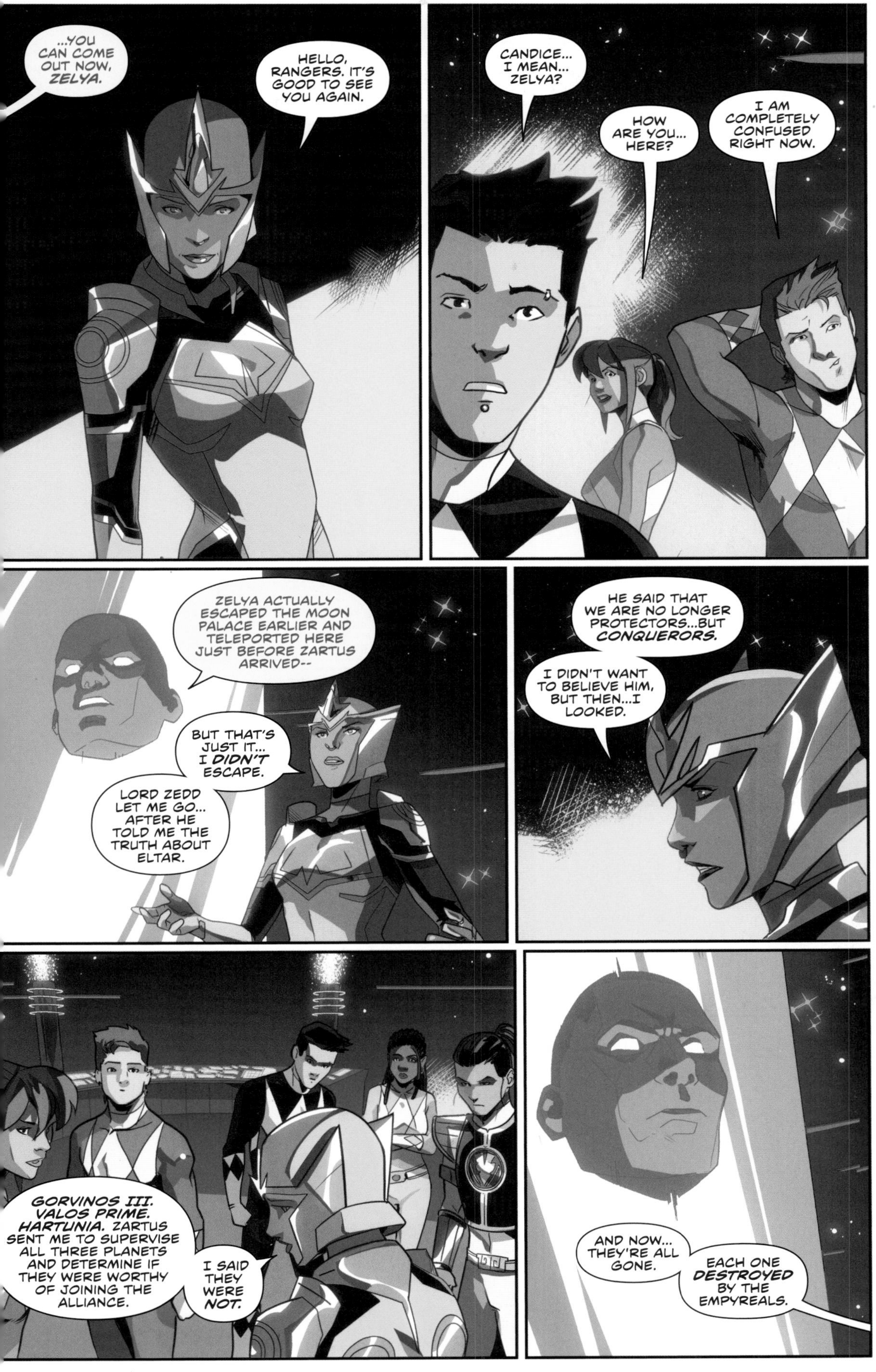
...YOU CAN COME OUT NOW, *ZELYA.*
HELLO, RANGERS. IT'S GOOD TO SEE YOU AGAIN.
CANDICE... I MEAN... ZELYA?
HOW ARE YOU... HERE?
I AM COMPLETELY CONFUSED RIGHT NOW.
ZELYA ACTUALLY ESCAPED THE MOON PALACE EARLIER AND TELEPORTED HERE JUST BEFORE ZARTUS ARRIVED--
BUT THAT'S JUST IT... I *DIDN'T* ESCAPE.
LORD ZEDD LET ME GO... AFTER HE TOLD ME THE TRUTH ABOUT ELTAR.
HE SAID THAT WE ARE NO LONGER PROTECTORS...BUT ***CONQUERORS.***
I DIDN'T WANT TO BELIEVE HIM, BUT THEN...I LOOKED.
GORVINOS III. VALOS PRIME. HARTUNIA. ZARTUS SENT ME TO SUPERVISE ALL THREE PLANETS AND DETERMINE IF THEY WERE WORTHY OF JOINING THE ALLIANCE.
I SAID THEY WERE ***NOT.***
AND NOW... THEY'RE ALL GONE.
EACH ONE ***DESTROYED*** BY THE EMPYREALS.

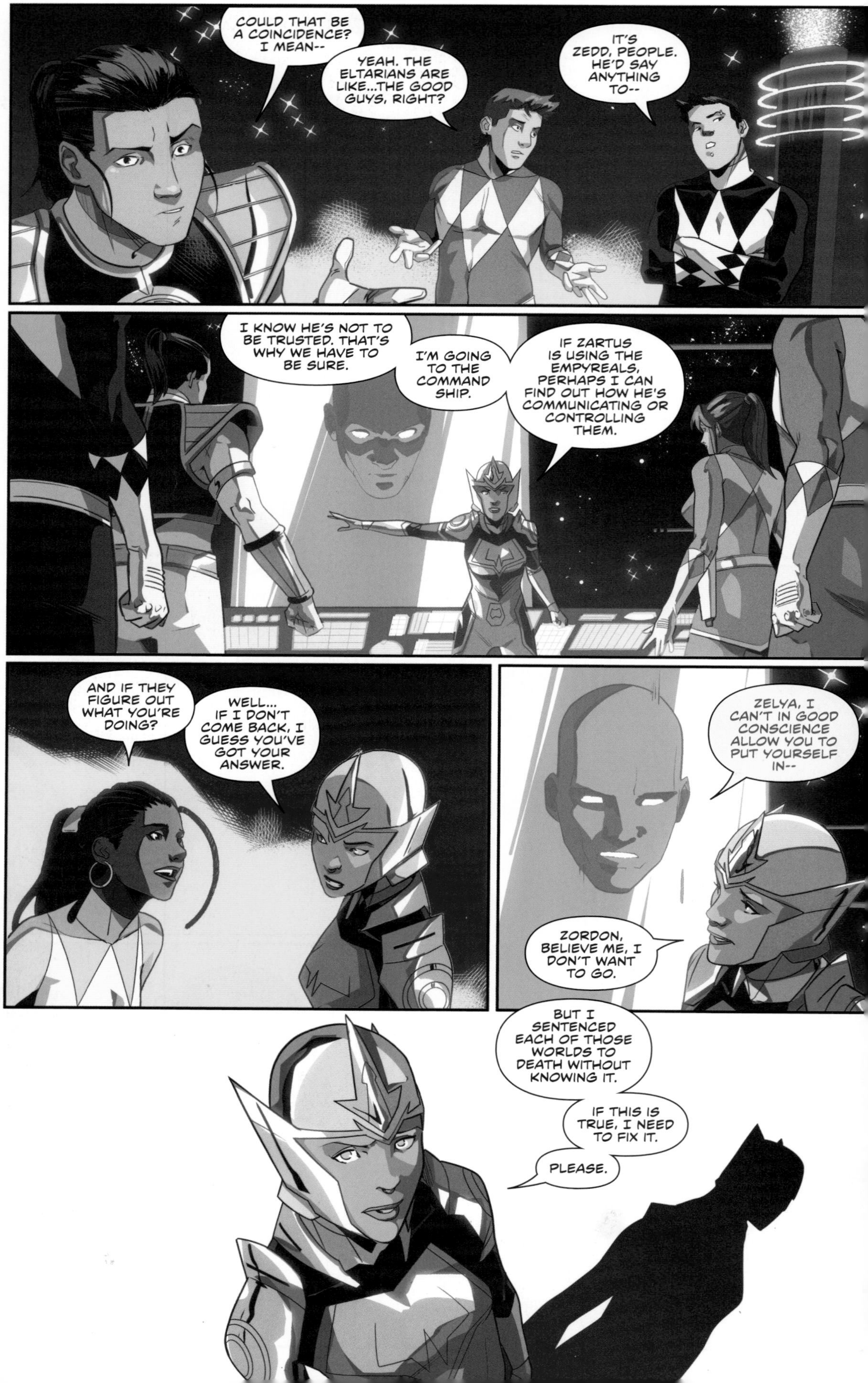
COULD THAT BE A COINCIDENCE? I MEAN--
YEAH. THE ELTARIANS ARE LIKE...THE GOOD GUYS, RIGHT?
IT'S ZEDD, PEOPLE. HE'D SAY ANYTHING TO--
I KNOW HE'S NOT TO BE TRUSTED. THAT'S WHY WE HAVE TO BE SURE.
I'M GOING TO THE COMMAND SHIP.
IF ZARTUS IS USING THE EMPYREALS, PERHAPS I CAN FIND OUT HOW HE'S COMMUNICATING OR CONTROLLING THEM.
AND IF THEY FIGURE OUT WHAT YOU'RE DOING?
WELL... IF I DON'T COME BACK, I GUESS YOU'VE GOT YOUR ANSWER.
ZELYA, I CAN'T IN GOOD CONSCIENCE ALLOW YOU TO PUT YOURSELF IN--
ZORDON, BELIEVE ME, I DON'T WANT TO GO.
BUT I SENTENCED EACH OF THOSE WORLDS TO DEATH WITHOUT KNOWING IT.
IF THIS IS TRUE, I NEED TO FIX IT.
PLEASE.

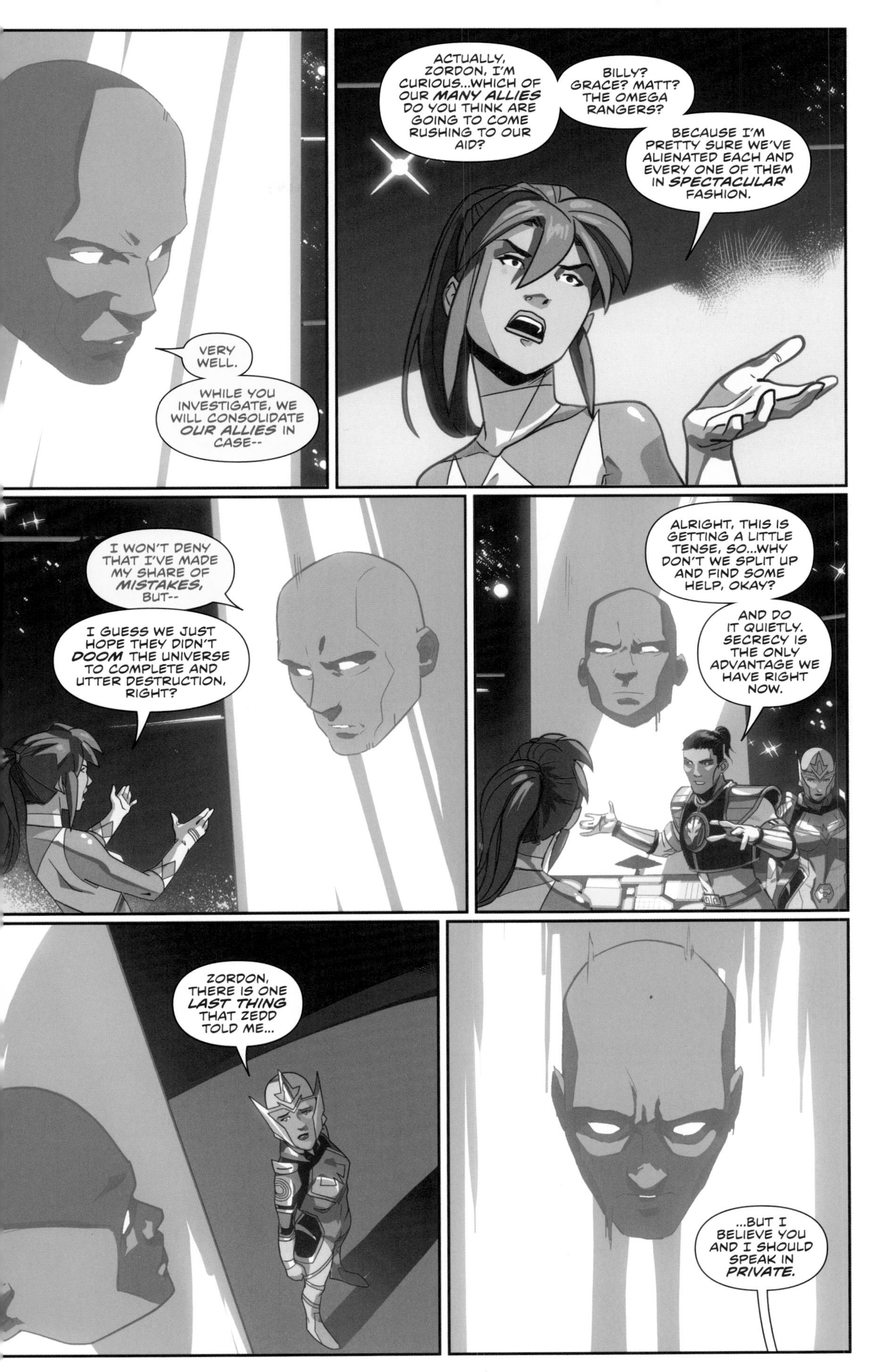
ACTUALLY, ZORDON, I'M CURIOUS...WHICH OF OUR MANY ALLIES DO YOU THINK ARE GOING TO COME RUSHING TO OUR AID?
BILLY? GRACE? MATT? THE OMEGA RANGERS?
BECAUSE I'M PRETTY SURE WE'VE ALIENATED EACH AND EVERY ONE OF THEM IN SPECTACULAR FASHION.
VERY WELL.
WHILE YOU INVESTIGATE, WE WILL CONSOLIDATE OUR ALLIES IN CASE--
I WON'T DENY THAT I'VE MADE MY SHARE OF MISTAKES, BUT--
I GUESS WE JUST HOPE THEY DIDN'T DOOM THE UNIVERSE TO COMPLETE AND UTTER DESTRUCTION, RIGHT?
ALRIGHT, THIS IS GETTING A LITTLE TENSE, SO...WHY DON'T WE SPLIT UP AND FIND SOME HELP, OKAY?
AND DO IT QUIETLY. SECRECY IS THE ONLY ADVANTAGE WE HAVE RIGHT NOW.
ZORDON, THERE IS ONE LAST THING THAT ZEDD TOLD ME...
...BUT I BELIEVE YOU AND I SHOULD SPEAK IN PRIVATE.

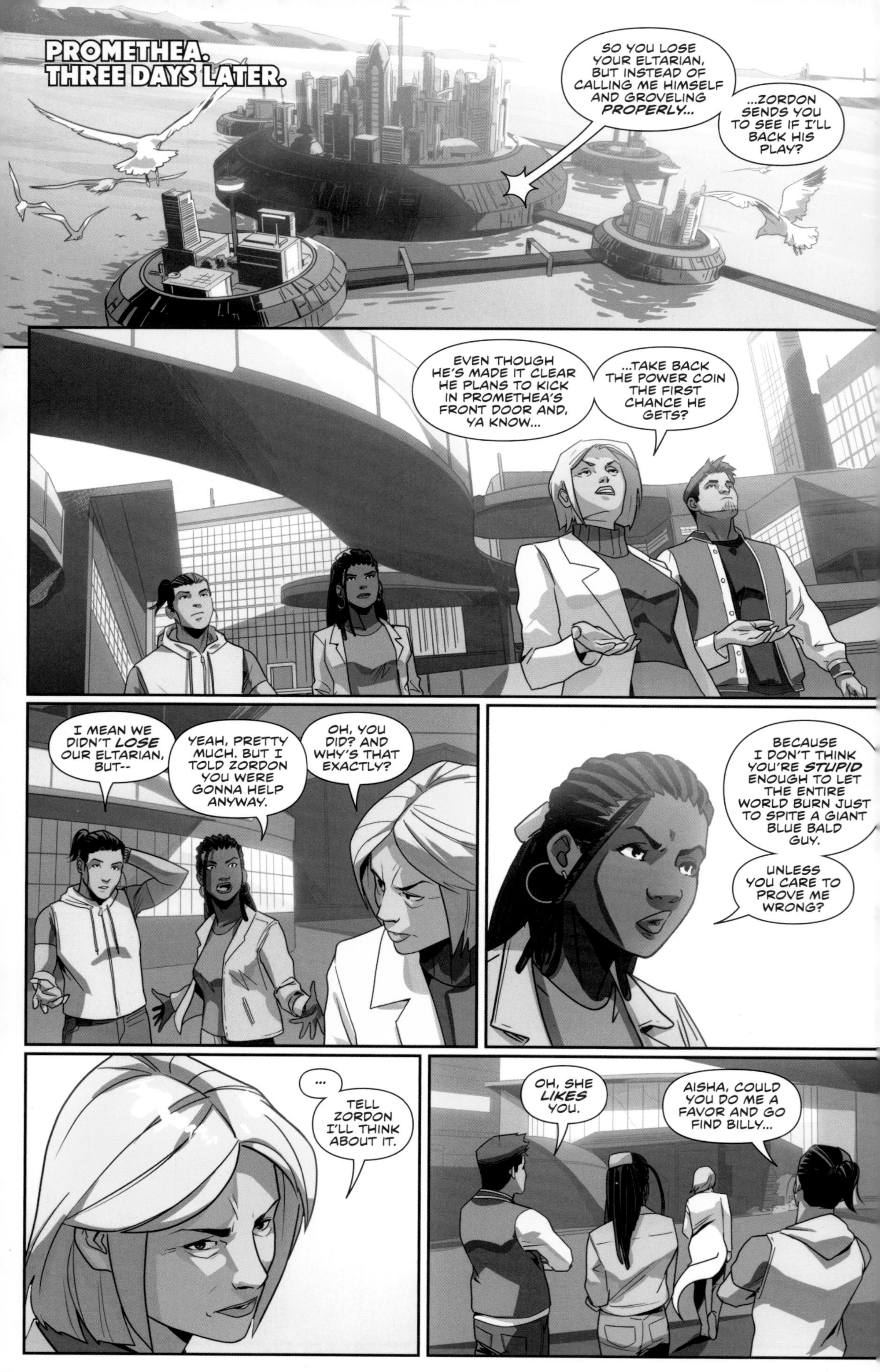
PROMETHEA. THREE DAYS LATER.
SO YOU LOSE YOUR ELTARIAN, BUT INSTEAD OF CALLING ME HIMSELF AND GROVELING PROPERLY...
...ZORDON SENDS YOU TO SEE IF I'LL BACK HIS PLAY?
EVEN THOUGH HE'S MADE IT CLEAR HE PLANS TO KICK IN PROMETHEA'S FRONT DOOR AND, YA KNOW...
...TAKE BACK THE POWER COIN THE FIRST CHANCE HE GETS?
I MEAN WE DIDN'T LOSE OUR ELTARIAN, BUT--
YEAH, PRETTY MUCH. BUT I TOLD ZORDON YOU WERE GONNA HELP ANYWAY.
OH, YOU DID? AND WHY'S THAT EXACTLY?
BECAUSE I DON'T THINK YOU'RE STUPID ENOUGH TO LET THE ENTIRE WORLD BURN JUST TO SPITE A GIANT BLUE BALD GUY.
UNLESS YOU CARE TO PROVE ME WRONG?
...
TELL ZORDON I'LL THINK ABOUT IT.
OH, SHE LIKES YOU.
AISHA, COULD YOU DO ME A FAVOR AND GO FIND BILLY...

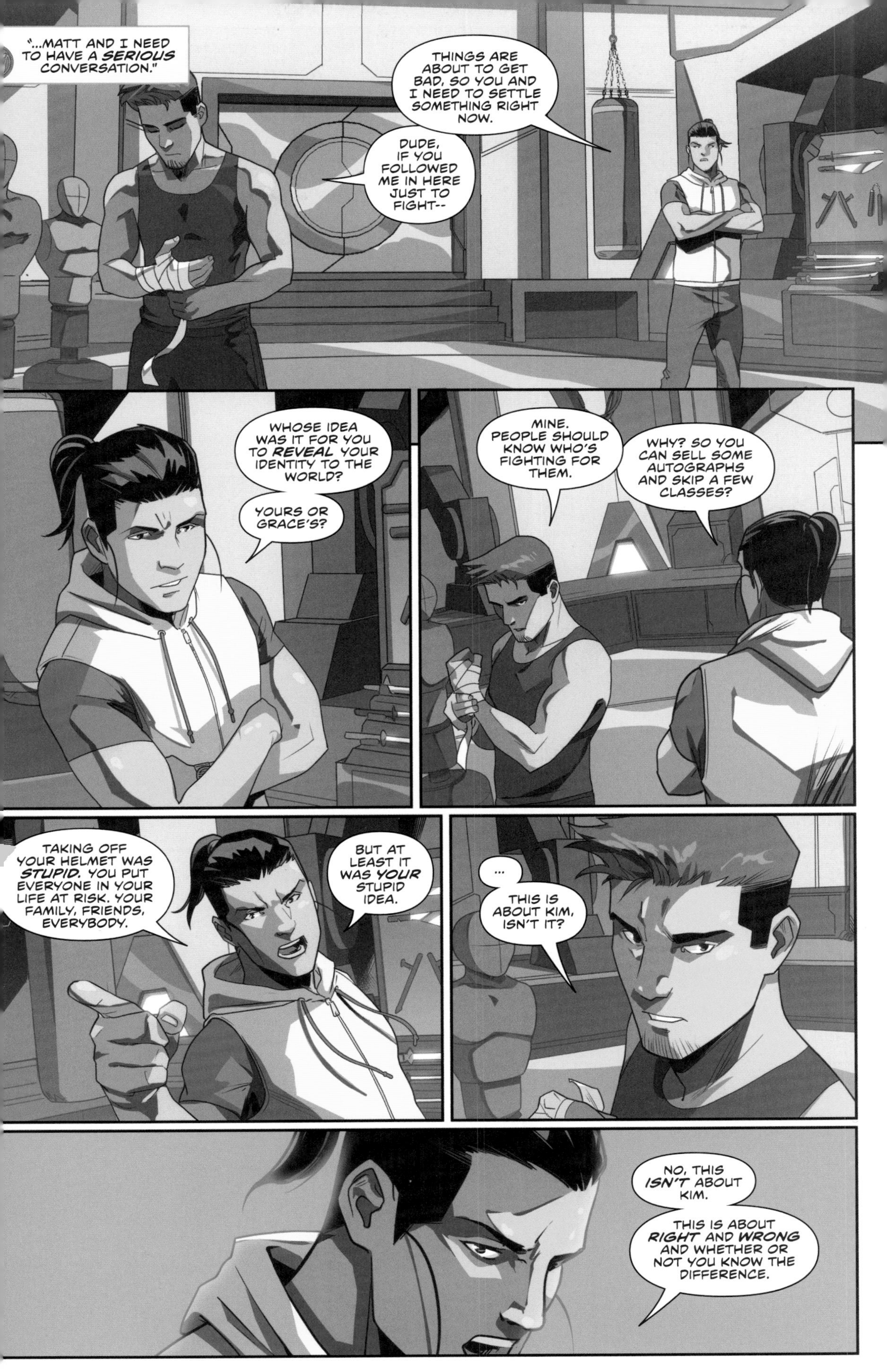
"...MATT AND I NEED TO HAVE A *SERIOUS* CONVERSATION."
THINGS ARE ABOUT TO GET BAD, SO YOU AND I NEED TO SETTLE SOMETHING RIGHT NOW.
DUDE, IF YOU FOLLOWED ME IN HERE JUST TO FIGHT--
WHOSE IDEA WAS IT FOR YOU TO *REVEAL* YOUR IDENTITY TO THE WORLD?
YOURS OR GRACE'S?
MINE. PEOPLE SHOULD KNOW WHO'S FIGHTING FOR THEM.
WHY? SO YOU CAN SELL SOME AUTOGRAPHS AND SKIP A FEW CLASSES?
TAKING OFF YOUR HELMET WAS *STUPID*. YOU PUT EVERYONE IN YOUR LIFE AT RISK. YOUR FAMILY, FRIENDS, EVERYBODY.
BUT AT LEAST IT WAS *YOUR* STUPID IDEA.
...
THIS IS ABOUT KIM, ISN'T IT?
NO, THIS *ISN'T* ABOUT KIM.
THIS IS ABOUT *RIGHT* AND *WRONG* AND WHETHER OR NOT YOU KNOW THE DIFFERENCE.

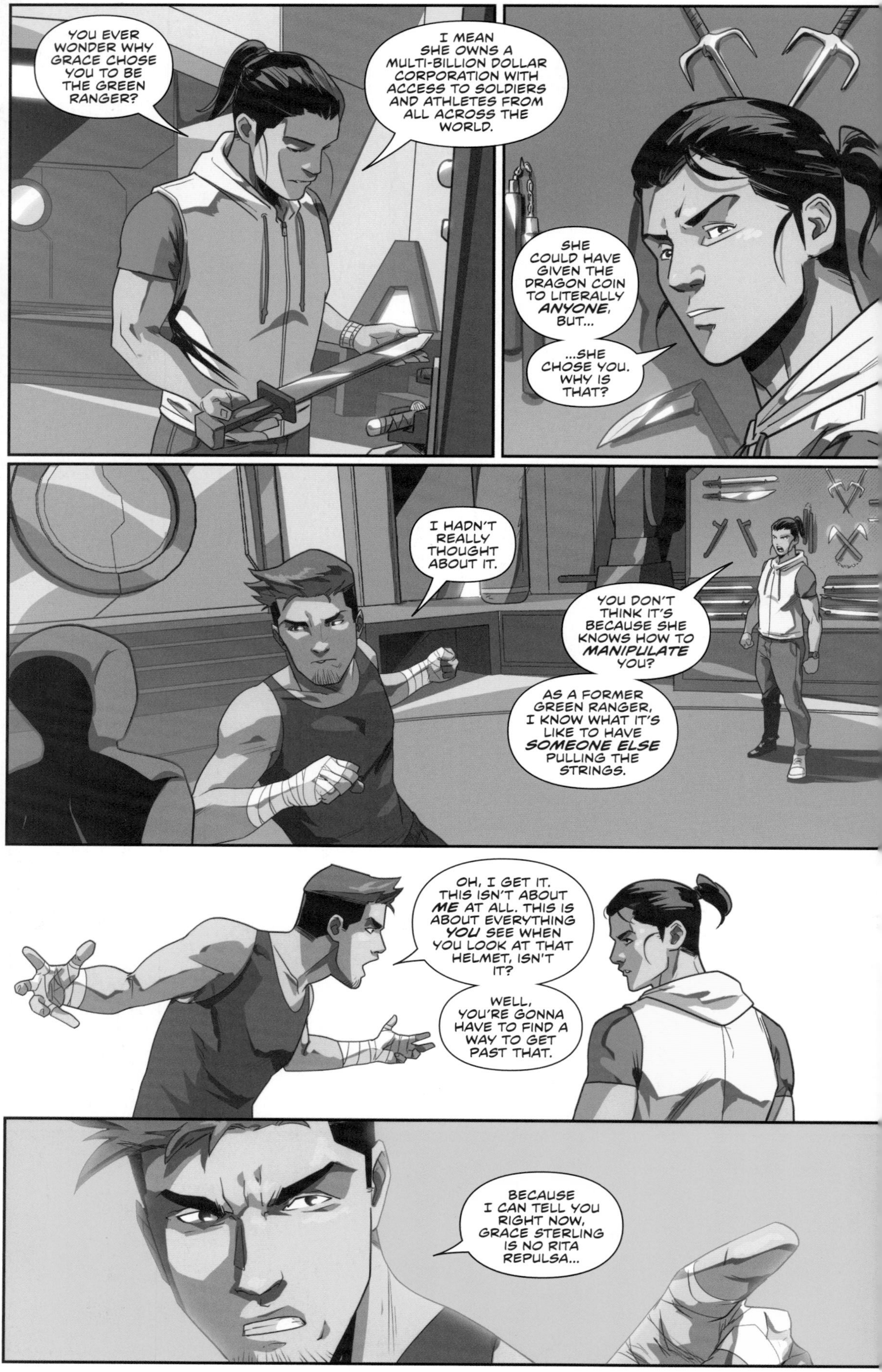
YOU EVER WONDER WHY GRACE CHOSE YOU TO BE THE GREEN RANGER?
I MEAN SHE OWNS A MULTI-BILLION DOLLAR CORPORATION WITH ACCESS TO SOLDIERS AND ATHLETES FROM ALL ACROSS THE WORLD.
SHE COULD HAVE GIVEN THE DRAGON COIN TO LITERALLY ***ANYONE***, BUT...
...SHE CHOSE YOU. WHY IS THAT?
I HADN'T REALLY THOUGHT ABOUT IT.
YOU DON'T THINK IT'S BECAUSE SHE KNOWS HOW TO ***MANIPULATE*** YOU?
AS A FORMER GREEN RANGER, I KNOW WHAT IT'S LIKE TO HAVE ***SOMEONE ELSE*** PULLING THE STRINGS.
OH, I GET IT. THIS ISN'T ABOUT ***ME*** AT ALL. THIS IS ABOUT EVERYTHING ***YOU*** SEE WHEN YOU LOOK AT THAT HELMET, ISN'T IT?
WELL, YOU'RE GONNA HAVE TO FIND A WAY TO GET PAST THAT.
BECAUSE I CAN TELL YOU RIGHT NOW, GRACE STERLING IS NO RITA REPULSA...

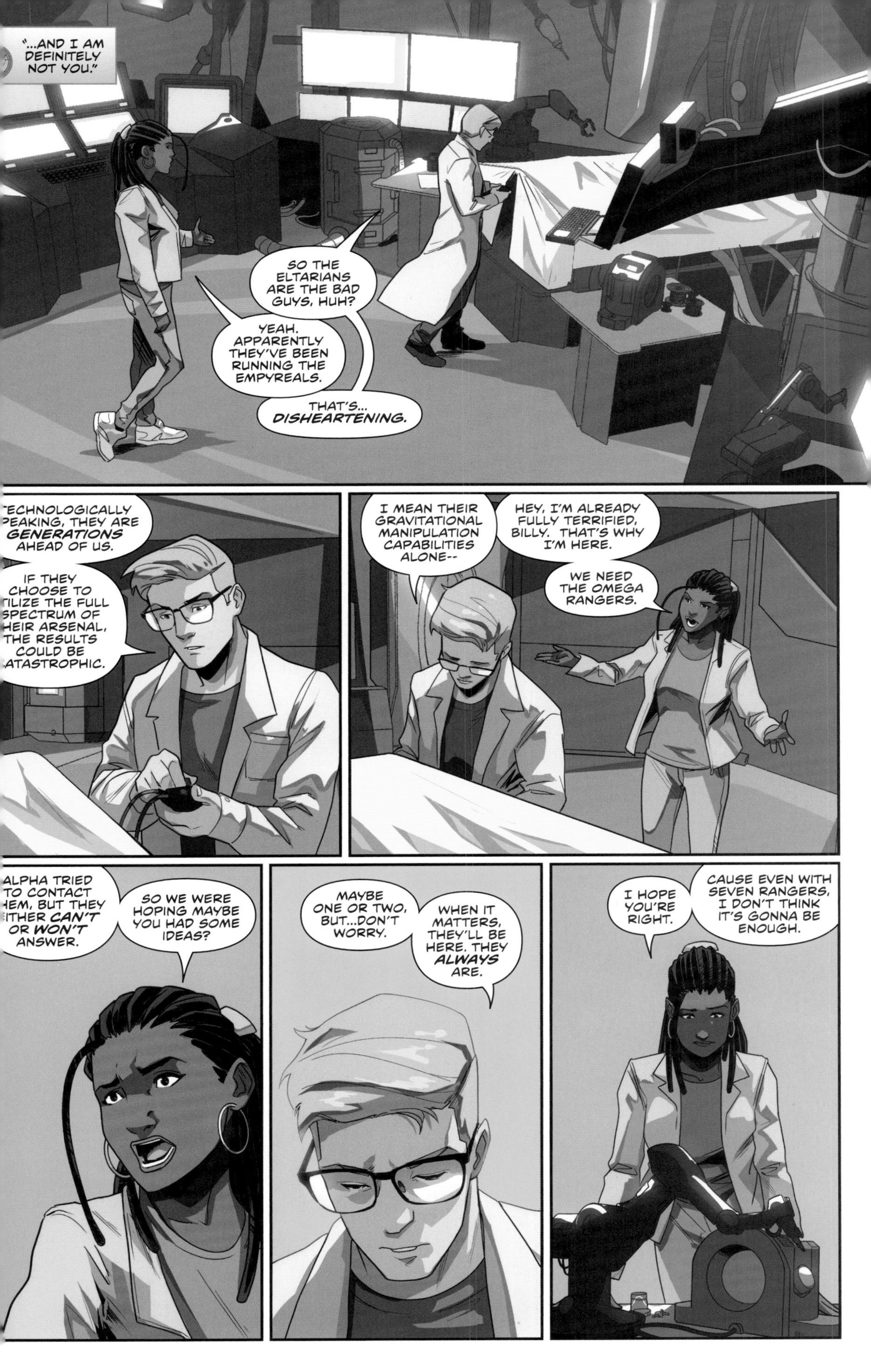
"...AND I AM DEFINITELY NOT YOU."
SO THE ELTARIANS ARE THE BAD GUYS, HUH?
YEAH. APPARENTLY THEY'VE BEEN RUNNING THE EMPYREALS.
THAT'S... DISHEARTENING.
TECHNOLOGICALLY SPEAKING, THEY ARE GENERATIONS AHEAD OF US.
IF THEY CHOOSE TO UTILIZE THE FULL SPECTRUM OF THEIR ARSENAL, THE RESULTS COULD BE CATASTROPHIC.
I MEAN THEIR GRAVITATIONAL MANIPULATION CAPABILITIES ALONE--
HEY, I'M ALREADY FULLY TERRIFIED, BILLY. THAT'S WHY I'M HERE.
WE NEED THE OMEGA RANGERS.
ALPHA TRIED TO CONTACT THEM, BUT THEY EITHER CAN'T OR WON'T ANSWER.
SO WE WERE HOPING MAYBE YOU HAD SOME IDEAS?
MAYBE ONE OR TWO, BUT...DON'T WORRY.
WHEN IT MATTERS, THEY'LL BE HERE. THEY ALWAYS ARE.
I HOPE YOU'RE RIGHT.
CAUSE EVEN WITH SEVEN RANGERS, I DON'T THINK IT'S GONNA BE ENOUGH.

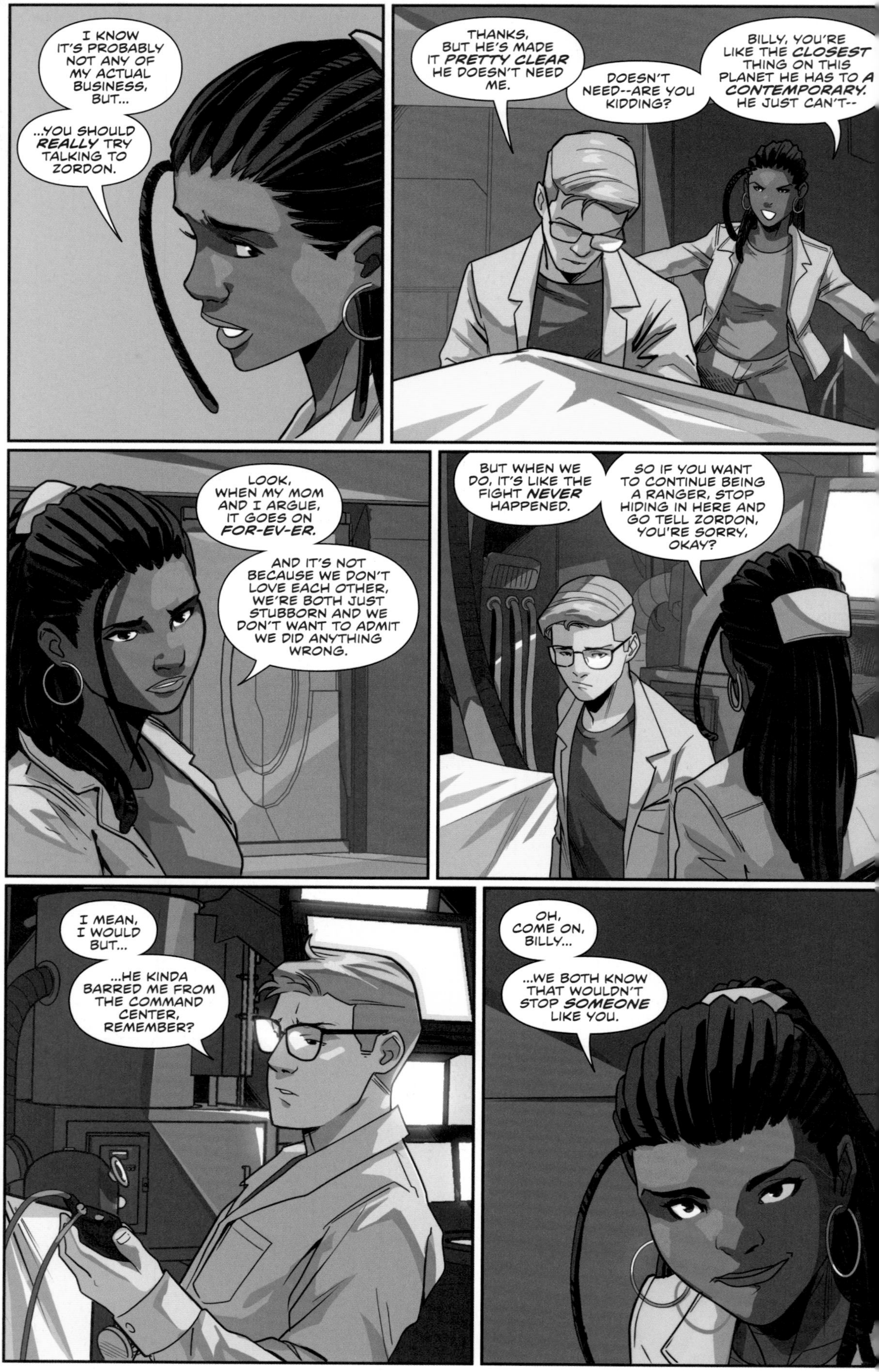

I KNOW IT'S PROBABLY NOT ANY OF MY ACTUAL BUSINESS, BUT...
...YOU SHOULD *REALLY* TRY TALKING TO ZORDON.
THANKS, BUT HE'S MADE IT *PRETTY CLEAR* HE DOESN'T NEED ME.
DOESN'T NEED--ARE YOU KIDDING?
BILLY, YOU'RE LIKE THE *CLOSEST* THING ON THIS PLANET HE HAS TO *A CONTEMPORARY.* HE JUST CAN'T--
LOOK, WHEN MY MOM AND I ARGUE, IT GOES ON *FOR-EV-ER.*
AND IT'S NOT BECAUSE WE DON'T LOVE EACH OTHER, WE'RE BOTH JUST STUBBORN AND WE DON'T WANT TO ADMIT WE DID ANYTHING WRONG.
BUT WHEN WE DO, IT'S LIKE THE FIGHT *NEVER* HAPPENED.
SO IF YOU WANT TO CONTINUE BEING A RANGER, STOP HIDING IN HERE AND GO TELL ZORDON, YOU'RE SORRY, OKAY?
I MEAN, I WOULD BUT...
...HE KINDA BARRED ME FROM THE COMMAND CENTER, REMEMBER?
OH, COME ON, BILLY...
...WE BOTH KNOW THAT WOULDN'T STOP *SOMEONE* LIKE YOU.

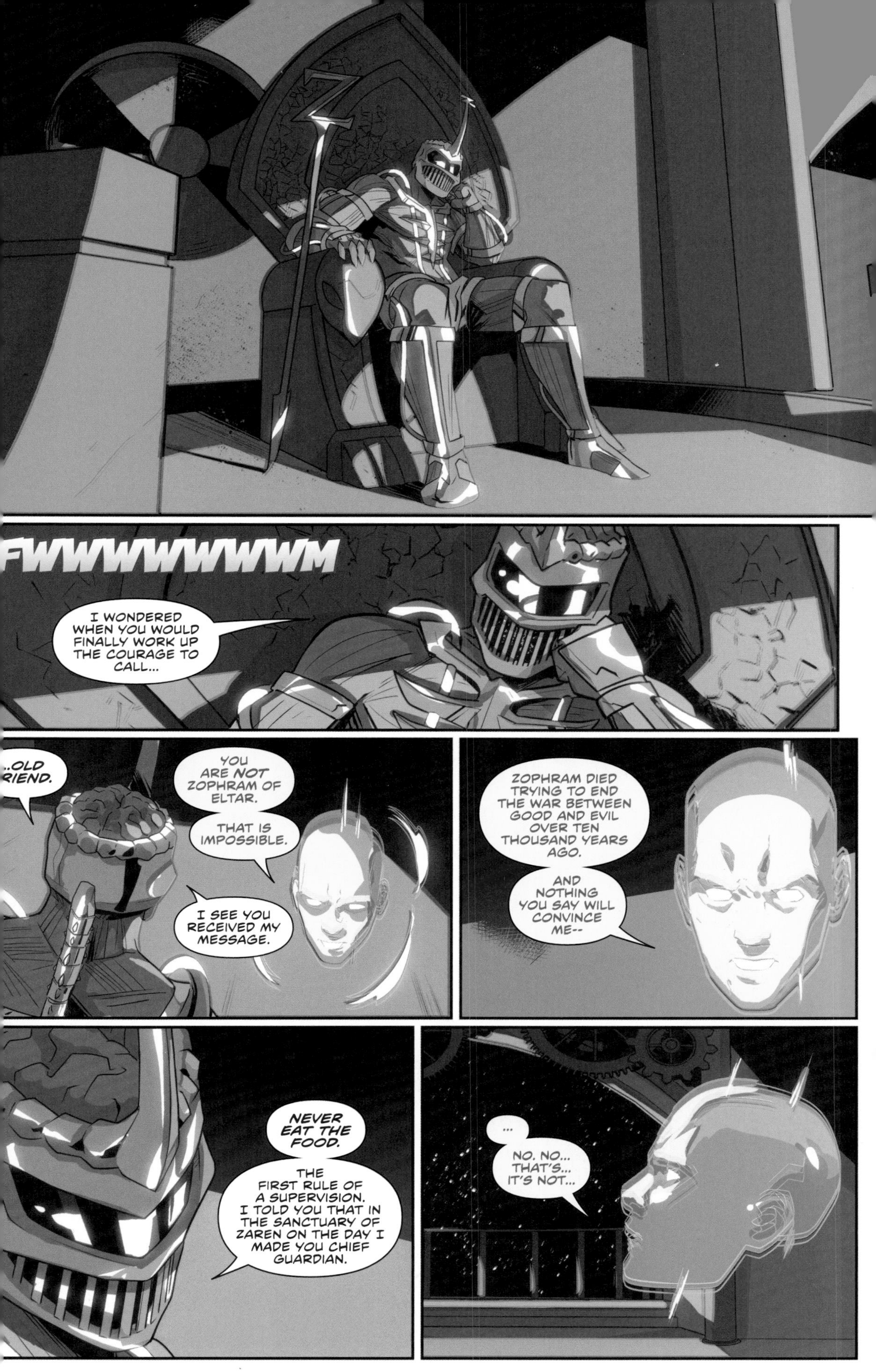
FWWWWWWWM
I WONDERED WHEN YOU WOULD FINALLY WORK UP THE COURAGE TO CALL...
...OLD FRIEND.
YOU ARE NOT ZOPHRAM OF ELTAR.
THAT IS IMPOSSIBLE.
I SEE YOU RECEIVED MY MESSAGE.
ZOPHRAM DIED TRYING TO END THE WAR BETWEEN GOOD AND EVIL OVER TEN THOUSAND YEARS AGO.
AND NOTHING YOU SAY WILL CONVINCE ME--
NEVER EAT THE FOOD.
THE FIRST RULE OF A SUPERVISION. I TOLD YOU THAT IN THE SANCTUARY OF ZAREN ON THE DAY I MADE YOU CHIEF GUARDIAN.
...
NO. NO... THAT'S... IT'S NOT...

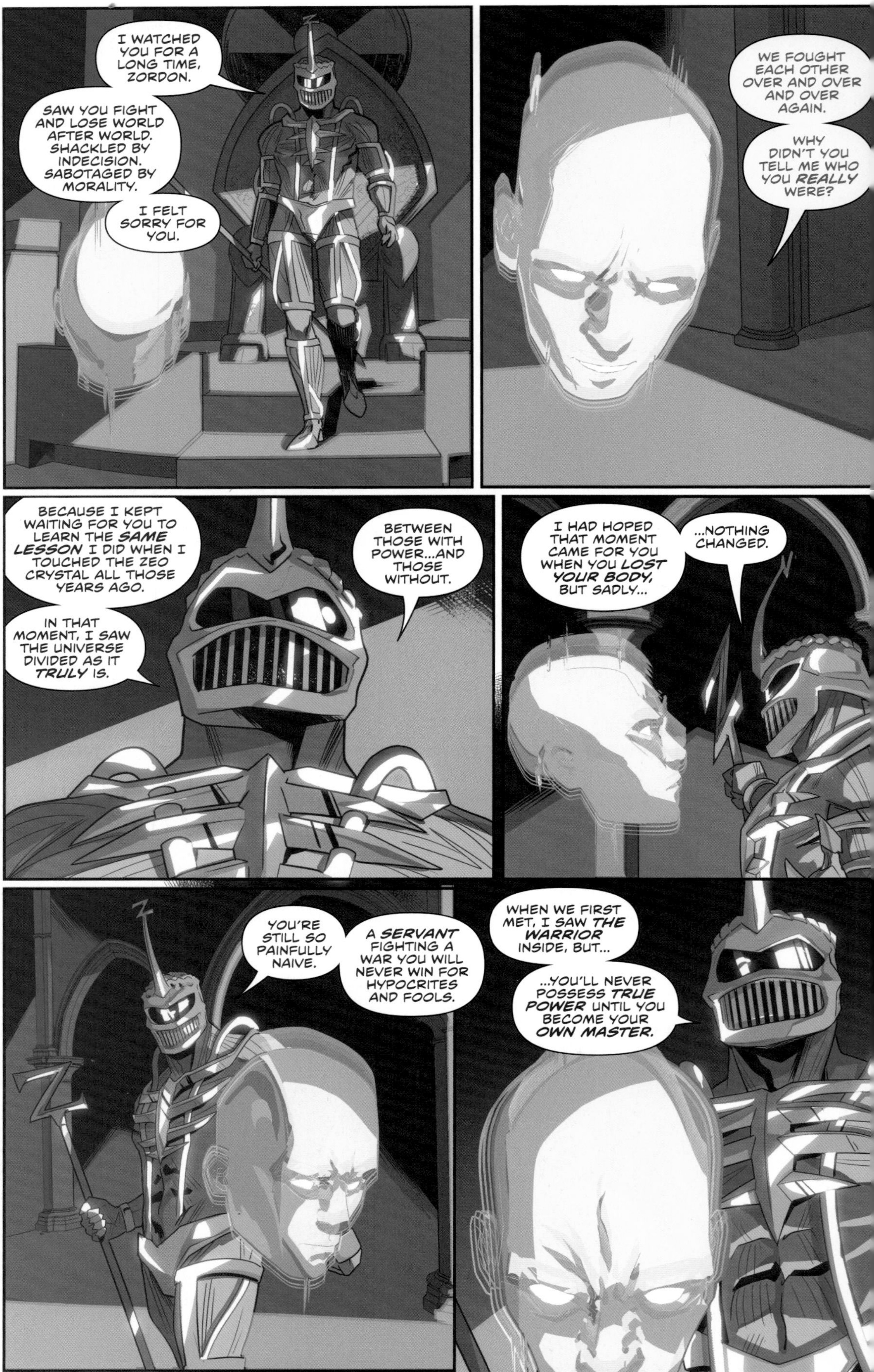
I WATCHED YOU FOR A LONG TIME, ZORDON.
SAW YOU FIGHT AND LOSE WORLD AFTER WORLD. SHACKLED BY INDECISION. SABOTAGED BY MORALITY.
I FELT SORRY FOR YOU.
WE FOUGHT EACH OTHER OVER AND OVER AND OVER AGAIN.
WHY DIDN'T YOU TELL ME WHO YOU *REALLY* WERE?
BECAUSE I KEPT WAITING FOR YOU TO LEARN THE *SAME LESSON* I DID WHEN I TOUCHED THE ZEO CRYSTAL ALL THOSE YEARS AGO.
IN THAT MOMENT, I SAW THE UNIVERSE DIVIDED AS IT *TRULY* IS.
BETWEEN THOSE WITH POWER...AND THOSE WITHOUT.
I HAD HOPED THAT MOMENT CAME FOR YOU WHEN YOU *LOST YOUR BODY,* BUT SADLY...
...NOTHING CHANGED.
YOU'RE STILL SO PAINFULLY NAIVE.
A *SERVANT* FIGHTING A WAR YOU WILL NEVER WIN FOR HYPOCRITES AND FOOLS.
WHEN WE FIRST MET, I SAW *THE WARRIOR* INSIDE, BUT...
...YOU'LL NEVER POSSESS *TRUE POWER* UNTIL YOU BECOME YOUR *OWN MASTER.*

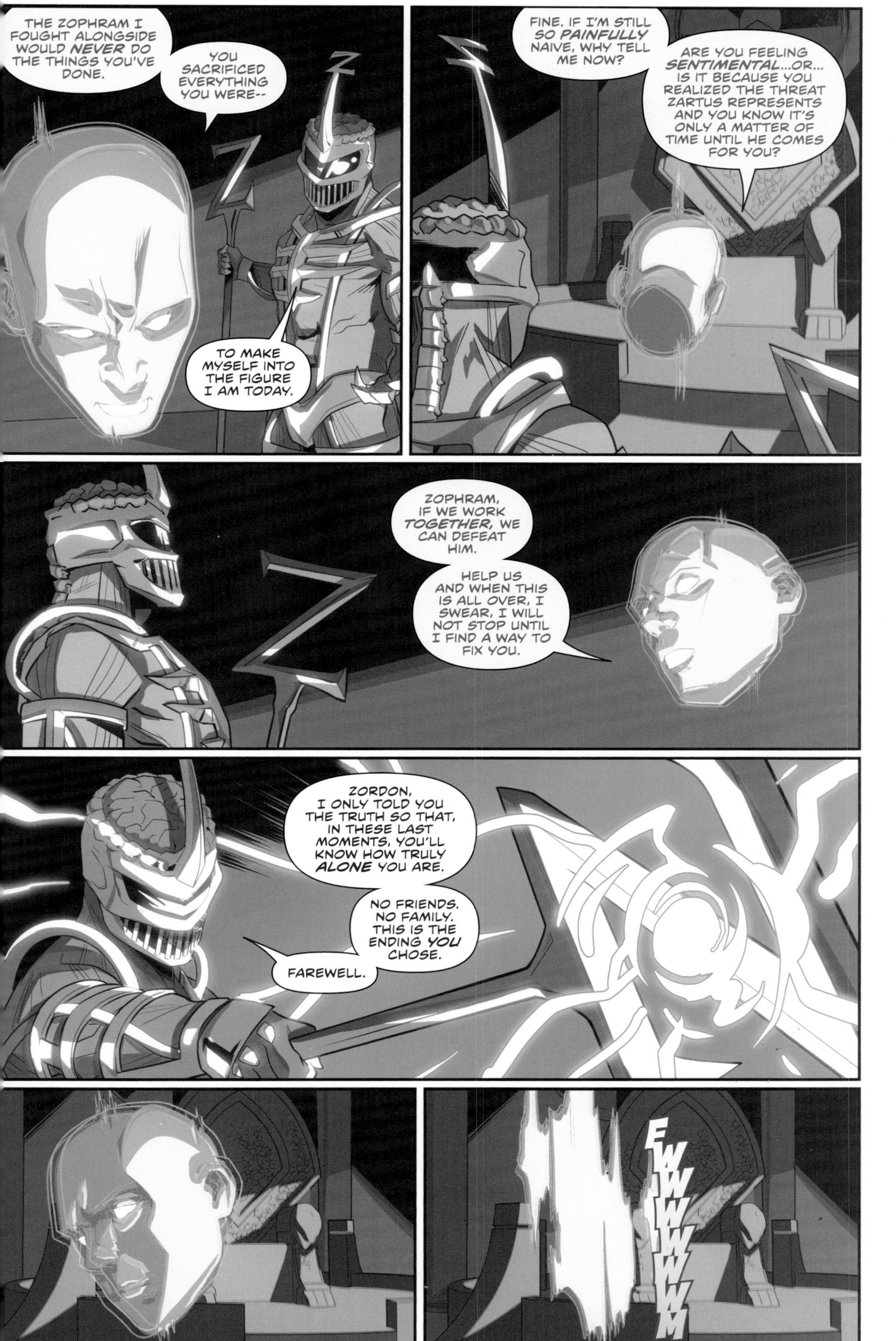
THE ZOPHRAM I FOUGHT ALONGSIDE WOULD NEVER DO THE THINGS YOU'VE DONE.
YOU SACRIFICED EVERYTHING YOU WERE--
TO MAKE MYSELF INTO THE FIGURE I AM TODAY.
FINE. IF I'M STILL SO PAINFULLY NAIVE, WHY TELL ME NOW?
ARE YOU FEELING SENTIMENTAL...OR... IS IT BECAUSE YOU REALIZED THE THREAT ZARTUS REPRESENTS AND YOU KNOW IT'S ONLY A MATTER OF TIME UNTIL HE COMES FOR YOU?
ZOPHRAM, IF WE WORK TOGETHER, WE CAN DEFEAT HIM.
HELP US AND WHEN THIS IS ALL OVER, I SWEAR, I WILL NOT STOP UNTIL I FIND A WAY TO FIX YOU.
ZORDON, I ONLY TOLD YOU THE TRUTH SO THAT, IN THESE LAST MOMENTS, YOU'LL KNOW HOW TRULY ALONE YOU ARE.
NO FRIENDS. NO FAMILY. THIS IS THE ENDING YOU CHOSE.
FAREWELL.
FWWWWWWM

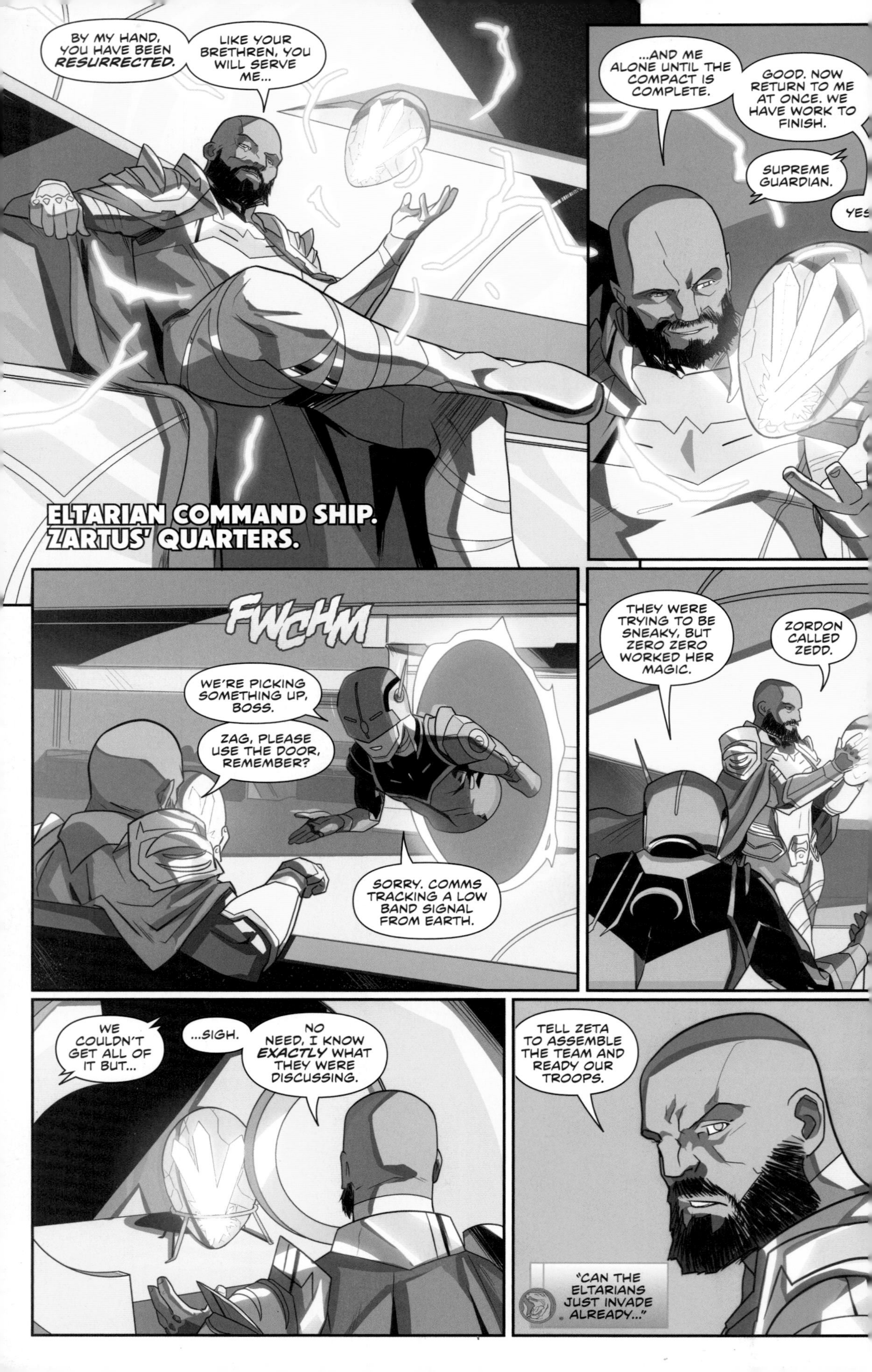
BY MY HAND, YOU HAVE BEEN RESURRECTED.
LIKE YOUR BRETHREN, YOU WILL SERVE ME...
ELTARIAN COMMAND SHIP. ZARTUS' QUARTERS.
...AND ME ALONE UNTIL THE COMPACT IS COMPLETE.
GOOD. NOW RETURN TO ME AT ONCE. WE HAVE WORK TO FINISH.
SUPREME GUARDIAN.
YES
FWCHM
WE'RE PICKING SOMETHING UP, BOSS.
ZAG, PLEASE USE THE DOOR, REMEMBER?
SORRY. COMMS TRACKING A LOW BAND SIGNAL FROM EARTH.
THEY WERE TRYING TO BE SNEAKY, BUT ZERO ZERO WORKED HER MAGIC.
ZORDON CALLED ZEDD.
WE COULDN'T GET ALL OF IT BUT...
...SIGH.
NO NEED, I KNOW EXACTLY WHAT THEY WERE DISCUSSING.
TELL ZETA TO ASSEMBLE THE TEAM AND READY OUR TROOPS.
"CAN THE ELTARIANS JUST INVADE ALREADY..."

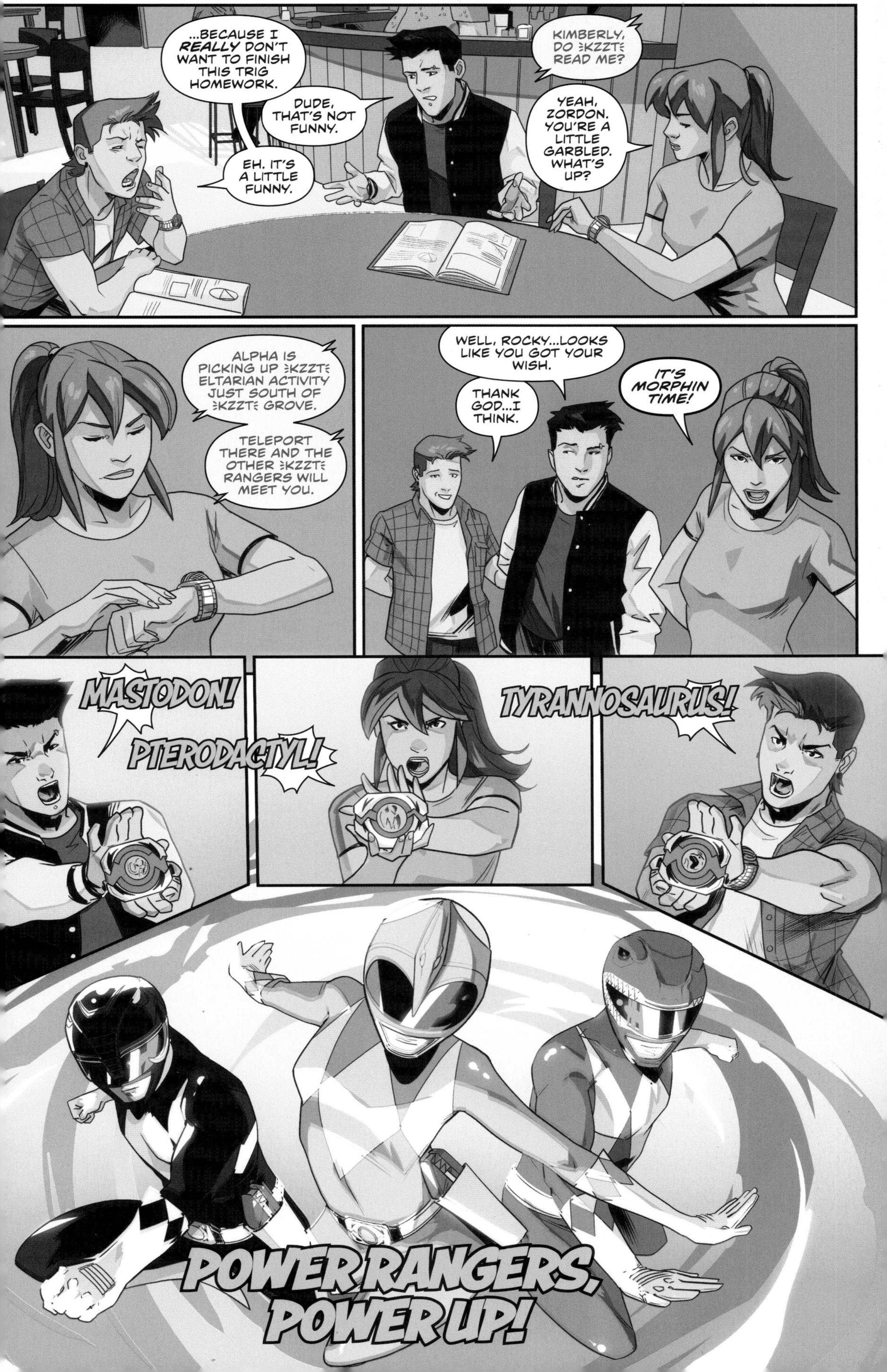
...BECAUSE I REALLY DON'T WANT TO FINISH THIS TRIG HOMEWORK.
DUDE, THAT'S NOT FUNNY.
EH. IT'S A LITTLE FUNNY.
KIMBERLY, DO ⋮KZZT⋮ READ ME?
YEAH, ZORDON. YOU'RE A LITTLE GARBLED. WHAT'S UP?
ALPHA IS PICKING UP ⋮KZZT⋮ ELTARIAN ACTIVITY JUST SOUTH OF ⋮KZZT⋮ GROVE.
TELEPORT THERE AND THE OTHER ⋮KZZT⋮ RANGERS WILL MEET YOU.
WELL, ROCKY...LOOKS LIKE YOU GOT YOUR WISH.
THANK GOD...I THINK.
IT'S MORPHIN TIME!
MASTODON!
PTERODACTYL!
TYRANNOSAURUS!
POWER RANGERS, POWER UP!

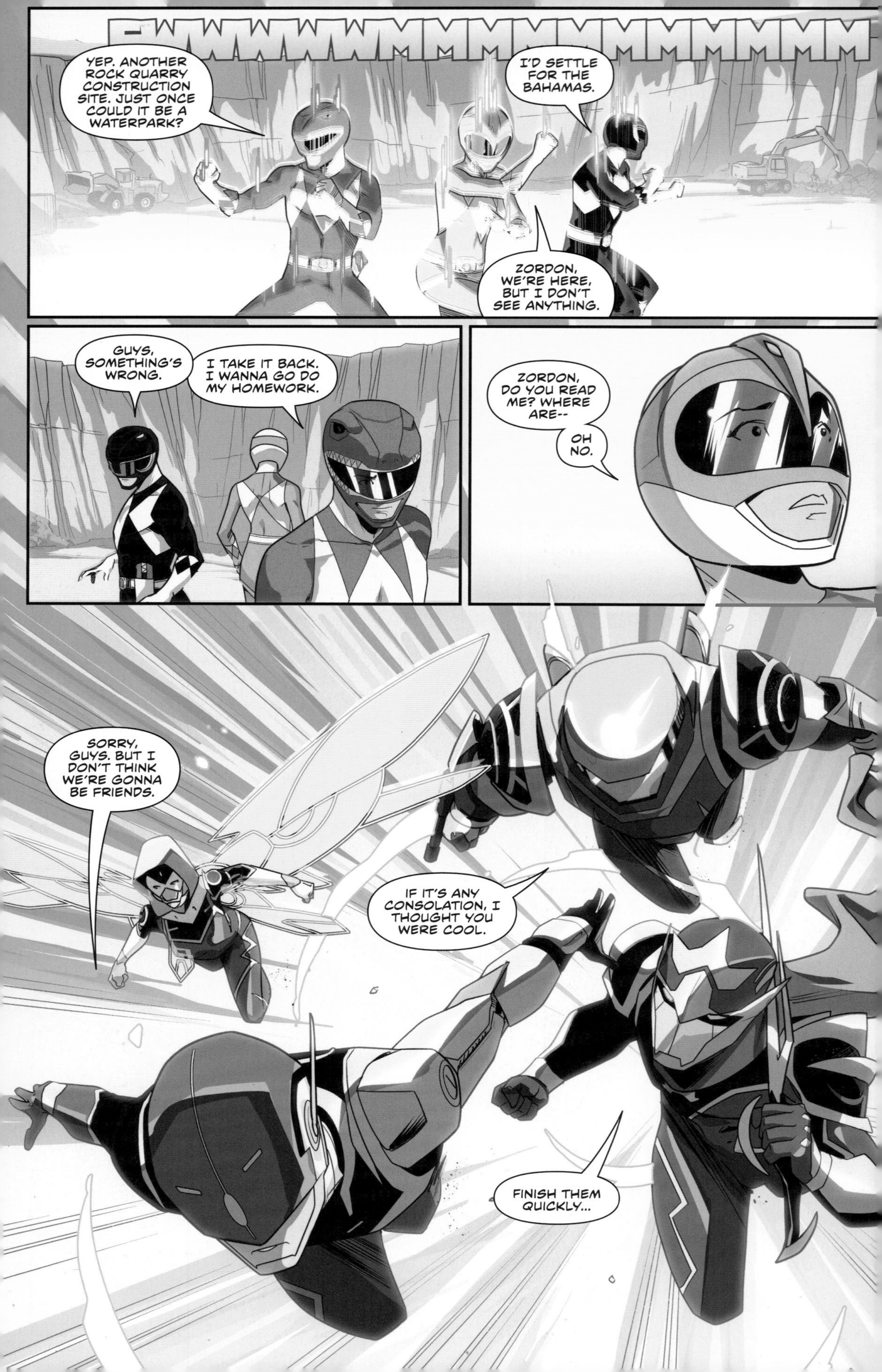
FWWWWWWWMMMMMMMMMMMMMMM
YEP. ANOTHER ROCK QUARRY CONSTRUCTION SITE. JUST ONCE COULD IT BE A WATERPARK?
I'D SETTLE FOR THE BAHAMAS.
ZORDON, WE'RE HERE, BUT I DON'T SEE ANYTHING.
GUYS, SOMETHING'S WRONG.
I TAKE IT BACK. I WANNA GO DO MY HOMEWORK.
ZORDON, DO YOU READ ME? WHERE ARE--
OH NO.
SORRY, GUYS. BUT I DON'T THINK WE'RE GONNA BE FRIENDS.
IF IT'S ANY CONSOLATION, I THOUGHT YOU WERE COOL.
FINISH THEM QUICKLY...

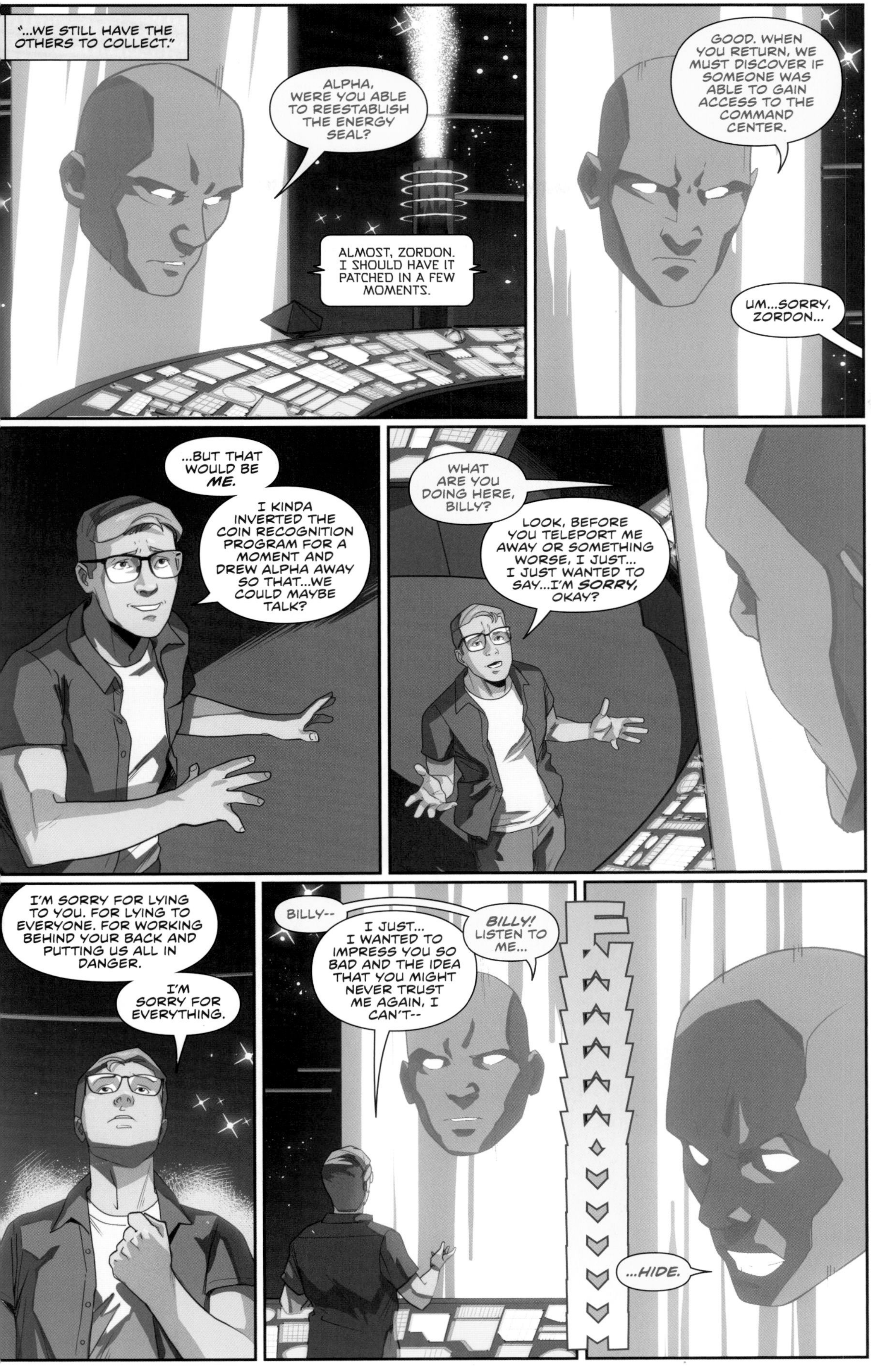
"...WE STILL HAVE THE OTHERS TO COLLECT."
ALPHA, WERE YOU ABLE TO REESTABLISH THE ENERGY SEAL?
ALMOST, ZORDON. I SHOULD HAVE IT PATCHED IN A FEW MOMENTS.
GOOD. WHEN YOU RETURN, WE MUST DISCOVER IF SOMEONE WAS ABLE TO GAIN ACCESS TO THE COMMAND CENTER.
UM...SORRY, ZORDON...
...BUT THAT WOULD BE *ME.*
I KINDA INVERTED THE COIN RECOGNITION PROGRAM FOR A MOMENT AND DREW ALPHA AWAY SO THAT...WE COULD MAYBE TALK?
WHAT ARE YOU DOING HERE, BILLY?
LOOK, BEFORE YOU TELEPORT ME AWAY OR SOMETHING WORSE, I JUST... I JUST WANTED TO SAY...I'M *SORRY,* OKAY?
I'M SORRY FOR LYING TO YOU. FOR LYING TO EVERYONE. FOR WORKING BEHIND YOUR BACK AND PUTTING US ALL IN DANGER.
I'M SORRY FOR EVERYTHING.
BILLY--
I JUST... I WANTED TO IMPRESS YOU SO BAD AND THE IDEA THAT YOU MIGHT NEVER TRUST ME AGAIN, I CAN'T--
BILLY! LISTEN TO ME...
...*HIDE.*

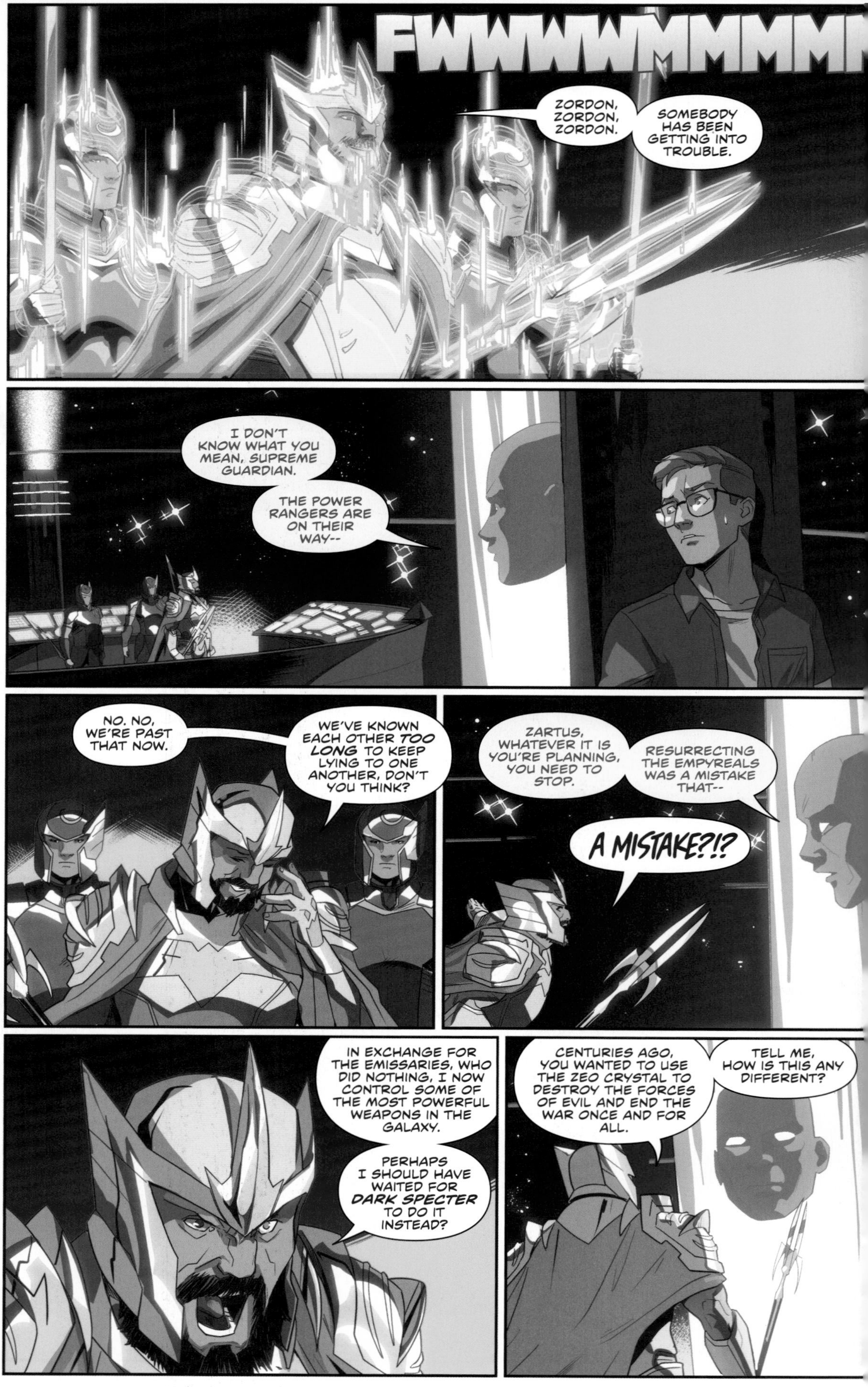
FWWWWMMMMM
ZORDON, ZORDON, ZORDON.
SOMEBODY HAS BEEN GETTING INTO TROUBLE.
I DON'T KNOW WHAT YOU MEAN, SUPREME GUARDIAN.
THE POWER RANGERS ARE ON THEIR WAY--
NO. NO, WE'RE PAST THAT NOW.
WE'VE KNOWN EACH OTHER *TOO LONG* TO KEEP LYING TO ONE ANOTHER, DON'T YOU THINK?
ZARTUS, WHATEVER IT IS YOU'RE PLANNING, YOU NEED TO STOP.
RESURRECTING THE EMPYREALS WAS A MISTAKE THAT--
A MISTAKE?!?
IN EXCHANGE FOR THE EMISSARIES, WHO DID NOTHING, I NOW CONTROL SOME OF THE MOST POWERFUL WEAPONS IN THE GALAXY.
PERHAPS I SHOULD HAVE WAITED FOR *DARK SPECTER* TO DO IT INSTEAD?
CENTURIES AGO, YOU WANTED TO USE THE ZEO CRYSTAL TO DESTROY THE FORCES OF EVIL AND END THE WAR ONCE AND FOR ALL.
TELL ME, HOW IS THIS ANY DIFFERENT?

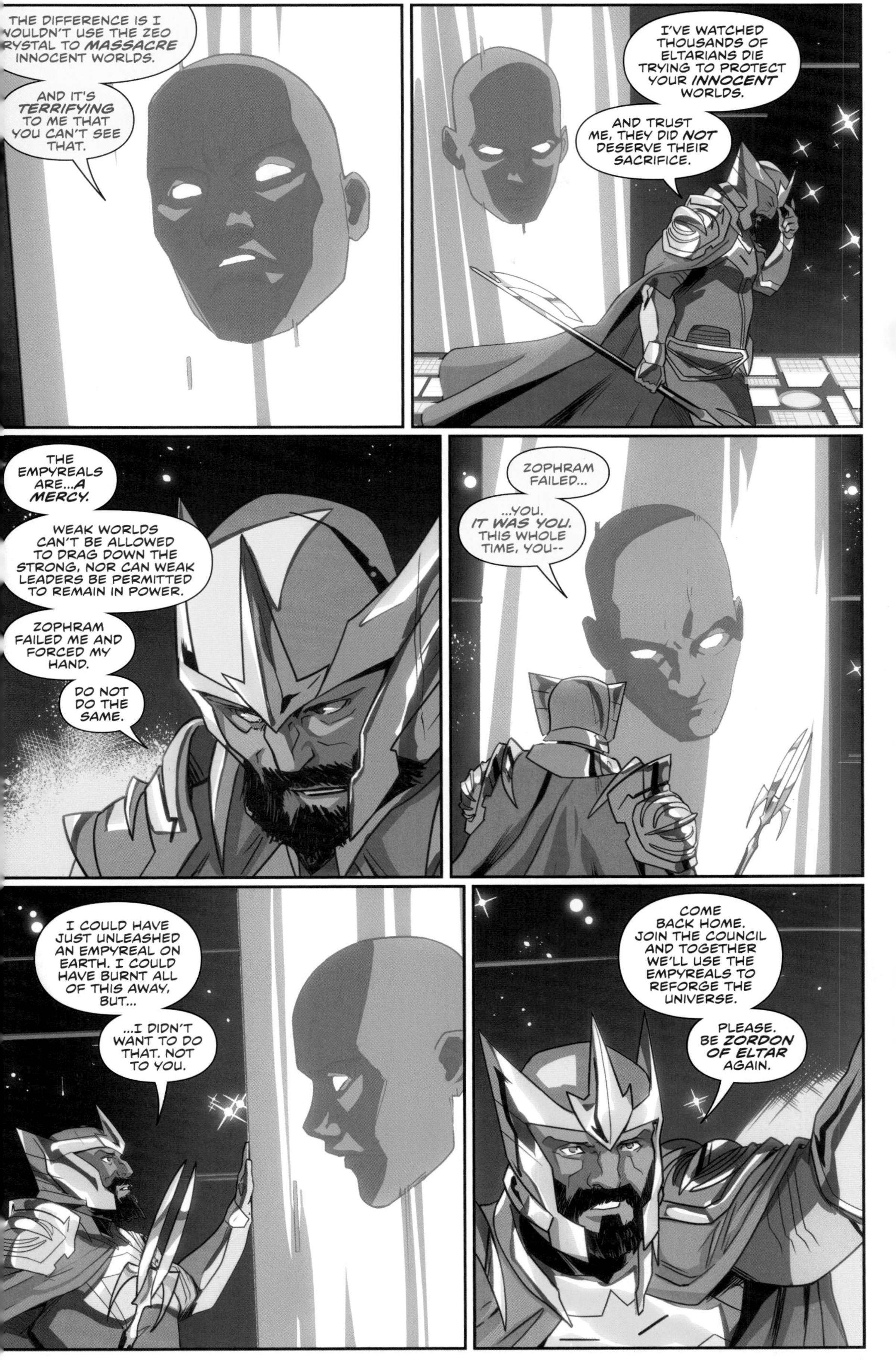
THE DIFFERENCE IS I WOULDN'T USE THE ZEO CRYSTAL TO *MASSACRE* INNOCENT WORLDS.
AND IT'S *TERRIFYING* TO ME THAT YOU CAN'T SEE THAT.
I'VE WATCHED THOUSANDS OF ELTARIANS DIE TRYING TO PROTECT YOUR *INNOCENT* WORLDS.
AND TRUST ME, THEY DID *NOT* DESERVE THEIR SACRIFICE.
THE EMPYREALS ARE...*A MERCY.*
WEAK WORLDS CAN'T BE ALLOWED TO DRAG DOWN THE STRONG, NOR CAN WEAK LEADERS BE PERMITTED TO REMAIN IN POWER.
ZOPHRAM FAILED ME AND FORCED MY HAND.
DO NOT DO THE SAME.
ZOPHRAM FAILED...
...YOU. *IT WAS YOU.* THIS WHOLE TIME, YOU--
I COULD HAVE JUST UNLEASHED AN EMPYREAL ON EARTH. I COULD HAVE BURNT ALL OF THIS AWAY, BUT...
...I DIDN'T WANT TO DO THAT. NOT TO YOU.
COME BACK HOME. JOIN THE COUNCIL AND TOGETHER WE'LL USE THE EMPYREALS TO REFORGE THE UNIVERSE.
PLEASE. BE *ZORDON OF ELTAR* AGAIN.

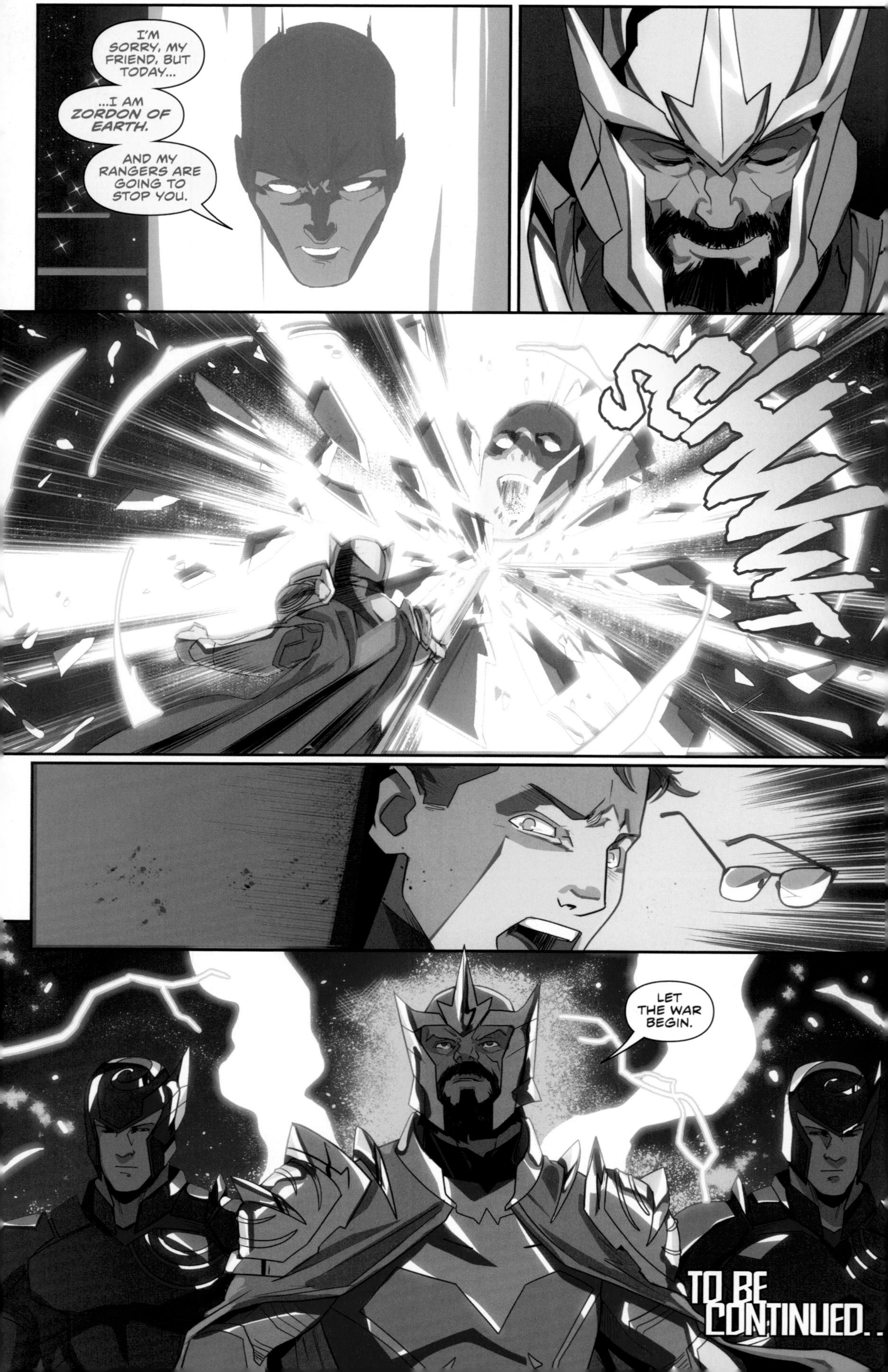
I'M SORRY, MY FRIEND, BUT TODAY...
...I AM ZORDON OF EARTH.
AND MY RANGERS ARE GOING TO STOP YOU.
SCHWA
LET THE WAR BEGIN.
TO BE CONTINUED...

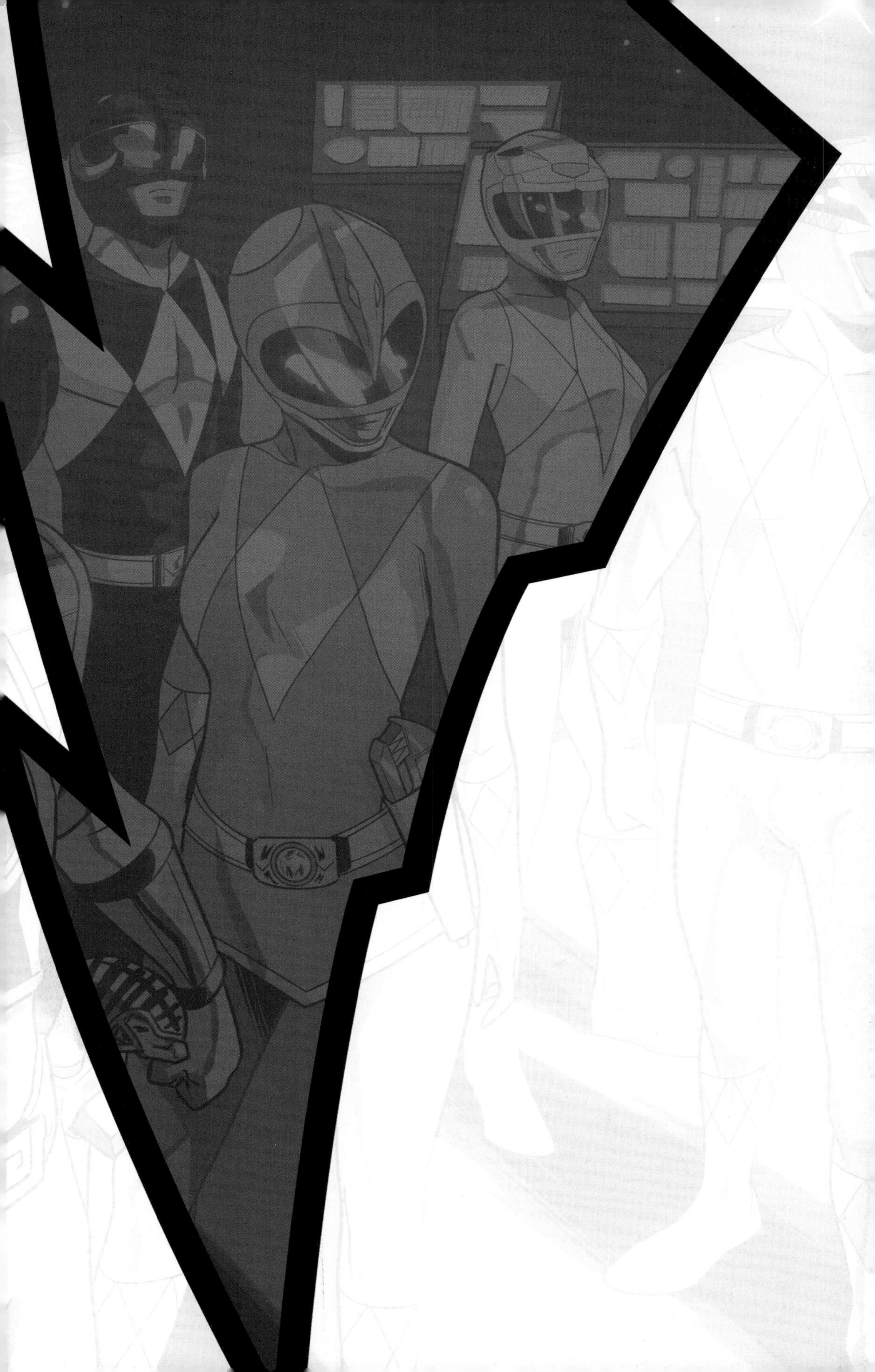

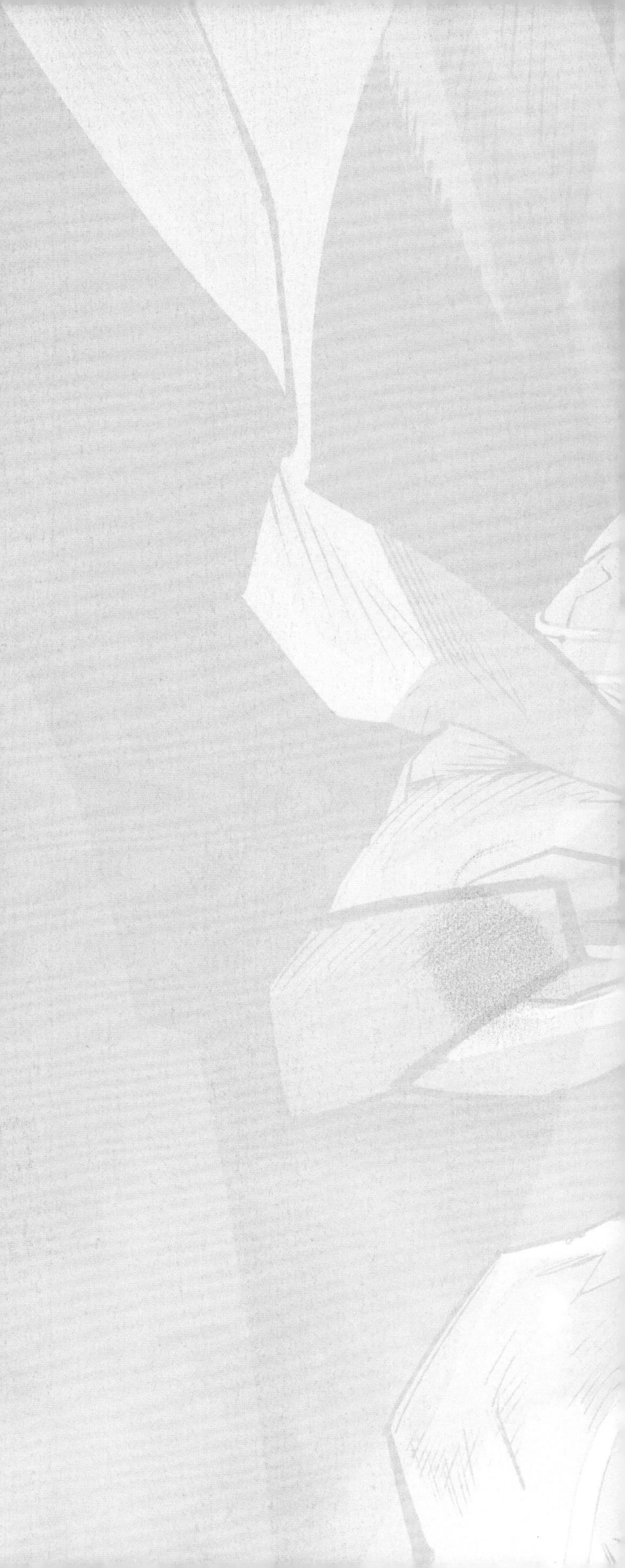

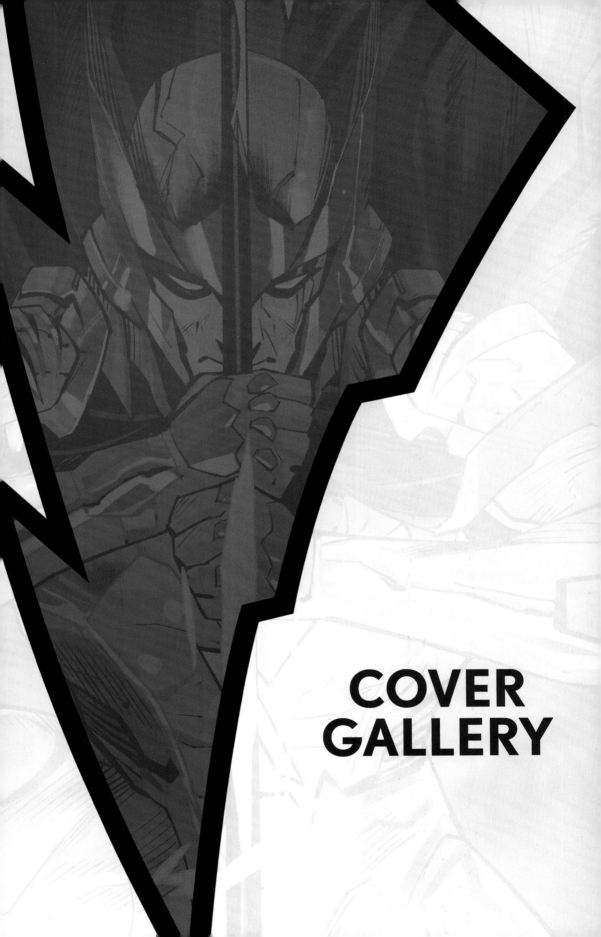

COVER
GALLERY

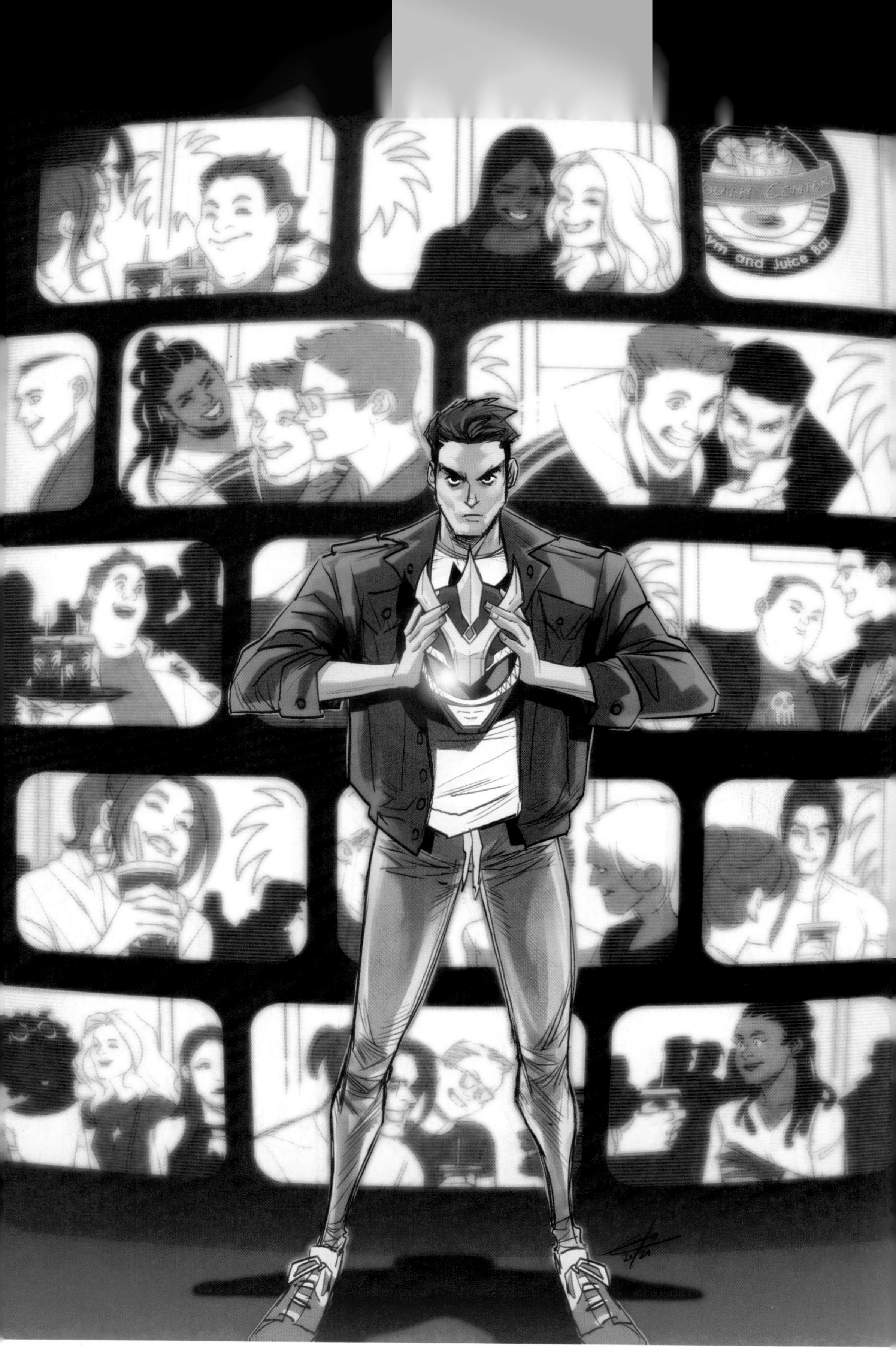
and Juice Bar

ELEONORA CARLINI | MIGHTY MORPHIN #9 VARIANT COVER

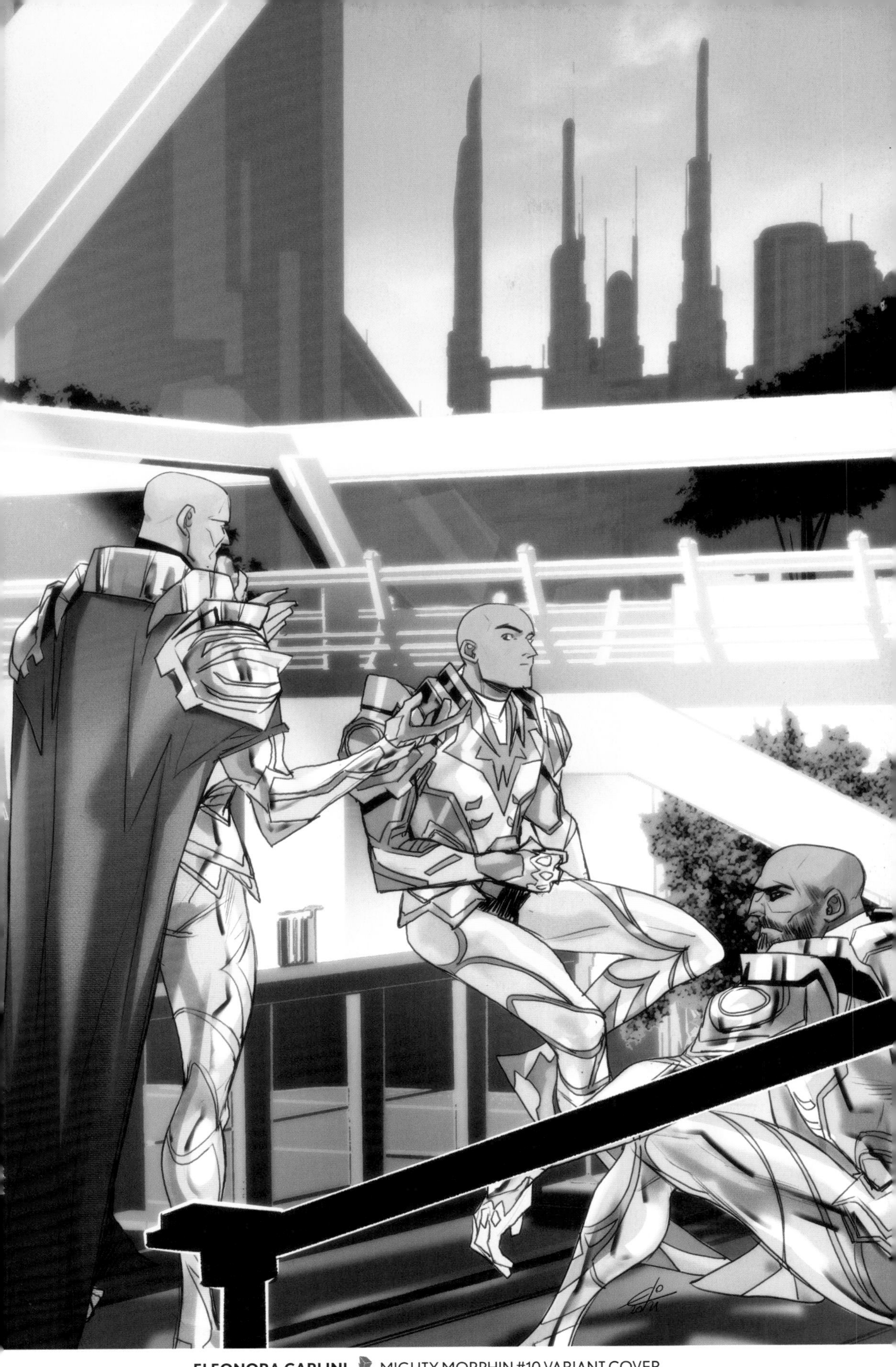

ELEONORA CARLINI MIGHTY MORPHIN #10 VARIANT COVER

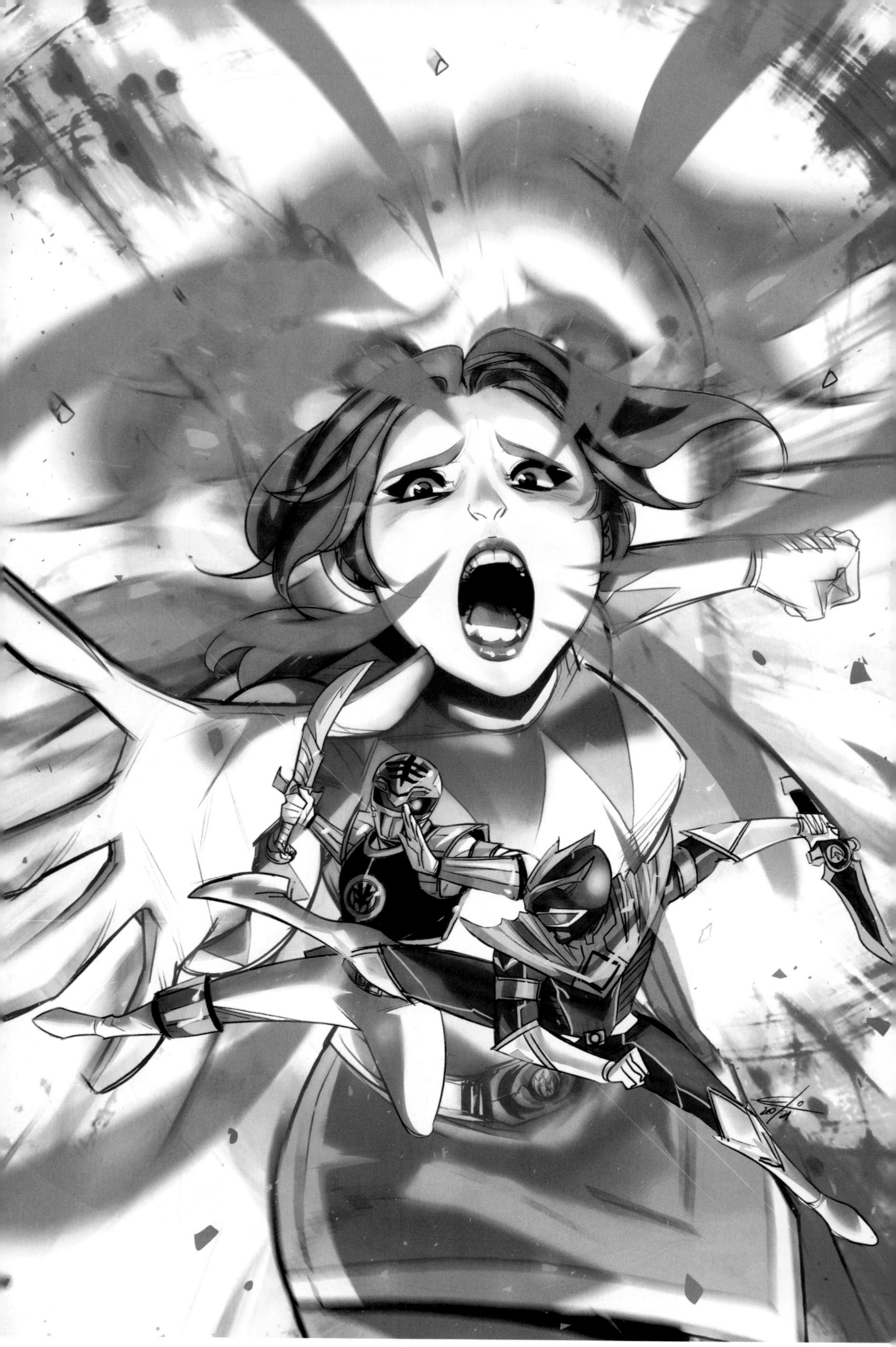

ELEONORA CARLINI MIGHTY MORPHIN #11 VARIANT COVER

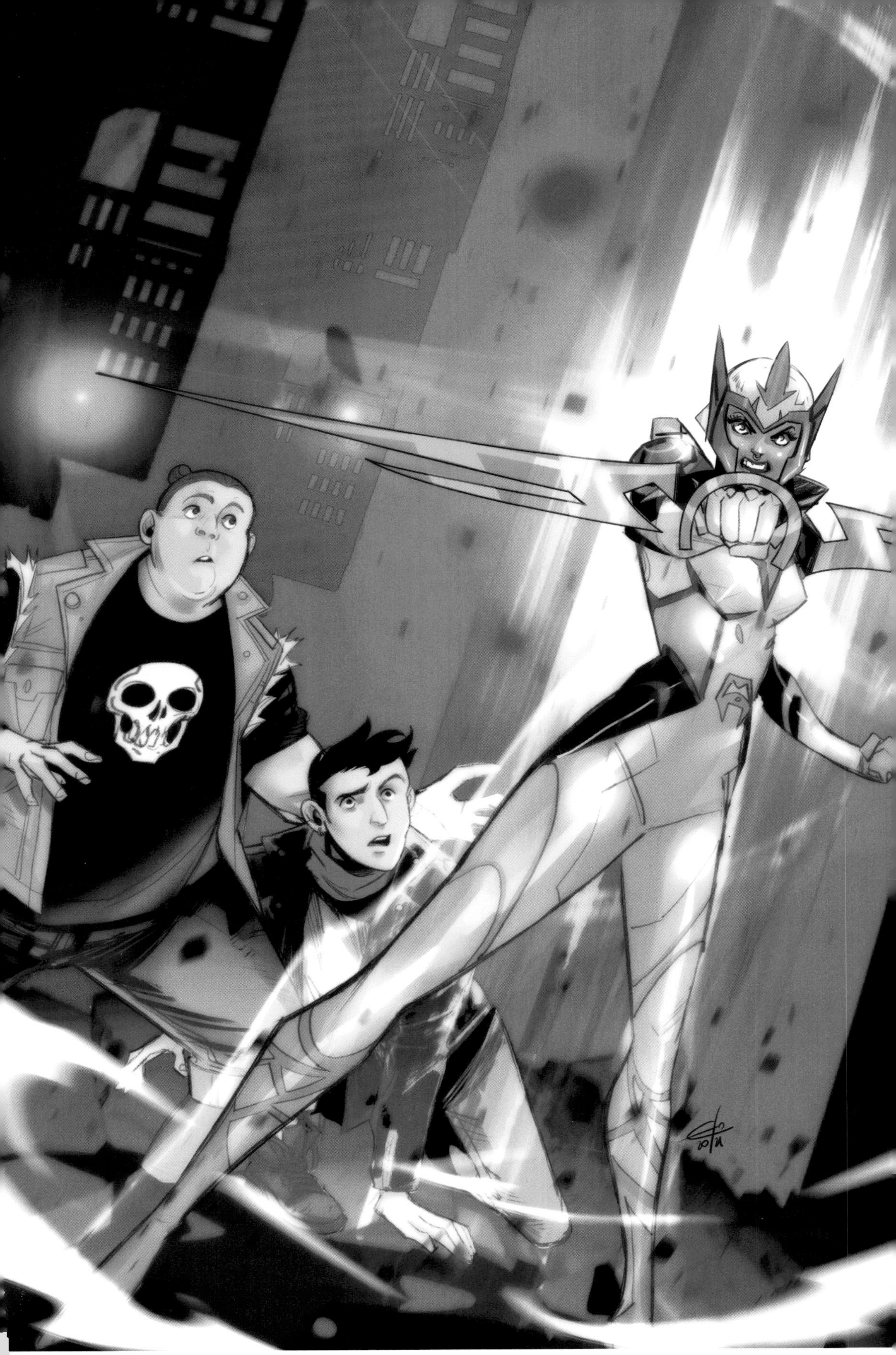

ELEONORA CARLINI MIGHTY MORPHIN #12 VARIANT COVER

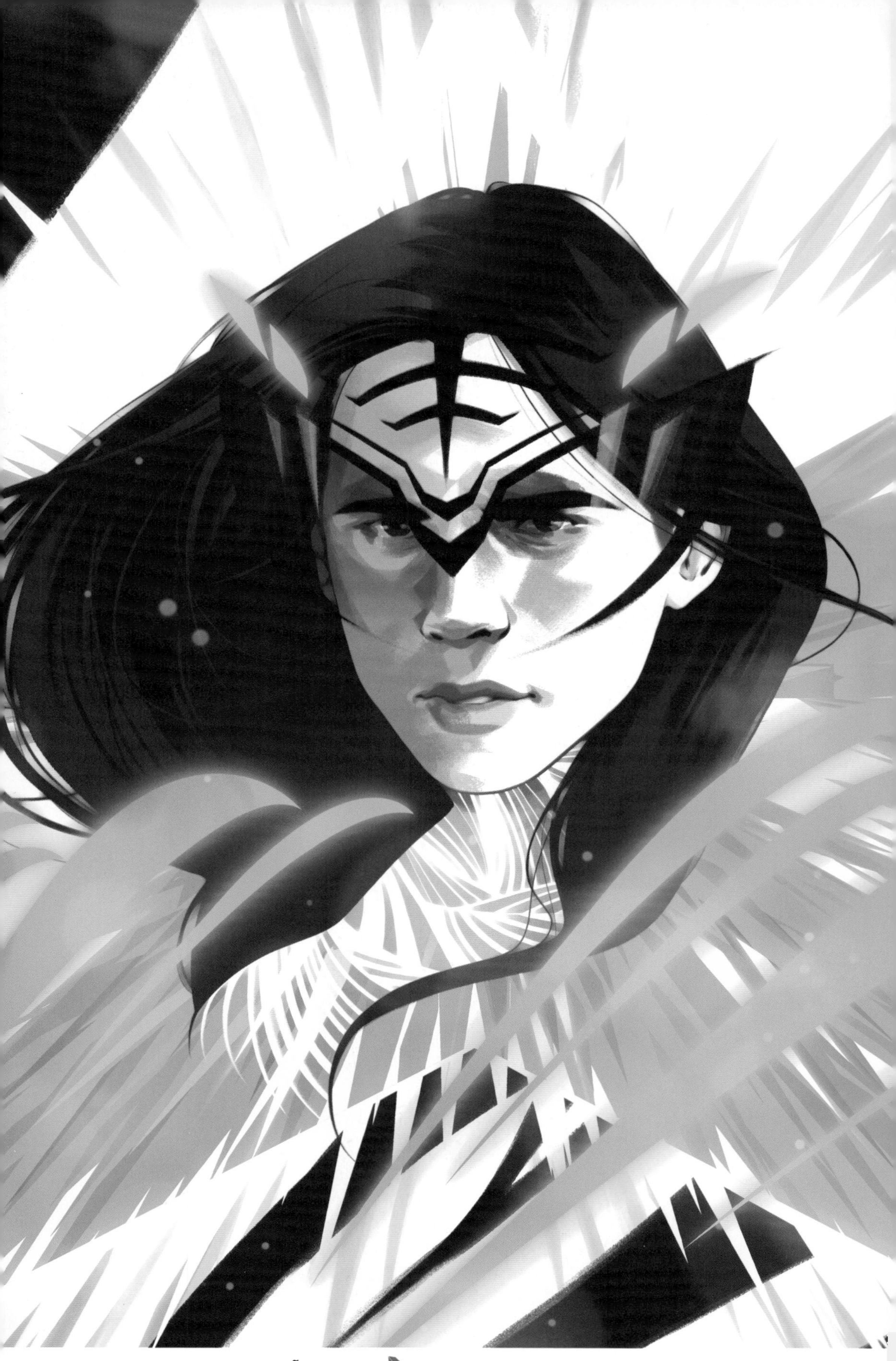

GOÑI MONTES MIGHTY MORPHIN #9 VARIANT COVER

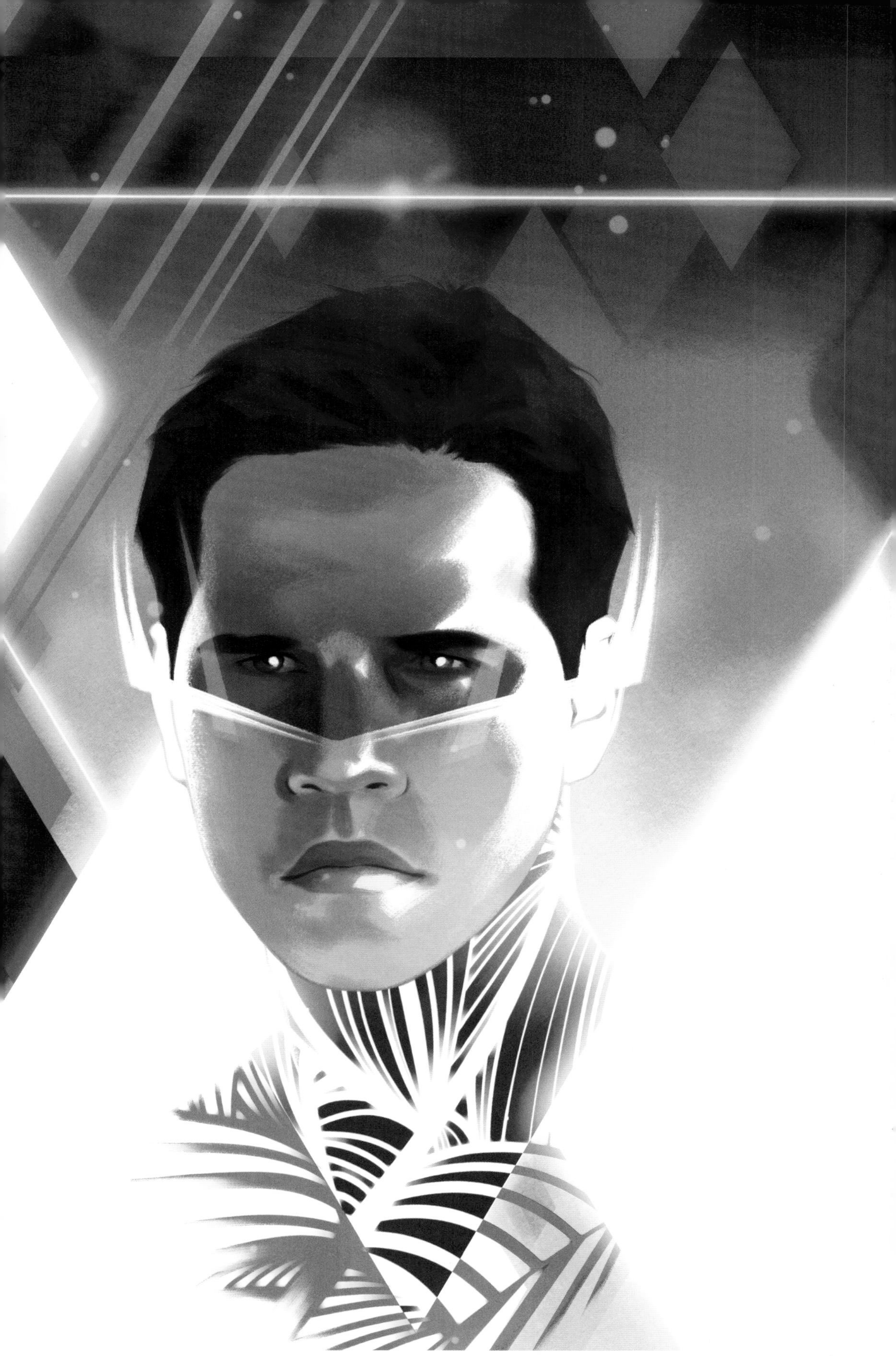

GOÑI MONTES MIGHTY MORPHIN #11 VARIANT COVER

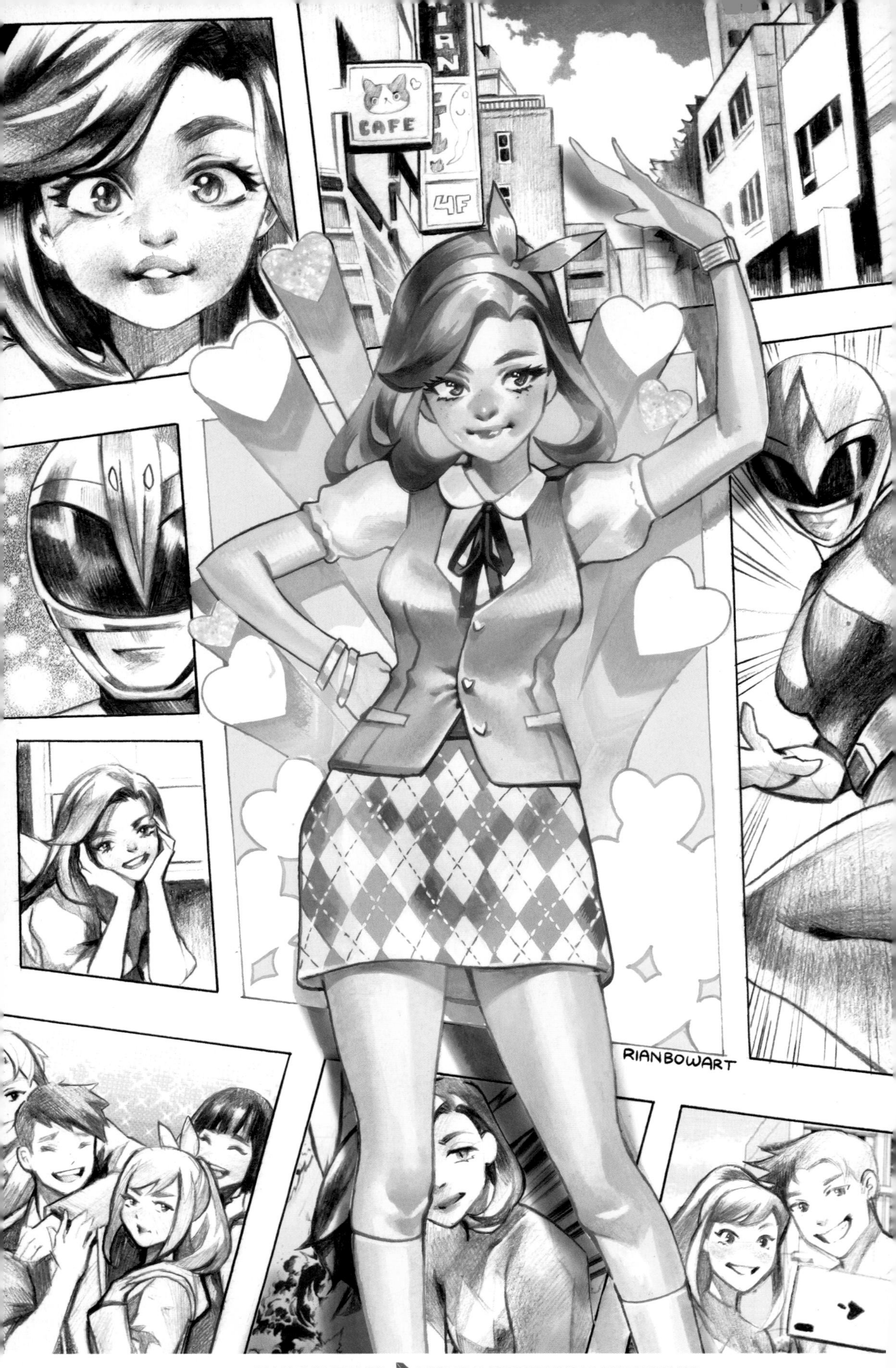
CAFE
4F
RIANBOWART

RIAN GONZALES MIGHTY MORPHIN #10 VARIANT COVER

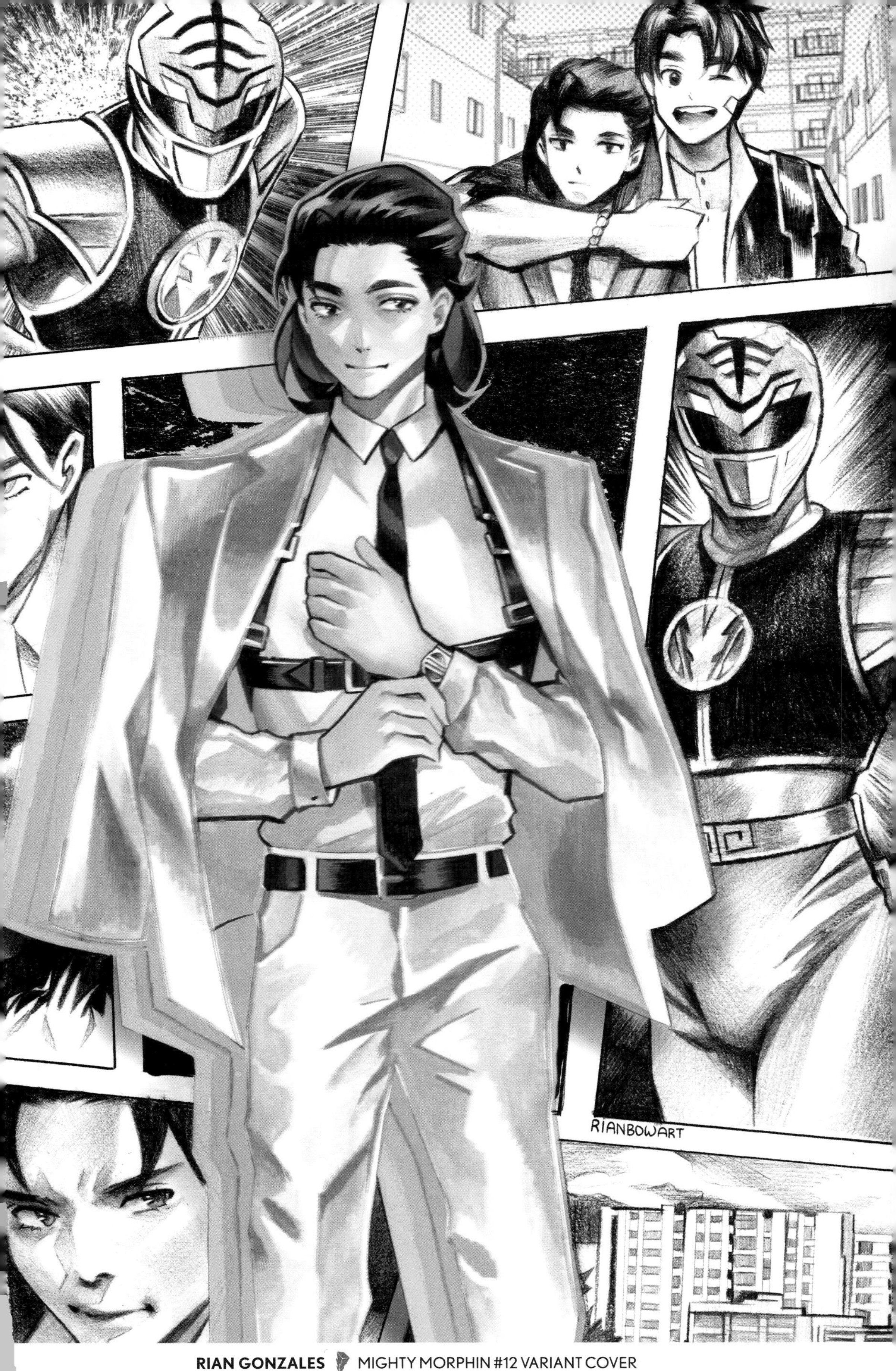
RIANBOWART

RIAN GONZALES MIGHTY MORPHIN #12 VARIANT COVER

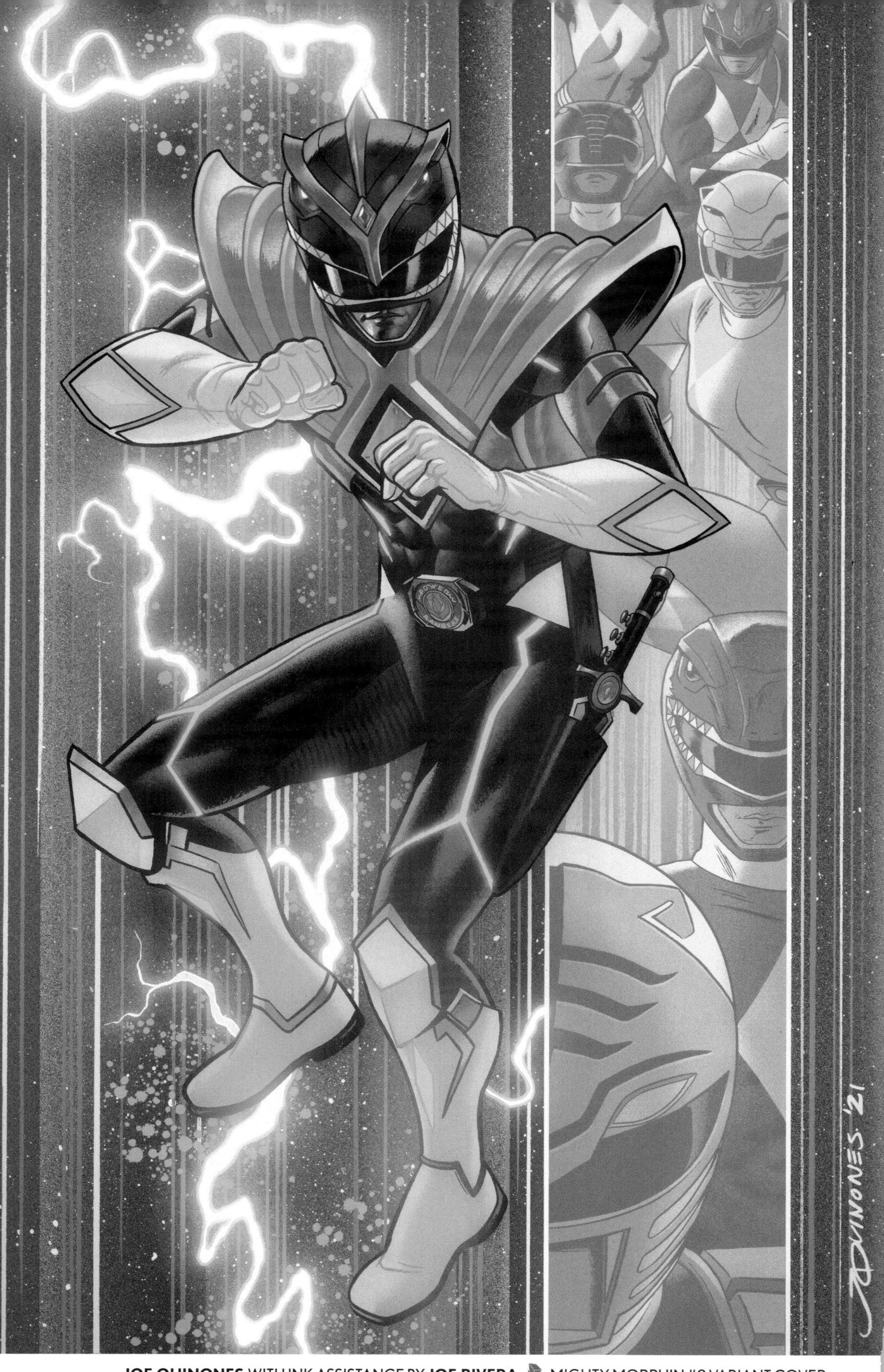
QUINONES '21

JOE QUINONES WITH INK ASSISTANCE BY **JOE RIVERA** MIGHTY MORPHIN #9 VARIANT COVER

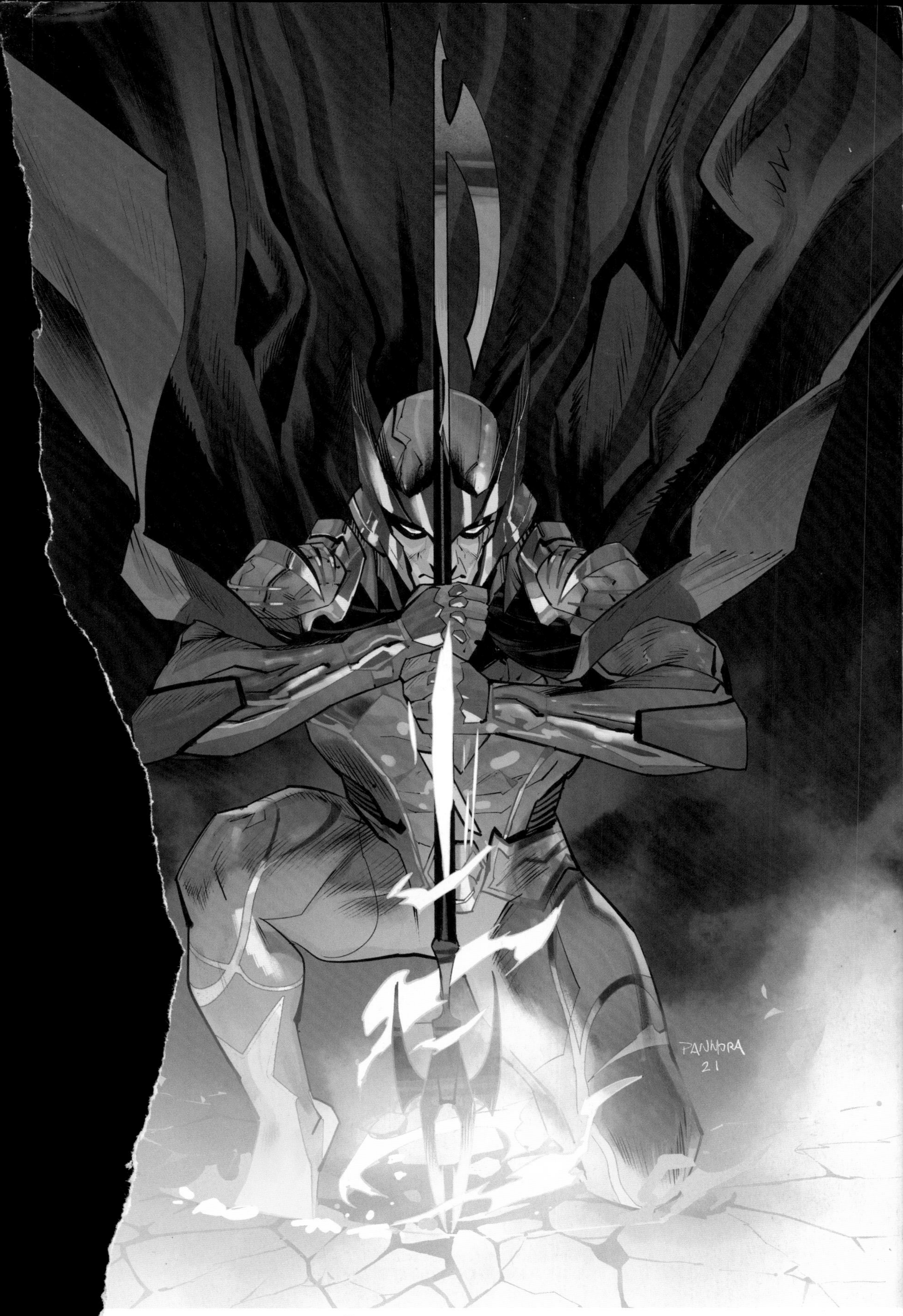
DANMORA
21

DAN MORA MIGHTY MORPHIN #10 VARIANT COVER

DISCOVER
MORE POWER RANGERS!

HIGGINS • PRASETYA • HERMS
ORLANDO • HOWELL • LAWSON
MIGHTY MORPHIN POWER RANGERS
VOLUME ONE
INTRODUCTION BY POWER RANGERS EXECUTIVE PRODUCER JUDD "CHIP" LYNN

HIGGINS • PRASETYA SILAS • HERMS
VALENZA • ORLANDO HOWELL • LAWSON
MIGHTY MORPHIN POWER RANGERS
VOLUME TWO

FLETCHER
THOMPSON
HOWARD
DI NICUOLO
STERN
MIGHTY MORPHIN POWER RANGERS
PINK
INTRODUCTION BY AMY JO JOHNSON KIMBERLY HART, THE ORIGINAL PINK RANGER

SABAN'S
POWER RANGERS
AFTERSHOCK
RYAN PARROTT
LUCAS WERNECK
JOANA LAFUENTE

MIGHTY MORPHIN POWER RANGERS
POSTER BOOK
FEATURING 20 REMOVABLE POSTERS

PARROTT • MORA • ANGULO
SABAN'S
GO GO POWER RANGERS
VOLUME ONE

Mighty Morphin Power Rangers
Kyle Higgins, Hendry Prasetya, Matt Herms
Volume 1
ISBN: 978-1-60886-893-3 | $19.99
Volume 2
ISBN: 978-1-60886-942-8 | $16.99
Volume 3
ISBN: 978-1-60886-977-0 | $16.99
Volume 4
ISBN: 978-1-68415-031-1 | $16.99

Mighty Morphin Power Rangers: Pink
Kelly Thompson, Brenden Fletcher, Tini Howard, Daniele Di Nicuolo
ISBN: 978-1-60886-952-7 | $19.99

Saban's Go Go Power Rangers
Ryan Parrott, Dan Mora
Volume 1
ISBN: 978-1-68415-193-6 | $16.99

Saban's Power Rangers: Aftershock
Ryan Parrott, Lucas Werneck
ISBN: 978-1-60886-937-4 | $14

Mighty Morphin Power Rangers Poster Book
Goñi Montes, Jamal Cam
Joe Quinones
ISBN: 978-1-60886-966-

Mighty Morphin Power Rangers Adult Coloring
Goñi Montes, Jama
Hendry Prasetya
ISBN: 978-1-60886-9

Mighty Morphin Power Rangers Year One: Deluxe
Kyle Higgins, Hendry Pras
Steve Orlando
ISBN: 978-1-68415-012-0

BOOM! STUDIOS

AVAILABLE AT YOUR LOCAL COMICS SHOP AND BOOKSTORE
Find a comic shop near you at www.comicshoplocator.com
WWW.**BOOM-STUDIOS**.COM

Licensed by: Hasbro